# PIERRE TALLET    MARK LEHNER

# THE
# RED SEA
# SCROLLS

## How Ancient Papyri Reveal
## the Secrets of the Pyramids

# CONTENTS

# PROLOGUE

It was 12 March 2013, and ten days had gone by since the start of the third season of fieldwork at a site called Wadi el-Jarf, on the shores of the Red Sea. As I (Pierre Tallet) was working on an area of excavation down by the coast, I noticed that someone from our team had been repeatedly trying to call me on my mobile phone. We had by now gained a greater knowledge of this remote site. Here we had already located the world's oldest harbour installation as well as numerous artificial galleries inland, carved into the rock of hillsides, where the ancient Egyptians had stored disassembled boats and other items. That day, however, a discovery of a different kind was made. It would lead on to others which would both revolutionize our understanding of how the early Old Kingdom state was organized and constitute a unique and unprecedented testimony relating to one of the world's most famous monuments – the Great Pyramid at Giza, over 150 km distant from our site.

We had experienced some difficulties with this archaeological project from the start. I and two colleagues had spent several years unsuccessfully seeking the site of Wadi el-Jarf, as part of a wider research programme that began in 2001 with the aim of studying the ancient Egyptians' navigation of the Red Sea and their expeditions to Sinai and the mysterious land of Punt. We knew of the site's existence from earlier explorers and suspected it might be an ancient Egyptian port like the one we had already excavated further north at Ayn Sukhna. Finally, in 2008, we found it. After three years spent putting together a team – a joint expedition from the French Institute of Archaeology in Cairo (IFAO – Institut français d'archéologie orientale), the University of Paris-Sorbonne and Asyut University – then gaining the necessary permissions from the Egyptian authorities and acquiring funding, we were able to complete two seasons of fieldwork in 2011–12, and we had already obtained crucial evidence.

We were almost certain that the complete assemblage of material we were finding at Wadi el-Jarf dated to the beginning of the 4th Dynasty, concentrated in particular in the reign of King Khufu (Cheops) (2633–2605 BC), whose Great Pyramid was the largest of all the Egyptian pyramids. His cartouche featured frequently, not only in the 'control marks' painted in red ink on the large blocks of limestone closing the entrances to the rock-cut storage galleries we had discovered, but also on inscribed potsherds found within them. We had also identified the different features that together made up the site as a whole. These elements extended from a spur at the edge of the mountains (some 5 km from the shore) down to the coast itself, where there was a very large artificial jetty. So we had already made a highly important discovery, because the site's date meant that it was the earliest port yet discovered on the Red Sea coast, or indeed in the world. We had also found evidence of the boats that had once been stored in the galleries, as well as other structures, and artifacts relating to the daily lives of the men who had temporarily lived and worked there.

More promising still, during the 2011 and 2012 seasons we had collected some small fragments of heavily used papyrus, spread

Map showing the principal sites discussed in the text, from Giza on the Nile (top left) to Wadi el-Jarf on the Red Sea coast.

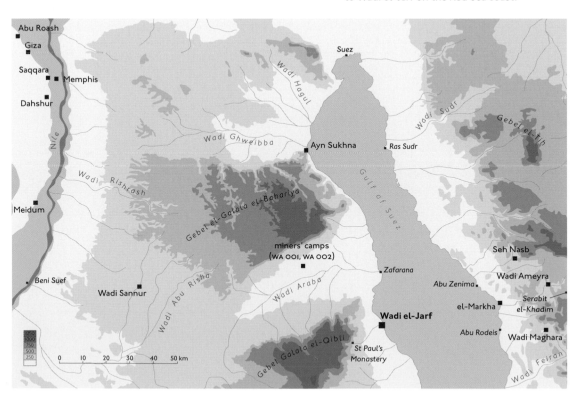

across the site – these bore traces of signs that had become too faint to read. Papyrus is a fragile material that tends only to be found in exceptional circumstances, especially at sites dating as early as the 4th Dynasty. Our fragments showed us that this type of document might actually have survived, against all the odds, at Wadi el-Jarf. However, we could never have anticipated what we would go on to discover.

In the 2013 field season we enlarged our workforce, taking on 60 workmen from Gurna, a village on the west bank at Luxor whose inhabitants have enjoyed a long tradition of collaboration with the French Institute of Archaeology over the last century. These extra workmen allowed us to focus on two separate areas of excavation simultaneously. In one zone we continued to explore the system of storage galleries we had already begun to investigate in previous years. The other area of excavation focused on an ancient camp, lying some 200 m from the coast, in association with the jetty, where we were uncovering an impressive assemblage of anchors. This was where I was working when I saw the repeated missed calls on my phone. I tried to call the team working on the galleries, but the signal was so bad that it was impossible to make contact. Had there been an accident or another serious incident on the dig? When I returned to our camp later that day, however, the surprise was of a completely different nature. Apparently on the first day of the new work on the galleries, just a few centimetres below the surface in front of gallery G2, the team had discovered six small fragments of papyrus, this time very nicely inscribed with perfectly clear signs in black and red ink.

Rapid deciphering revealed that some of the signs on the papyrus fragments were numbers, suggesting that these were probably small sections of accounts texts, which were already known to make up the bulk of papyri so far documented from the Old Kingdom. Other fragments, however, included sections of text arranged in columns, but the preservation was not good enough to be able to identify anything other than the cartouche of Khufu, which seemed to appear several times. This new discovery, albeit modest, was already of great significance: the archaeological context showed that the papyrus fragments could only date to the beginning of the 4th Dynasty, so it was immediately clear that we had unearthed fragments of what were probably the oldest inscribed papyri in the world.

Entrance to the storage galleries G1 and G2 after excavation. It was here that we unearthed the world's oldest documents: papyri from the time of King Khufu, builder of the Great Pyramid at Giza.

The next day, excavation resumed in the same area, but with increased numbers of workmen. The area in front of two of the storage galleries (G1 and G2) was examined meticulously, and, day by day, it gradually yielded regular batches of small fragments of papyri, many of which were only millimetres across, although a few rare pieces, mostly accounts texts, were a little larger, at around the size of the palm of a hand. Between 21 and 24 March we uncovered a rather more impressive accumulation of documents, still concentrated very near the surface, 5 m in front of gallery G2. One of them stood out instantly as a truly momentous find: it was the first section of an accounts papyrus, 21 cm high and with a surviving length of 31 cm.

More than just its size, its real significance lay in the fact that the first column featured a specific date in the reign of King Khufu. The text, inscribed in black ink and comprising very careful and detailed hieroglyphic signs, mentioned 'the year after the 13th census of large and small cattle', which can probably be equated with the 26th year of Khufu's reign. The second column contained the king's *serekh*, a device used in ancient Egypt to frame the royal 'Horus name' – part of the royal titulary. In this case, Khufu's rather mysterious Horus name is Medjedu, which may be translated as 'The one who crushes'. The rest of the document then identified a naval work-gang as 'The Escort Team <of the ship named> "The Uraeus of Khufu is its Prow"'. This particular crew of sailors was already known to us, because the gang's name also featured on dozens of marks painted on pottery found at the site. But the new evidence from the papyri allowed us to connect the archives with this one particular work-gang, thus enabling us to make a direct link between the documents and what we were finding at the port of Wadi el-Jarf.

It was at this point in the 2013 season that we began to recognize the truly exceptional nature of our discoveries, and as a result our momentum slowed down a little over the next few days. We completed the excavation of the area in front of the two galleries, and even of the galleries themselves, without any fresh discoveries of papyri. We considered ourselves already very fortunate to have uncovered this group of papyrus fragments, including three or four documents that were genuinely of great interest, and one that was totally outstanding. Our general view, therefore, was that we had probably collected the entire batch of archives that had been inexplicably abandoned at the site. How wrong we were!

On 28 March we began to clear a narrow space between two large blocks of limestone that served as a kind of portcullis for sealing the entrance to the G1 gallery. This was one of the few parts of the galleries that had not yet been excavated – and from the very beginning we were dealing with an absolute flood of papyrus fragments. A pit between the blocks was completely full of remains of papyri: hundreds of pieces, belonging to several dozen different texts, some almost completely disintegrated but others still preserved to lengths of over 50 cm, including sections that could sometimes be joined with others. It was within this batch from the entrance to G1 that we found the sheets we would later call 'Papyrus A' and 'Papyrus B'. These were excavated in an exceptional state of preservation, and we immediately knew that we were in the presence of a logbook filled in by a scribe day by day. It recorded the activities of the team of sailors whom we had already identified

Aurore Ciavatti excavates the main cache of papyri at Wadi el-Jarf.

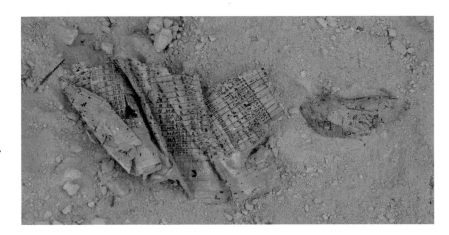

Accounts papyri from Wadi el-Jarf at the time of the discovery, before conservation. The major surviving papyri record the activities of an official called Inspector Merer, in charge of a work-gang whose activities included delivering stone down the Nile to the Great Pyramid construction site at Giza.

in the G2 papyri and the pot-marks. From 28 March to 4 April, at the very end of our 2013 season, we extracted the papyri from this pit, cleaned, unrolled and laid them out under glass, and even partially translated them.

The most important fragments repeatedly referred to Khufu's funerary complex at Giza and focused on the work of a minor official, an inspector called Merer, who for several months was responsible for transporting limestone blocks to the massive building site around the Great Pyramid. Astonishingly, for the first time, we had the direct written testimony of a contemporary eyewitness who had participated in the construction of the pyramid complex of Khufu. Until now it had stood silent and enigmatic on the Giza

Plateau, with no known contemporary documentary references to it at the time it was built. But what is more, these papyri would link in wholly unexpected ways with ongoing excavations conducted by my friend and fellow Egyptologist Mark Lehner in the vicinity of the pyramid itself. In the following pages we tell the incredible story of how our parallel research has totally transformed what we know about one of the greatest construction projects ever undertaken, and how that project shaped the creation of the ancient Egyptian state.

Back at Wadi el-Jarf our discovery in 2013 was beyond our wildest dreams. Yet the desperate need to conserve and transfer these documents to ensure their preservation meant that at the time we hardly had a moment to think about the significance of it all. We had begun to realize that all the papyri found so far had originally been placed in this pit, probably at the end of the reign of Khufu. The pit had then no doubt subsequently been disturbed and the fragments scattered in antiquity. This showed us that our collection of papyri was not only exceptional but was also a perfectly coherent archive. The careful process of excavation had literally kept us spellbound for nearly a month. It was an extraordinary archaeological event and I knew I would be unlikely ever to experience anything like it again.

# INTRODUCTION

One of the most appealing things about archaeology is that we can never fully predict what we will find, especially when starting work at a site that has not previously been scientifically studied. The excavation of Wadi el-Jarf on the west coast of the Gulf of Suez promised from the very beginning to provide new information on the nature of ancient Egyptian seagoing in the Red Sea, and particularly on the maritime expeditions of the early Old Kingdom; but we could never have anticipated that it would yield the oldest papyri yet discovered, dating to *c.* 2607–2605 BC, at the end of the reign of Khufu, the second king of the 4th Dynasty. Not only that, but no one would have expected that these documents – uncovered at an obscure site in Egypt, a very long way from the centre of Old Kingdom administration – would provide us with information concerning the construction of Khufu's Great Pyramid, one of the most famous monuments in the world. Ultimately our work at Wadi el-Jarf showed that this remote port on the Red Sea had to be taken into consideration as one of the essential components in the massive building works of this king, and that the teams of specialist workers active at the port were also to be found, at certain times of the year, in the Giza Plateau region.

The site of Wadi el-Jarf lies on the Red Sea coast, 23 km south of the small modern city of Zafarana and about 10 km east of St Paul's Monastery. Founded in the 5th century, this monastery has long been an important sacred place for Egyptian Christians; even today it is still a major pilgrimage destination as well as a tourist attraction. The relative proximity of a remarkable freshwater spring in the midst of the desert, which is currently within the enclosure of the monastery, was probably one of the major reasons for the choice of Wadi el-Jarf as the location for a port by the Egyptians at the beginning of the 4th Dynasty. The port was in use only during a very specific period, probably for around 70 years, from the reign of Sneferu, founder of the 4th-Dynasty royal family, to that of Khafre, the fourth ruler of the dynasty. Wadi el-Jarf is the earliest and probably most informative example of the so-called 'intermittent ports' which were set up by the Egyptians on the Red Sea coast

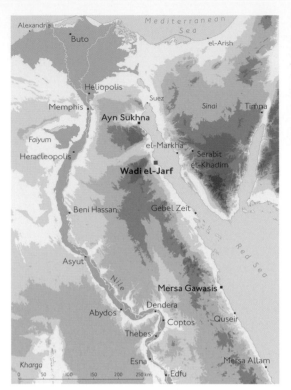

ABOVE LEFT Map showing
the location of the three
pharaonic harbours that
have so far been identified
on the Red Sea shore:
Ayn Sukhna, Wadi el-Jarf
and Mersa Gawasis. The
Wadi el-Jarf harbour is
the oldest, having been
used exclusively from
c. 2650 to 2600 BC, at
the beginning of the
4th Dynasty.

ABOVE RIGHT View of one
of the galleries at Wadi
el-Jarf before excavation.

for maritime missions sent out to acquire necessary raw materials
during the pharaonic period. They are known as 'intermittent'
because they were occupied only periodically, when the expeditions
were in operation. The most important of these raw materials was
copper, obtained at this period from copper mines in Sinai, across
the Red Sea. Copper tools were essential for many tasks, such as
the finishing of stone blocks used in the pyramids (see Chapter 3).
It should be remembered that this was a time before the invention
and widespread introduction of other metals, in particular bronze
and then, much later, iron. During the Old Kingdom, therefore,
besides the extensive use of copper, Egyptians were still employing
stone tools.

One notable feature of Wadi el-Jarf is that its remains are
so widely dispersed, extending for a distance of more than 5.5 km,
from the foothills of the Gebel el-Galala el-Bahariya mountain
range in the west, which dominates the region, to the shore of the
Gulf of Suez in the east. The most spectacular aspect of the site is
the set of 31 elongated galleries carved into the limestone rock of
a small hillock and the side of a wadi, which stored the equipment

needed for the Red Sea maritime expeditions during periods of the port's inactivity, quite possibly over several years. The fleet of boats, which initially would have had to be transported in pieces by land along desert tracks stretching from the Nile Valley and rebuilt before setting sail, could be disassembled again into separate sections for storage once an expedition had been completed. The boats then awaited the commissioning of a new expedition, when they would once more be required.

This cache of wood was particularly valuable as it consisted of coniferous timber, which had to be imported from the Levantine coast as such trees did not grow in the Nile Valley. Before the work-gangs headed back to the Nile Valley after each mission, they therefore took great pains to prevent looting by sealing up the entrances to the galleries with large limestone blocks, each weighing several tonnes. In addition to the group of rock-cut galleries, the site as a whole incorporates three separate zones of ancient encampments, each several kilometres apart, and an imposing north-facing L-shaped jetty, forming a maritime port that is currently the oldest known example in the world.

View of the Wadi el-Jarf jetty at low tide, part of the world's oldest seaport dating from the time of King Khufu.

## Early explorers

Forgotten for millennia, the site of Wadi el-Jarf had already been visited and identified twice previously before we managed to relocate it in 2008. The first person to provide a description of it was the English explorer Sir John Gardner Wilkinson, who encountered it in 1823 as part of a larger expedition along the west coast of the Gulf of Suez. The narrative of his journey was published nearly ten years later, in 1832, in the second volume of the *Journal of the Royal Geographical Society*. Wilkinson described the galleries, which he called 'excavated chambers', noting the presence of pottery and burnt wood inside them. On the basis of the burning that had taken place, he identified them as Greco-Roman catacombs, as this was the only period in Egyptian history when the cremation of bodies was regularly practised by some of the population. The site was also visited at about the same time by another British explorer, James Burton, who unfortunately did not publish his observations, although his archives include a series of notes regarding the site. In our investigations we found some physical traces of the presence of these English explorers, including early 19th-century imported European pottery, Ottoman pipes and a small note, perhaps written by Wilkinson, indicating the route to follow to reach the site from the direction of St Anthony's Monastery in the Wadi Araba.

After this, the site fell back into obscurity, until two French boat pilots working for the Suez Canal Company – François Bissey and René Chabot-Morisseau – rediscovered it in the 1950s, doubtless following the descriptions provided by Wilkinson and Burton. These amateur archaeologists then spent several years exploring the area of rock-cut galleries, which they called Rod el-Khawaga (literally 'The Garden of the Foreigner' in Bedouin dialect), surveying several of them and drawing some of the ceramics. Although they succeeded in correctly dating the galleries and pottery to the Old Kingdom, when it came to a more precise chronology they suggested attributing the site to its final phase, the 6th Dynasty, rather than the beginning. They were very curious about the system of galleries, and suggested that they represented a mining site, although they were unable to determine what was being extracted. Bissey published a brief note about their investigations in 1960, focusing on the ancient jetty situated directly below the site in the Red Sea. For over half a century, this half-page article, in a relatively specialized journal, was the only information available on the structures and remains at Wadi el-Jarf. The French boat pilots, deeply intrigued by all they had found, even submitted a request to the Egyptian government to take on an archaeological concession there, but the Suez Crisis put an end to their planned project in 1956. With France and Egypt then at war, the two pilots-turned-archaeologists were forced to leave the country, and the site of Wadi el-Jarf was lost once more.

In the years following 2001, I and two colleagues, Georges Castel and Grégory Marouard, undertook the study of Ayn Sukhna, another coastal site in the Gulf of Suez, as part of wider research into the maritime activities of the ancient Egyptians in the Red Sea. Thanks to the excavations carried out at this other ancient port, from the beginning we knew something that our predecessors who had explored Wadi el-Jarf could not have guessed – namely that the existence of tunnels carved out of rock near the coastline probably indicated the presence of a pharaonic port. These rock-cut installations were in fact the most visible sign of the system of 'intermittent ports' set up along the Red Sea coast and used by the Egyptians over a period of more than a thousand years, and so we determined to find and investigate Wadi el-Jarf ourselves.

It took us some years of searching to rediscover the site, but we were ultimately able to do so thanks to the information provided by these earlier explorers, and in particular by consulting a file in the archives of the French Institute of Archaeology in Cairo (IFAO), which was published by Ginette Lacaze and Luc Camino in 2008 as *Mémoires de Suez: François Bissey et René Chabot-Morisseau à la découverte du désert oriental d'Égypte (1945–1956)*. It was through the analysis of Google Earth satellite photos that the settlements near the galleries were identified, as well as the jetty, and, finally, a mysterious large building located halfway between the mountains and the sea. A little initial reconnaissance was then all that was needed to relocate the system of galleries reported by previous researchers, some of which had been subjected to recent looting, probably by Bedouin. In 2008 we applied to the Egyptian authorities for permission to work at the site as a collaboration between the University of Paris-Sorbonne, IFAO and Asyut University (represented by my colleague and friend El-Sayed Mahfouz, a specialist in Red Sea studies, who was also part of the mission working at Mersa Gawasis, the third pharaonic port discovered on the Red Sea).

## Excavations begin

Following the long initial stage of the project, which involved applying for the necessary official permissions and preparations for our mission, the first field season was scheduled for March 2011. However, in January–February of that year, we really began to think that this site was cursed, and that we were going to suffer the same fate as the Suez Canal pilots. The Egyptian revolution of 2011 (part of the so-called Arab Spring), which we could not possibly have anticipated, interrupted all archaeological fieldwork in Egypt at that time. Nevertheless, Adel Farouk, a member of the Suez office of the Ministry of Antiquities who had already overseen work at the site for several years, patiently set about the task of requesting the necessary military security permissions, despite a state of national disorganization that made such operations very delicate, and at a time when no one was particularly interested in facilitating archaeological work.

As a result of Adel's dedication, we were able to carry out our first campaign at the site in June, with a small team consisting of myself, Georges Castel (architect at IFAO), Grégory Marouard (then an archaeologist based at the Oriental Institute of the University of Chicago) and Damien Laisney (topographer at the Maison de l'Orient et de la Méditerranée, University of Lyons). From this initial work, we could determine that the site dated to the very beginning of the 4th Dynasty, both from the analysis of the pottery found at the site and by the study of some of the first inscriptions discovered there, particularly the storage jars bearing one of the royal names of Khufu. The port at Wadi el-Jarf now appeared to be the prototype

The excavation team at Wadi el-Jarf in 2015.

of similar installations established on the Red Sea coast throughout the pharaonic period, with its creation and initial use dating to *c.* 2650 BC. It was therefore already evident that this was the oldest known seaport.

However, our continued fieldwork at Wadi el-Jarf was telling us one other thing: the site was not just a new addition to the list of ancient ports on the Red Sea, but, more significantly, in Khufu's time it was actually an essential component in the process of construction of the king's pyramid at Giza. This was demonstrated first by the seal impressions we had discovered, which consist of the imprint left by an official's seal in a small lump of clay used to seal documents or boxes. They mentioned personnel attached to the king's funerary complex, known as Akhet Khufu ('Horizon of Khufu'). In addition, the abundant archive of papyri that we discovered from the 2013 season onwards consisted partly of accounts texts, recording the royal administration's deliveries of supplies to groups of full-time specialized workers, and partly also logbooks presenting daily reports of the work carried out by these teams, in particular one led by a middle-ranking official, Inspector Merer.

Through these papyri we can follow in detail the activities of a group of elite boatmen working permanently in the employ of the royal court, undertaking several different missions in different places throughout the year. The documents provide extremely valuable information about the first pyramid at Giza, in particular the organization of the teams who worked there and the supply of raw materials for its construction. Moreover, they also, for the first time, provide us with an illuminating picture of internal administration at that time, allowing us to see how the pharaonic state actually worked at the beginning of Egyptian history.

Locally made storage jar found at Wadi el-Jarf, inscribed with the Golden Horus name of Khufu. It refers to the royal work-gang who were called 'Those who are Known to the Double Golden Horus'.

This book is an account, step by step, of the detective work both by Pierre that resulted in the discovery and interpretation of the Wadi el-Jarf complex and papyri, and by Mark at Giza, where his team has identified the ancient harbour, port city, workers' barracks and quarry. It is remarkable how well the revelations from the papyri found in an obscure site far from Giza fit with and amplify our knowledge of the Great Pyramid complex gained in recent years from archaeology. These new discoveries are revolutionizing our understanding of the Golden Age of the pyramids, the first great high point of Egyptian civilization.

# PART I

# ON THE TRAIL OF THE PYRAMID BUILDERS

# CHAPTER 1

# RICHES IN EGYPT'S REMOTE DESERTS

I (Pierre) have always been fascinated by the deserts that surround Egypt, and which nowadays make up the vast majority of its territory. This is a world of minerals, one that changes constantly. In some places sharply contrasting mountainous reliefs rear up, and in others rather monotonous plains are peppered with hillocks or rocky mounds serving as landmarks, occasionally engulfed by sand dunes. It is also a world crisscrossed by tracks, and sometimes still inhabited by people adapted to the conditions of life in this harsh environment. The energy and skill with which the ancient Egyptians exploited these difficult areas are deeply impressive. Very early on in their history, they colonized the oases – those rare green, living spaces that are scattered through the Western Desert – and they systematically extracted desirable materials for making precious objects, artifacts or monumental constructions.

From the Old Kingdom onwards, expeditions were sent as far south as Gebel el-Asr (in the Western Desert, in the region where the Abu Simbel temples would later be constructed) in order to bring back one particular variety of stone: anorthosite gneiss. The bluish glint of this stone when seen in a certain light was considered especially suitable for the creation of royal sculptures. A single large block was used to carve the famous statue of Khafre (Chephren) (*c.* 2597–2573 BC) discovered by George Reisner in the king's valley temple at Giza, which is now one of the greatest masterpieces in the Egyptian Museum, Cairo. The Egyptians also sent expeditions to the area around Dakhla Oasis, deep in the Western Desert, in search of a pigment called *mefat*, which was used in decoration. They obtained basalt from the edge of the Faiyum region; greywacke, amethyst and gold from the Eastern Desert; and copper and turquoise from Sinai. Indeed, very few natural deposits were not exploited by these expeditions, which were sent from the very beginning of pharaonic history.

Such forays were initially led by a group of geological prospectors, described as the *sementiu*, who were responsible for identifying mineral deposits that could be mined or quarried in the most remote areas, probably with the help of the populations already living there. Signs of their activities can be found all

The ancient Egyptians exploited precious minerals in desert regions. They obtained turquoise for use in jewelry from mines in Sinai, such as at Serabit el-Khadim shown here (see pp. 26–31).

over the deserts, including caravan routes that are still visible, sometimes millennia after they were first created. These routes can be traced by observing areas where the ground surface is disturbed and alignments of pebbles indicate tracks worn by the passage of pack-animals, which can be reminiscent of the glacial moraines found in other latitudes. In addition, there are remnants of encampments near areas that were being exploited, as well as the mines and quarries themselves, and sometimes ancient workshops where mineral deposits, such as copper or gold ores, were being processed *in situ*. At many of these sites rock inscriptions were left by the teams who worked there. These can be very important historical sources – the texts frequently give dates and the names of expedition leaders, and very often cite the rulers who sponsored these missions into the desert. Such inscriptions may also provide unique chronological details that contribute to the writing of ancient Egyptian history. Some kings are known solely through these texts, and the lengths of the reigns of others may be indicated by the dates given. They can also sometimes have important ideological implications: their positions along routes or at places of mineral exploitation could have served as proclamations that the Egyptian ruler owned the surrounding territory as well as the populations who lived there. Evidence from rock inscriptions thus provides immediate information, often on several levels, concerning the nature of the places in which they were located.

Although deserts were comparatively overlooked by archaeologists in the past, over the last 30 years they have been studied by numerous expeditions using new tools such as GPS and satellite imagery. The resulting greater understanding of desert activities has contributed immensely to the advance of Egyptology. It is often from these remote areas of the Egyptian landscape that the most groundbreaking, fresh information has come, either because they had previously escaped the attention of scholars, or because their very remoteness had – until recently – preserved them from the destructive effects of the modern world.

## Surprises in Dakhla and Bahariya Oases

It is in any case surprising to observe how a particular scientific investigation that may involve decades of work can sometimes hinge on the sheer luck of a simple discovery, the true importance of which may not even be fully appreciated at the time. At the end of the 1990s, I was a regular participant in the excavation of the palace built by Old Kingdom governors at Balat, in the Dakhla Oasis, an IFAO project directed by Georges Soukiassian. On Fridays, our weekly day off, I often went walking with two colleagues, Michel Baud and Frédéric Colin, in the area of Tenida, a little further to the west, at the ends of several desert tracks leading into the oasis. Here, at the entrance to the oasis depression, over the millennia the sharp jagged shapes of sandstone outcrops had been carved with thousands of inscriptions and drawings by travellers passing through Dakhla, but at that time no text from the pharaonic period had yet been reported there. This was all about to change.

One lunchtime, as we were sitting surrounded by a tangled mass of drawings of all periods, I suddenly recognized the outline of a small carved stela, on which was depicted a wine-jar. The image was preceded by a few hieroglyphic signs spelling out the name of an individual called Wenu – a personal name that was typical of the Egyptian Middle Kingdom (*c.* 2045–1700 BC). Despite the relative modesty of this stela, I was utterly captivated by it, and particularly struck by the directness and immediacy of the inscription. I could not escape the feeling that I was suddenly in direct touch with another person who had stood in the same spot as me and had left behind this rock-cut graffito nearly four thousand years earlier for reasons known only to him. More than 20 years later, I am still drawn to these places and deeply immersed in the search for this type of textual record in the Egyptian deserts.

Totally hooked, the three of us then spent all our free time exploring that area of Dakhla, eventually discovering a coherent group of about thirty inscriptions, each of which either mentioned the administrative staff based at the oasis or represented the provincial governors (*haty-a*) who were in post during this period of Egyptian history. The governors wore strange headgear surmounted by snakes imitating the uraeus worn by the king, and their loincloths were decorated with royal emblems, no doubt indicating a certain autonomy in their management of the oasis. Their inscriptions dealt with such issues as the setting up of their funerary cults, the succession from father to son of two of them (Ameny and Mery), the sinking of wells in the region, and the movements of troops along the routes passing through Dakhla. Virtually nothing had previously been known about Dakhla in the Middle Kingdom, but now these discoveries were sufficient to provide us with at least a page of history. I have probably never felt quite such intense joy as the feeling I experienced when identifying each of these rock inscriptions. That fraction of a second when something we see in front of us suddenly begins to make sense and we have an idea of its significance provides a sensation of pure discovery that is then repeated with each new revelation.

A few years later I went in search of rock inscriptions in the Bahariya Oasis, situated much further north than Dakhla in the Western Desert. This area had never yielded anything in the way of rock inscriptions of this type, but in 1973, Ahmed Fakhry, the great Egyptian oases specialist, had reported finding three rock inscriptions in the el-Harra region, at the northern end of the Bahariya depression. This was in fact the year of Fakhry's death, so he had no time to publish them fully, and the small amount of information he provided, within a general article, was insufficient for anyone else to locate them precisely. In April 2000, along with my colleague Georges Castel, I spent several days in a serious attempt to track the inscriptions down. We first questioned the Bedouin based in the region, but they had no knowledge of the inscriptions, so we then made enquiries among the workers employed at some important iron mines at Bahariya. Our theory was that perhaps Fakhry had been alerted to the inscriptions, more than 25 years earlier, by the geologists conducting initial prospection for the mining company.

Thanks to the guidance of some of the older staff at the company, we were given a rough idea of the areas that they had explored in the 1970s, and this, along with a little luck, enabled us to discover a small 'hanging valley' (a tributary valley with a mouth above the floor of the main valley), into which several passages had been cut by ancient miners. Six sandstone rocks were inscribed with 12th-Dynasty (c. 1974–1781 BC) inscriptions of varying length. The most complex were rock-cut stelae identifying members of the mining administration at this date – a 'seal-bearer' named Nehetet and an 'overseer of stores' called Senebtify, both probably sent to supervise the extraction of some unknown mineral product here. Several of the texts also included the name of a local governor called Hebi. At the time of our discovery, these Middle Kingdom inscriptions were the earliest evidence for pharaonic activities at Bahariya.

## Survey in Sinai

Ever since these discoveries, my passion for rock inscriptions has endured, sometimes leading to important discoveries. For example, our documentation of rock inscriptions at Ayn Sukhna – discussed later – led to that site's identification as a pharaonic port in the Red Sea, where we began excavations in 2001. From 2004 onwards, I initiated a survey project in southern Sinai, carrying out one or two field seasons per year until 2013, when the political situation in the peninsula brought an end to this fieldwork due to insecurity. The main aim of our work had been to find traces of the pharaonic mining expeditions that regularly travelled to Sinai from the ports on the Red Sea. By examining the areas where turquoise and copper had been exploited, we aimed to produce the most accurate archaeological map possible of the ancient mining activities across a vast region.

It was a truly exhilarating research project: we operated in this remote region with a very small team, mostly limited to five or six people, including myself, Damien Laisney (IFAO topographer) and three Bedouin from North Sinai who helped us to set up camp and organize our supplies for periods varying between a fortnight and a month. Our camps throughout each season were very basic – apart from small individual tents they included a kind of canvas awning that served, depending on the time of the day, either as kitchen or work place. The camp allowed us to function virtually

A view in South Sinai: Wadi Baba, in the ancient Egyptian mining zone, west of the plateau of Serabit el-Khadim.

independently. We survived on stocks of food purchased before leaving Cairo – mostly pasta and tins of tuna, sardines and corned beef – as well as petrol for the generator we needed for the nightly recharging of our devices, including the computers and differential GPS through which we built up our topographic map of the sites studied. Life was rather austere, and no outside communication was possible in this mountainous region with no mobile phone masts. But we were surrounded by such stunning, varied landscapes that we felt constantly grateful for the opportunity to work there, amid precipitous, multicoloured sandstone cliffs at the bottoms of wadis cutting deep into the mountains, sometimes offering the shade of a secret palm grove hidden away in a rocky recess.

The epicentre of our survey zone was the Serabit el-Khadim plateau, the site of the largest complex of turquoise mines ever exploited by the Egyptians, who prized this mineral for use in jewelry and adornment. In addition to the mines, Serabit el-Khadim is also home to an astounding Middle Kingdom temple dedicated to Hathor, Mistress of Turquoise, one of the few temples to have survived from the Middle Kingdom. (Hathor is often seen as the protector of Horus, god of kingship, and was associated with foreign sources of materials, quarries and mines.) Built on the eastern side of the plateau, in the midst of the largest concentration of turquoise mines, the temple's appearance is unique. Most of it is surrounded by a rectangular dry-stone wall, while a circular wall encloses the sanctuary at the eastern end, roughly following the local topography. The temple as a whole consisted of two distinct elements, the most important of which was a pair of *speoi* (rock-chapels) cut into the mountain at the eastern end of the sacred space. One of the shrines contained a statue of the goddess Hathor, whose cult was celebrated here as the 'Mistress of Turquoise', while an image of the creator god Ptah (a deity from the Memphite area, closely linked with craftsmen and frequently associated with Hathor in the Sinai Peninsula) stood in the other, secondary chapel. These two deities served to ensure the success of the royal turquoise-mining expeditions and also played a role in the temple's other holy place, the so-called Chapel of Kings. Set on a terrace on the northern side of the temple, this provided a theatrical backdrop for royal rituals designed to ensure the stability and continuity of kingly power. Finally, the temple also contained dozens of stone stelae, some almost 3 m high. Each had been erected by one of the expeditions sent to Sinai to

View of Gebel Reglein ('The Mountain of the Two Legs'), two twin peaks to the south of the plateau of Serabit el-Khadim. It was on the Serabit plateau that the ancient Egyptians exploited the largest turquoise mines in Sinai.

Horurrê Stela in the Hathor Temple. This monument, commissioned by an expedition leader named Horurrê, gives an account of a mission sent to Sinai during the Middle Kingdom (6th year of the reign of Amenemhat III, c. 1832 BC). Horurrê complains about the summer heat, but explains that because he was obedient to the king, he had won the favour of the goddess Hathor, Mistress of Turquoise, and was able to bring back more precious stone than anyone before him.

commemorate their arrival at this place so far from the Nile Valley and to seek divine protection for their mission. From an Egyptian perspective this site lay at the very edge of the known world. These stelae are extremely important historical sources. They preserve the names of the main participants in the expeditions, helping us to understand the methods of organization, and sometimes even give an indication (naturally always of a positive nature) of the unfolding events of the actual expedition.

With its sheer cliffs, Serabit el-Khadim – at an average altitude of 800 m above sea level (asl) – has the appearance of a kind of natural citadel, accessible only by the routes created by wadis that have carved channels out of its flanks. Its sprawling overall shape, stretching out rocky fingers towards other summits in the region, has been aptly compared to 'a hand spread out over the sand'. On top of the plateau are tracks that were mostly worn by pharaonic work-gangs passing back and forth between the temple, the encampments and the different mining areas scattered across the site. Following in their footsteps today can feel like travelling along high mountain paths.

Serabit has been investigated by several archaeological expeditions in the past. The Hathor Temple was excavated by the British archaeologist Flinders Petrie in 1905, while the commemorative stelae from the site were initially documented and published by the Egypt Exploration Society in 1917, and subsequently republished in a two-volume revised edition by the great Czech Egyptologist Jaroslav Černý in 1952–55. The site was then the subject of several Harvard University expeditions in the

Inscriptions on a rock wall at Rod el-Air, the pass giving access to the Serabit el-Khadim plateau. Made either by professional scribes or by semi-literate members of the mining teams, some inscriptions record an offering formula seeking divine favour to ensure a safe return journey to the Nile Valley.

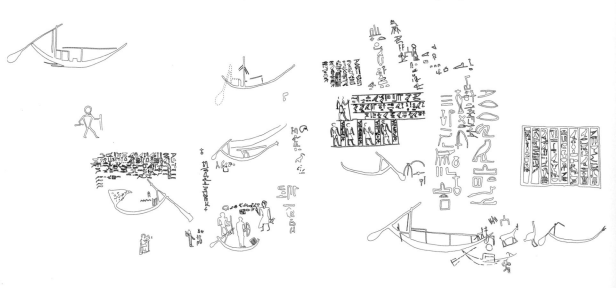

PART I    On the Trail of the Pyramid Builders

1920s and 1930s, followed by a number of seasons of exploration by Israeli teams during the period when the entire Sinai Peninsula was occupied by Israel (1967–79). Finally, a detailed archaeological study of the remains was undertaken by Dominique Valbelle and Charles Bonnet in the early 1990s, on behalf of the universities of Lille and Geneva respectively. Our own objective was therefore not to work on the temple, which is already clearly well studied, but to complete the map of the whole region through the documentation of many subsidiary sites that had not previously been the subject of real archaeological study. These included dry-stone encampments, a turquoise-processing area, mineshafts, minor ritual structures (often in the form of small stone circles originally surrounding stelae) or simple cairns that may have served as guides to gain access to the plateau.

Our surveys were also opportunities for us to systematically record all the rock inscriptions left by the ancient expeditions passing through. These clustered in well-defined areas, particularly at Rod el-Air (literally in Bedouin dialect 'Garden of the Donkey'), a pass forming the main access to the summit of the plateau. It seems to have been a stopping-off place for the pharaonic teams, probably because the donkeys accompanying them could climb no higher. At this place, which effectively marks the gateway to the plateau, we recorded dozens of rock-cut images and inscriptions. Most of the major texts were published after the discovery of Rod el-Air in 1935, but numerous more modest graffiti had been overlooked, as well as a large number of rock-drawings that probably reveal aspects of the cognitive universe and beliefs of an entire set of illiterate individuals

Detail of a boat inscribed in the rock at Rod el-Air, made by one of the Sinai mining teams, aware that it was in such vessels they could cross the Red Sea and return home.

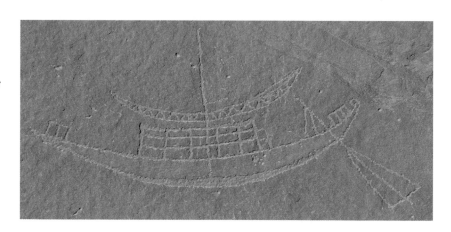

who passed through in the Middle Kingdom. Members of mining teams who were not able to write their names left traces of their presence either by carving symbols identifying their specific work-gang, or occasionally by hammering or chiselling the rock to pick out the outlines of an axe – probably their own personal mining tool. We also recorded a huge abundance of representations of sail-boats, which brings us back to the Red Sea. The fastest way for expeditions to return home to Egypt would certainly have been by crossing the Gulf of Suez (rather than travelling overland north and then west), and these drawings of ships – no doubt illustrating seagoing vessels of the time – clearly show the miners' desire for a rapid return to the welcoming Nile Valley. In the course of our work we also discovered several new rock stelae dating to the reigns of Amenemhat II and III (third and sixth kings of the 12th Dynasty, respectively *c.* 1900–1865 and 1838–1794 BC) carved in the entrance-ways of turquoise mines to commemorate the opening of new mineshafts.

Many other sites were investigated in the course of our survey, spread over the entire area, some of which had been occupied from the Old Kingdom. Notable among them were Wadi Kharig (marked by a monumental inscription of Sahure, second ruler of the 5th Dynasty, *c.* 2534–2515 BC) and Seh Nasb, where we uncovered a set of spectacular ore-processing facilities, discussed in Chapter 3. The most satisfying discovery, however, resulting in evidence that significantly affected our picture of the general history of pharaonic Egypt, was the Wadi Ameyra site, a little to the north of the mining zone that we were methodically surveying.

For several years, one of the Bedouin who worked with us, Rabia Barakat, had offered to show me some inscriptions he knew of in South Sinai. However, he wanted us to go out alone with him, outside the restrictions of our official fieldwork, to visit places that seemed to him to be interesting. At the end of June 2012, Damien Laisney and I accompanied him as tourists, sleeping under the stars near Bedouin encampments, systematically checking all the places where rock drawings and inscriptions appeared, moving east to west from the border with Israel to the coast of the Gulf of Suez. This trip was in many ways a unique and exciting opportunity to make a transect through the varied landscapes of the Sinai Peninsula. Initially, from an Egyptological point of view, our interest was limited: the inscriptions and drawings we discovered mostly dated to prehistoric or Nabataean times, or were even medieval or modern

Wadi Kharig: general
view of this copper-
mining site with a stela
of the 12th-Dynasty ruler
Senwosret I (c. 1940 BC).

Inscription of the
5th-Dynasty ruler Sahure
(c. 2530 BC), engraved on
a rock above the workers'
camp at Wadi Kharig.

General view of the inscribed rock wall at Wadi Ameyra,
a little to the north of the main area of our mining survey.

A rock panel at Wadi Ameyra shows Iry Hor, a ruler of
so-called 'Dynasty 0', *c.* 3100 BC. The hieroglyphs spell
his name; the boat probably symbolizes his power.

Wadi Ameyra rock panel of Djer, third ruler of the
1st Dynasty, showing the Horus name of the king,
in a *serekh* surmounted by a falcon, smiting a foe.

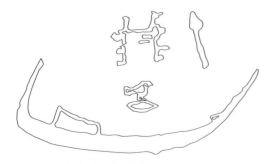

Bedouin, with occasional, much rarer occurrences of Greek or Coptic inscriptions. However, on the penultimate day of the trip we were back in the general vicinity of the pharaonic mining area, and Moussa Abu Rashid, one of our two guides, remembered a site that he thought might prove interesting, close to his home village.

He led us to a kind of rocky terrace, marked by hundreds of small piles of stones, mostly consisting of just three or four slabs placed on top of each other. The site was of some interest because these cairns were highly reminiscent of those we had seen on the Serabit el-Khadim plateau, at the beginning of the track leading up to the summit. Still a little disappointed, we nevertheless made a note of the coordinates of the site and were about to leave when we saw that Moussa was beckoning to us to come and see one more thing. We approached the western edge of the plateau, where a small wadi stretched for a few metres. I felt my heart racing: on a wide, flat, weather-beaten rock face, almost down at ground level, we could see dozens and dozens of engraved motifs and signs, combining together into more complex compositions. The images included large boats surmounted by archaic-style *serekh*s framing the names of kings from the beginning of Egyptian history, sometimes accompanied by hieroglyphic inscriptions that were among the earliest yet known.

I counted five discrete sections, arranged in chronological order from right to left on the rock face. These images and texts demonstrated that Egyptian mining expeditions had already been regularly passing through the area more than 500 years earlier than previously thought. The style of the earliest section of images and signs suggested a date of around 3200 BC, most likely indicating a ruler from the beginning of the Naqada IIIA period, when political control in the lower Nile Valley was just beginning to become unified. Then came compositions of Iry-Hor and Narmer, who ruled at the transition between 'Dynasty 0' and the 1st Dynasty, around 3100 BC, both of which were accompanied by hieroglyphic captions. The inscription of Iry-Hor, the penultimate ruler before Narmer, included the first mention of the city of Memphis, then known as Ineb-hedj ('The White Walls'), thus moving the date of this important city's foundation – which Herodotus attributed to Menes/Narmer – back by at least 50 years. Further to the left, the final tableau included the name of King Djer, the third ruler of the 1st Dynasty, commemorating a military triumph accomplished by him in the western Delta, and mentioning a queen-regent called Neithhotep. This text also

What could be the first sentence written in hieroglyphs: 'The Horus, he is Ity'– a detail of the rock panel of the ıst-Dynasty ruler Djer at Wadi Ameyra.

incorporates the earliest known instance of a hieroglyphic sentence taking the form of a proclamation: 'The Horus, he is Ity'. Though brief, it has been interpreted as the phrase spoken in order to confer full royal status on the king while he was still prince, calling him, somewhat exceptionally, by his 'birth name' (as opposed to his royal Horus name, Djer).

Together, these inscriptions have enabled us to amend or improve our knowledge of these first reigns of pharaonic history in a whole variety of ways – not only chronologically but also in terms of political and administrative perspectives. In the excitement of that moment, I remember thinking that I would never again make an archaeological discovery of such importance in my entire career as a researcher. This was precisely ten months before we discovered the papyri at Wadi el-Jarf.

# CHAPTER 2

# FINDING THE
# RED SEA PORTS

Certain Egyptologists long believed – and indeed some still do – that as the ancient Egyptians were essentially a farming people they were not great sailors. In order to venture beyond the Nile and out to sea they therefore had to draw on the skills and know-how of peoples more naturally suited to maritime activities, such as the inhabitants of the Levantine coast in the eastern Mediterranean. However, one of the greatest classic texts of the Middle Kingdom – known to Egyptologists as the *Tale of the Shipwrecked Sailor* – tells the story of someone setting out on a voyage across the Red Sea, which is described as Wadj-wer: literally 'The Great Green'. The sailor's aim is to reach the 'royal mines', probably the Sinai mining area. He is overtaken by a storm, and a wave 8 cubits high wrecks his ship and casts him up on a mythical island, which is clearly regarded by the ancient narrator as lying halfway between fantasy and reality. Even so the island is evidently regularly accessible to Egyptian boats sailing over the Red Sea. It is inhabited by an imaginary creature, a giant snake whose body is plated with gold and lapis lazuli and who calls himself the Lord of Punt.

The story's mythical setting has led many scholars to doubt the veracity of the events and places it contains (we do not, after all, usually seek to treat fairy tales as if they were history or geography), but criticism of the tale has often been rather excessive. Some scholars argue that there is no reference to the sea in the text, and suggest instead that 'The Great Green' (Wadj-wer) might correspond to the fertile expanses of the Nile Delta region. Similarly, these scholars also reject any possibility that the Egyptians at this date were capable of expeditions by sea to the land of Punt – a very real but much debated geographical location within the Egyptian world, discussed below. Instead, they argue that contact with Punt would have been achieved solely by sailing up the Nile. However, the identification of the remains of three ports on the Red Sea has obliged us to carefully reconsider all the evidence. Several years of excavation at each of these ports have resulted in a large body of archaeological evidence which shows that they specifically facilitated Egyptian voyages by sea, either to the coast of Sinai or the land of Punt. This therefore places the *Tale of the Shipwrecked Sailor* in a new cultural context, making its narrative seem much more plausible in terms of the geopolitics of the Middle Kingdom.

PREVIOUS PAGE
Inscriptions on a rock face overlooking Ayn Sukhna, the Red Sea port used from the time of King Khafre as a base from which to reach the Sinai mines (see pp. 44–52).

PART I   On the Trail of the Pyramid Builders

## Mersa Gawasis: a Middle Kingdom port

The first, and farthest south, of the Red Sea ports to be located was Mersa Gawasis, a short distance to the south of the modern coastal town of Safaga. It was discovered in 1976 by the Egyptian archaeologist Abd el-Moneim M. Sayed (of the University of Alexandria) who undertook two seasons of survey and excavation of the numerous pharaonic remains there, mostly found on a small rocky prominence overlooking the sea. The site included several small chapels, probably erected by teams of sailors returning from voyages across the Red Sea. Two of these structures contained commemorative stelae that provided information allowing the site to be dated to the Middle Kingdom, between the 20th and 19th centuries BC. In addition they give some indication of the reasons why Egyptians were active here at that time.

One monument, erected by an official named Ankhu, was built entirely of limestone anchors, piled up to create a kind of small votive alcove. It was decorated with stone-carved hieroglyphic texts describing an expedition sent to the land of Punt during the reign of Senwosret I, the second ruler of the 12th Dynasty (c. 1944–1900 BC). Given that various hypotheses locate Punt on the coasts of southern Sudan, Eritrea or Yemen, this set of inscriptions suggests that Mersa Gawasis could be seriously regarded as an embarkation point for long-distance expeditions intended to reach the southern reaches of the Red Sea. Another of the chapels contained the stela of the well-known vizier Antefoker, who held office during the reign of Senwosret I. Although the upper part of the text has unfortunately been lost due to erosion, his stela gives some sense of the fundamental motivations for Egyptian activities at this port. The surviving lines of the inscription can be translated as follows:

> His majesty ordered the prince, count, overseer of the city, vizier, overseer of the six courts of justice, Antefoker, to assemble this fleet from the arsenal (dockyards) of Coptos and to travel to the mining region of Punt, in order to reach it unhindered and to come back safely, with all their work having been achieved with exceptional efficiency, superior to anything that had been done in this country before. And he achieved this perfectly, according to what had been ordered by the majesty of the palace. Then the herald Ameny was on the coast of the Great Green (the sea) to assemble these boats with the great council of the Head of the South from the Thinite Nome that was with him.

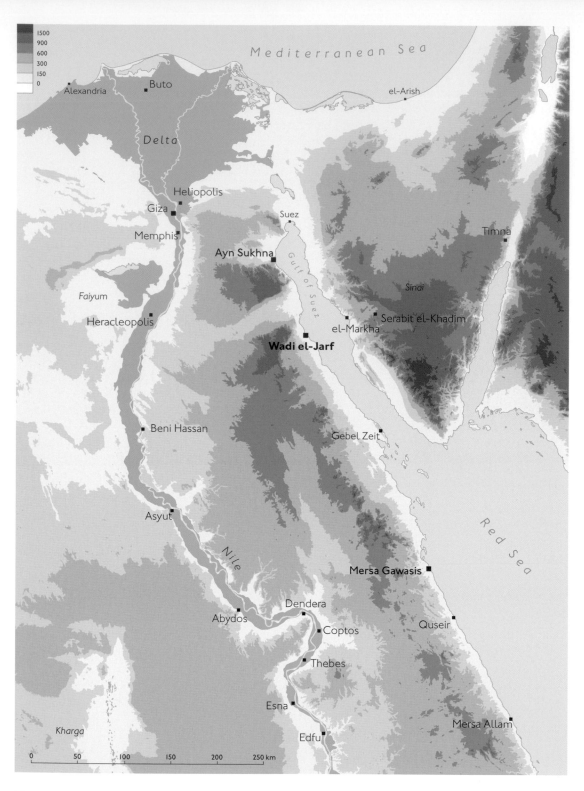

Map showing the three ancient
'intermittent ports' on the Red Sea:
Old Kingdom Wadi el-Jarf, Ayn Sukhna,
in use from the Old to Middle Kingdoms,
and Middle Kingdom Mersa Gawasis.

A small dry-stone structure at Mersa Gawasis, incorporating a stone anchor.

Detail of the Mersa Gawasis anchor.

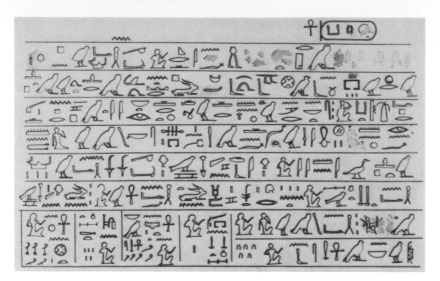

Inscription from the stela of the vizier Antefoker, who held office during the reign of the 12th-Dynasty ruler Senwosret I. Drawing by Abd el-Moneim M. Sayed.

This text focuses on two successive phases of work, showing that, in the initial stage, a fleet was assembled in dockyards in Coptos, at a point in the Nile Valley where desert tracks headed out towards the Red Sea. This fleet was then rebuilt on the coast, after it had been transported in the form of dismantled sections.

A number of Egyptologists later disputed the identification of Gawasis as a port, despite the discovery there of the texts and the marine anchors. However, renewed excavations at the site by an Italian-American team led by Rodolfo Fattovich of the University of Naples L'Orientale and Kathryn A. Bard of Boston University, beginning in 2001, provided confirmation of the maritime nature of the pharaonic activities along the coast. In 2003 this new team discovered a system of galleries cut into the limestone below the plateau where the votive shrines were located. The galleries still contained large quantities of nautical equipment, including more anchors and well-preserved coils of thick rope that had been stored there. From the same area of the site they also collected numerous pieces of wood deriving from boats, including several well-preserved rudders. The location had probably been chosen for the port because of a natural lagoon which would have sheltered the fleet from the north wind that blows regularly throughout this region. Evidence relating to the site's chronology came in the form of many more commemorative stelae, originally embedded in the cliff face in which the galleries were cut, but found by the excavators in different levels of erosion deposited at its base.

Entrance to the artificial storage galleries at Mersa Gawasis, with carved niches for commemorative stelae.

Gallery 4a/b

Gallery 3

Gallery 2

Gallery 5

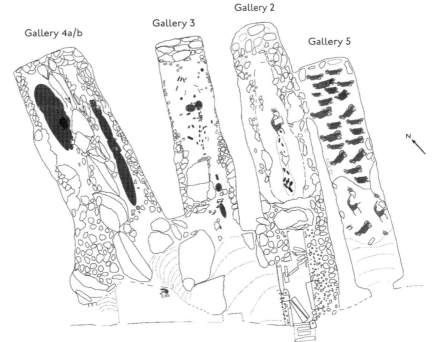

Plan of the Mersa Gawasis galleries showing the nautical material still kept inside; for instance, Gallery 5 contained large bundles of rope.

Some of the stelae included the names of kings Senwosret II and III, and Amenemhat III (the fourth, fifth and sixth rulers of the 12th Dynasty respectively), while material dating from the reign of Amenemhat IV (seventh in the sequence) has also been discovered. Clearly, the port was regularly used for most of the period between 1920 and 1785 BC. The excavations also revealed substantial evidence that confirmed the existence of direct contacts between the Egyptian coast and areas in the far south of the Red Sea at this time. Fragments of obsidian were found that can be geologically provenanced to Yemen or Ethiopia, as well as small quantities of 'exotic' pottery deriving from both Ethiopia and the Aden region of Yemen that can be accurately dated to the 2nd millennium BC. All the work so far carried out at the site therefore indicates the prolonged operation of a complex port structure, which was probably used intermittently. The galleries cut into the rock face were used to store the disassembled boats during the periods of inactivity between each of the maritime expeditions, sometimes lasting several years. In this way the ancient Egyptians were spared the effort of constantly transporting the boats back and forth from the Nile Valley each time they were required. Such a system seems to have been in operation from a very early date, as evidenced by the two other Red Sea port sites that have been identified further north in the Gulf of Suez.

## Ayn Sukhna: a port of the Old and Middle Kingdoms

The second port on the Red Sea coast to be discovered was Ayn Sukhna, located at almost exactly the same time as excavations were renewed at Mersa Gawasis in 2001 under Fattovich and Bard. Ayn Sukhna lies on the western coast of the Gulf of Suez at the end of the shortest desert route to the Red Sea from Memphis, Egypt's administrative capital for much of the pharaonic period. The site's sheltered position and the presence of a hot-water spring, which gives the area its modern Arabic name, as well as a small oasis arising from the water source, all certainly played an important role in the choice of this location. Probably from as early as the first few dynasties, Ayn Sukhna began to be used as a key intermediate staging-post along the route adopted by Egyptian mining expeditions heading to the southern Sinai Peninsula in search of copper and turquoise, some 100 km across the sea.

Ayn Sukhna first came to the attention of Egyptologists in the 1990s, when Mahmoud Abd el-Raziq (of the University of Ismailia) published an important series of inscriptions found on a rock face overlooking the site. Among these inscriptions, which dated from the Old Kingdom to the Coptic period, were the official records of missions sent during the reigns of Mentuhotep IV and Amenemhat I, at the turn of the 11th and 12th Dynasties (around 1981–1970 BC). These texts show that particularly large expeditions, involving respectively 3,000 and 4,000 men, passed through Ayn Sukhna. One of the inscriptions even refers to the specific purpose of the expedition that was being thus commemorated: 'Bring back turquoise, copper, *hesemen*, and other fine products of the desert'. The Egyptian word *hesemen* can designate several kinds of products. Here – from the context – it is likely to be either natron, found in the Red Sea/Sinai area, or bronze, which Egyptians at this time made by adding arsenic to copper.

Another in this group, dating to the 9th year of the reign of Senwosret I, mentions that an official was sent to the 'mining land

Rock stela at Ayn Sukhna of the 12th-Dynasty ruler Amenemhat III.

An inscription at Ayn Sukhna of the 11th-Dynasty ruler Mentuhotep IV.

of the King of Upper and Lower Egypt, Kheperkare', a recognized term for the Sinai region from which the Egyptians extracted mineral wealth. Moreover, a small rock-cut stela, dated to the second year of Amenemhat III's reign, provides us with the names of several individual expedition members, at least one of whom, 'the repeller of scorpions, Ity son of Isis', reappears in inscriptions found at Wadi Maghara in Sinai. Inscriptions dating from the later reigns of Amenhotep I and Amenhotep III show that the port at Ayn Sukhna was still visited during the 18th Dynasty (1539–1295 BC) at least occasionally. A man named Panehsy, overseer of an expedition, is twice mentioned at Ayn Sukhna, and his presence is also recorded at the Serabit el-Khadim mining site, establishing a further connection between this coastal port and the mining area of South Sinai.

The excavations undertaken by our joint team from IFAO and the University of Paris-Sorbonne in 2001 soon revealed a large-scale settlement at Ayn Sukhna, extending westwards for 400 m inland from the Red Sea coast up to the Gebel el-Galala el-Bahariya mountain, the peak of which reaches an altitude of about 1,000 m. The upper (western) part of the site is dominated by a set of ten large storage galleries cut into the sandstone at the foot of the rock face bearing the inscriptions at a height of about 14 m asl. These galleries varied between 14 and 24 m in length, with an average width and height of 2.5–3 m and 1.8–2 m respectively. The earliest examples were created in the Old Kingdom, between the second half of the 4th Dynasty and the 5th Dynasty. Just as at Mersa Gawasis, the galleries were clearly used to store dismantled seagoing boats *in situ* during the periods between each of the expeditions. Some of their walls still bore official inscriptions (either written in ink or carved into the stone), commemorating the passage of expeditions through the site, notably in the time of the 5th-Dynasty rulers Niuserre (specifically in the year corresponding to the 2nd census of his reign) and Djedkare-Isesi (in the year of his 7th census). The Djedkare-Isesi texts also include what is so far the first known mention of the term *kebenet*-boats (translating literally as 'Byblos-style boats'), which seem to have been particularly used for the longest seafaring expeditions. Seal impressions of many Old Kingdom rulers (Khafre, Sahure, Niuserre, Djedkare-Isesi, Unas, Pepi I and Pepi II) were also discovered in the galleries, demonstrating the regular use of the site throughout most of the Old Kingdom over a period of more than three centuries (*c*. 2597–2260 BC).

During the Middle Kingdom, nine of the ten galleries at Ayn Sukhna were brought back into service at various times, having been abandoned during the First Intermediate Period (*c*. 2250–2045 BC), a time of crisis and political division for the rulers of Egypt. In some cases the gallery ceilings partially collapsed during the time they were not in use. The renewed activity usually took place a few metres from the original entrance, so a new access corridor was generally created, consisting of low mud-brick walls fitted with a door set within a wooden threshold and door-frame. The galleries' functions seem to have varied, with some obviously serving as stores for different foodstuffs, while the adjoining galleries G2 and G9 were both clearly used as boat storage buildings since each contained a dismantled vessel. On the basis of the ceramic assemblage in the stratigraphic level associated with the boats they can be precisely dated to the beginning of the 12th Dynasty.

Within the map:

60.00
55.00
50.00
45.00
40.00
35.00
30.00
25.00
20.00
G1
Memorial
15.00
G11  G6
G3
G9  G7
G2      G5
G4
G8
G10
barrage
S122
10.00

ABOVE Topographical map of the system of storage galleries at Ayn Sukhna, in use for some three centuries during the Old Kingdom (from Khafre to Pepi II), and periodically during the Middle Kingdom. It was even visited occasionally as late as the New Kingdom, c. 1350 BC.

OPPOSITE, ABOVE Plan of the galleries at Ayn Sukhna and of the rectangular building built around three of them. The archaeological remains found within the galleries are shown, including the remnants of two dismantled ships in G2 and G9, which were stored there and later burned by looters.

OPPOSITE, BELOW Official inscription of 5th-Dynasty ruler Djedkare-Isesi at the entrance of Ayn Sukhna gallery G1. It refers to a general Sed-Hetep, who also appears in a similar inscription found at Wadi Maghara, the turquoise mine in Sinai, giving the number of 1,400 men involved in this expedition.

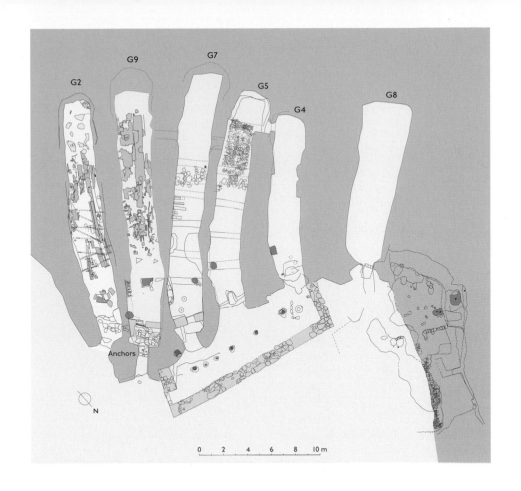

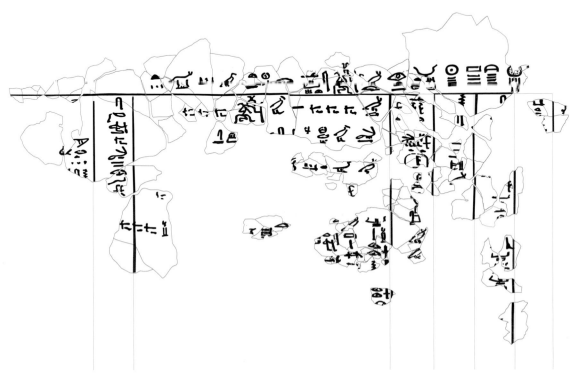

Seal impressions of various Old Kingdom rulers – from left to right, top to bottom: Khafre, Niuserre, Unas and Pepi I – found in the storage galleries at Ayn Sukhna.

Two Old Kingdom anchors stored at the entrance to gallery G9 at Ayn Sukhna.

Remains of a burnt boat in gallery G9, one of two found at Ayn Sukhna.

The two boats in G2 and G9 had been carefully taken to pieces after their last use, and their thick cedar planks, each averaging 10 cm thick and 30 cm wide, were stored in piles, sometimes roped together into bundles. Great care was taken in storing these valuable components in order to ensure their preservation: the larger pieces were lifted up above the ground on small wooden rods (perhaps reused oar-handles) to insulate them from contact with the moisture in the soil below. They were also covered with plant-fibre mats to protect them from sand and dust. Following a previous incident of looting, in the course of which some of the other items kept in the galleries had been thrown outside, the two boats had been deliberately burned at the beginning of the Middle Kingdom. This destruction probably took place shortly after the major expeditions that were sent out during the reigns of Mentuhotep IV and Amenemhat I. Paradoxical as it may seem, the burning of these vessels actually allows us to understand more clearly the details of how they had been stored and the techniques used to assemble them. The heat generated by the burning planks caused the roofs of the two galleries to collapse onto them, which in turn smothered the combustion and thus helped to preserve the original forms of the stored boat parts, while simultaneously sealing the archaeological deposit for posterity. Patrice Pomey, a specialist on ancient boats, has studied the scale of these vessels – mostly comprising sections of the hull – and estimates that the original fully assembled boats would each have been about 14–15 m in length. From all the evidence it can be concluded that the remains discovered at Ayn Sukhna include the oldest known seafaring boats found in a maritime setting. Other examples of ships have been discovered in funerary or religious contexts, such as the boats, possibly solar barques, found similarly disassembled next to the Great Pyramid of Khufu.

In the lower (eastern) part of the site, in a very large zone bordering the coastline, an area of occupation emerged. Buildings constructed from dry-stone walls were associated with evidence of craftwork, food production and habitation. Camps were established in this zone from the Old Kingdom onwards. A large-scale facility, 'Kom 14', undoubtedly functioned as the headquarters during this phase of occupation. A large boat-shaped pit dug into the ground, the exact purpose of which remains unknown, was probably used during the process of assembling or dismantling the boats at the site. At the beginning of the Middle Kingdom – probably contemporary

View of the large facility known as 'Kom 14' at
Ayn Sukhna, probably used as a headquarters
by the expedition leaders.

with the official inscriptions of Mentuhotep IV and Amenemhat I
carved in the rock-face overlooking the site – the whole area
experienced a major change of use. Metallurgical workshops enabled
the *in situ* smelting of copper ore, probably imported from Sinai, and
small cell-like residential buildings were constructed, sometimes
built up against formations of so-called 'pudding stone', a type of
conglomerate rock deriving from the ancient coastline. Numerous
hearths were used for baking bread, and a multitude of grain-storage
vessels were also discovered in these occupation strata.

The excavations undertaken at Ayn Sukhna therefore identified
a second intermittent Red Sea port, obviously organized on the
same basis as the one at Mersa Gawasis. Ayn Sukhna seems to
have taken over from the port of Wadi el-Jarf, which we discovered
subsequently, as the main Red Sea port, perhaps because it was
closer to the ancient Egyptian capital. It also operated over a much
longer period, covering about a millennium, between the middle of
the 4th Dynasty (*c.* 2600 BC) and the late 18th Dynasty (*c.* 1350 BC).

A boat pit at the foot of
'Kom 14' at Ayn Sukhna.

## Wadi el-Jarf: King Khufu's port

Wadi el-Jarf lies on the western coast of the Gulf of Suez, about
100 km south of Ayn Sukhna and 23 km south of the modern city of
Zafarana. From the shore, the coast of the Sinai Peninsula is visible
on the horizon, and a fortress was built by the Egyptians at Tell Ras
Budran (el-Markha), at the point directly across the sea, 50 km away.
This was the last of the three pharaonic ports on the Red Sea to be
formally identified when our team began work there in 2011, but it
is perhaps the earliest in date, with activity there concentrated in
the reign of King Khufu. As previously remarked, the port's remains
had been noted at least twice before, the first time in 1823, when
the English explorer Sir John Gardner Wilkinson made a brief
exploration there, and then in the 1950s, when it was examined by
two pilots, François Bissey and René Chabot-Morisseau, who were
based in the Gulf of Suez. However, these earlier explorers of the
site misinterpreted its essential characteristics, being misled both
by the relative proximity of the site to the Coptic monastery of
St Paul and by the fact that the most significant remains at Wadi
el-Jarf were situated so far from the sea. Wilkinson identified it as

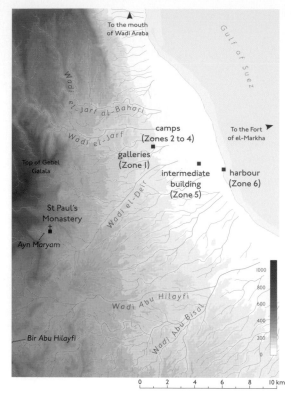

Map showing the location of the different parts of the Wadi el-Jarf site, from the storage galleries inland to the harbour with its jetty on the Red Sea.

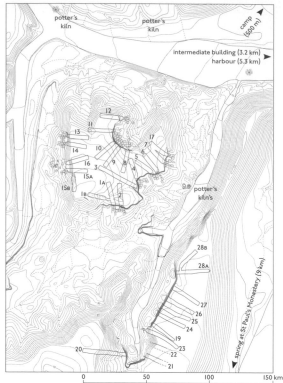

Plan of the system of storage galleries cut into the limestone escarpment at Wadi el-Jarf.

a Greco-Roman necropolis, and the two French pilots viewed it as a mining site, but were unable to ascertain the mineral that was supposedly being extracted.

Fortunately, knowledge of pharaonic activities on the Red Sea has progressed a great deal since the 1950s. Even before the beginning of our own archaeological study of the site, three years after we had relocated it in 2008, it was already obvious to us that the facilities corresponded in every way with the major features now recognizable as characteristic of Egyptian ports on the Red Sea, with Mersa Gawasis and Ayn Sukhna forming the main blueprints.

Remains at the site at Wadi el-Jarf are spread across an area extending over a little more than 5 km between the coast and the first mountainous peaks forming the edges of the South Galala massif. Moving from west to east the site includes a number of different elements. First, there are the 31 galleries cut into the limestone rock, which can themselves be divided into two groups: 19 radiate out from a small limestone mound, while further south another 12 were dug into the slopes of a south–north wadi. Secondly, about 500 m east of the gallery area and constructed on top of the rocky hills that dominate the area is a set of encampments, securely dated to the beginning of the 4th Dynasty by surface ceramics. Thirdly, at a distance of 2 km from the shore, in the centre of the vast plain adjoining the coast, an area with a very rough topography, rutted by numerous wadis, is a large rectangular structure (60 × 40 m), labelled the 'intermediate building'. Built of dry-stone walls and almost buried in sand, it was subdivided into 13 elongated sections, 3.3 m to 3.7 m wide, and was certainly created for residential purposes. After excavation, all the occupation levels in this structure were dated to the beginning of the 4th Dynasty. Finally, on the coast itself are the port facilities, as well as a further significant area of settlement and storage buildings.

Excavations at Wadi el-Jarf began in 2011 and have so far mainly focused on the gallery zone and the set of structures on the coast. After 9 seasons of fieldwork, 23 of the galleries have been explored. These vary in length from roughly 16 to 34 m and were carved out of the rock to a considerable height and width (ranging from 2.2 to 2.5 m and 3 to 3.5 m respectively). Almost all the galleries contained

Kite view of the rectangular structure we labelled the 'intermediate building' at Wadi el-Jarf after excavation.

View of the Wadi el-Jarf galleries photographed from a kite,
with galleries G1 and G2 at left and G4–G6 centre right.

large quantities of fragments of wood and cordage, confirming their likely use as stores for dismantled boats. Most featured small internal transverse walls, each usually comprising a single layer of limestone blocks embedded in a slot cut into the bedrock of the gallery floor. These walls seem to have been part of the method of storage by serving as supports below the wooden boat-planks, thus insulating them from contact with moisture from the ground. Rather than containing boats, some galleries served specifically for the storage of large quantities of locally produced pottery vessels. Very often marked with the names of the specific work-gangs for whom they were intended, these jars would have been used to hold supplies on the boats.

Access to each of the galleries had been carefully sealed up at the time of their last use. The initial stage took the form of positioning a stone block to narrow the entrance. In the second stage a system usually of large blocks of limestone was set in front to form a narrow corridor. One or more stone portcullis blocks were then inserted into the corridor in order to seal up the gallery completely, reminiscent of the plugging blocks used to seal passages in Old Kingdom pyramids. It was in a pit between two portcullis blocks sealing the entrance to one of the galleries that we discovered the most significant cache of papyri. One of the gallery-blocking systems still incorporated a slipway or access ramp formed of wooden rails beneath the large stones. Numerous control marks mentioning work-gangs had been inscribed on these massive blocks of limestone before they were placed in front of the galleries. The most commonly found mark refers to a group of workers called 'Khufu Brings it (i.e. a ship) his Two Uraei', providing further proof that the activities took place during Khufu's reign. In the areas in front of the galleries – especially within the filling of the gallery-blockage system – many other types of material were excavated, including fragments of boats (such as a 'midship frame', 2.95 m wide, found in front of the G5 gallery), as well as large quantities of pottery and fragments of textiles.

Excavation of the facilities on the seashore, 180 m from the coast, revealed a very large complex comprising two rectangular buildings constructed of stones held together with mortar. The two structures, which were probably contemporary, were built in parallel along a west–east axis, with their rear walls to the north in order to shelter the interior from the prevailing winds and prevent

Views from the outside and inside showing how gallery G1 was closed off.

Slipway or access ramp formed of wooden rails at the entrance to gallery G5.

them being sanded up. Originally they would have been roofed with light materials supported by wooden posts, the post-holes for which were clearly seen in the excavations. The general plan of these buildings is typical of known storage spaces for early Old Kingdom expeditions. All the finds in this coastal area, especially the huge quantities of pottery in lower occupation levels that had been locally manufactured in the 'galleries' zone, demonstrate that the buildings date to the beginning of the 4th Dynasty. The northern building consisted of five parallel rooms, each measuring around 20 m long on their east–west axis and with widths varying from 12.5 to 15 m. Numerous seal-impressions bearing both the 'Horus name' and cartouche of Khufu (and sometimes mentioning the name of his pyramid complex, 'Horizon of Khufu') were discovered on the original ground surface of each of the rooms. As well as providing dating for the building, these also suggest that this facility was specifically used to store various products in sealed bags or boxes.

The southern building also consisted of a row of ten parallel rooms, oriented north–south and opening at the southern end, with a length of 36.25 m and widths ranging from 7.6 to 8.5 m. This complex seems to have been used for housing and domestic activities, as indicated by the presence of numerous hearths, both in the entrances of the rooms and across a large open area south of the building. In the area between the northern and southern buildings an assemblage of more than 100 stone anchors was found where they had been carefully collected during the final phase of use of the two complexes. Some of the anchors, which vary widely in shape, still had ropes tied to them, presumably originally used to attach them to the boats. A significant number also bear marks in red or black ink, probably indications of the name of the boat for which they were intended, or the name of the work-gang that was responsible for it. Already in the early part of the Old Kingdom, sand had encroached and almost entirely engulfed the stores. A more modest rectangular structure was then built in the southeastern corner of the area using stone blocks taken from the earlier constructions. In the northeastern part of the area, some remains of small cellular installations, consisting of two rooms side by side, also belong to this second phase of Old Kingdom occupation, which still clearly dates to the 4th Dynasty.

Finally, one of the most remarkable elements of the Wadi el-Jarf site is a large L-shaped mole or jetty, ingeniously constructed

Control mark on one of the gallery blocking stones naming the team of the workers of the boat called 'Khufu Brings it his Two Uraei'.

The landward part of the Wadi el-Jarf harbour jetty after excavation.

During the final phase of occupation at Wadi el-Jarf, more than 100 anchors had been carefully collected and deposited between the two rectangular buildings that made up the shoreline settlement.

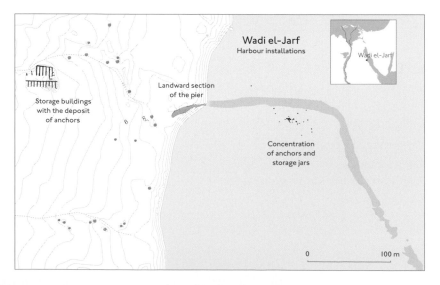

Wadi el-Jarf
Harbour installations

Wadi el-Jarf

Landward section
of the pier

Storage buildings
with the deposit
of anchors

Concentration
of anchors and
storage jars

0          100 m

General map of the camps and the jetty or pier and settlement facilities on the seashore at Wadi el-Jarf.

at a point on the coast where an opening in the coral formation is situated directly in front of the shore. At the end of the 2015 season we were able to obtain a complete picture of the jetty, thanks to the excavation of its landward section, which had been totally preserved by sand. The west–east leg (the most significant structural section) of the jetty measures 205 m in length, providing protection against the prevailing wind which generally comes from the north in the Gulf of Suez; the other section, running roughly north to south/southeast, stretches for a further 200 m. At the point where the jetty joins the shore it is about 6 m wide on average, and it is possible to see how its north face was built up using large limestone pebbles in a succession of slightly concave layers, about 6 m in length. The interior of the jetty consisted of finer material bonded together with clay, firmly packed and compacted at the time it was built. A zone of calm water extending for about 5 ha is created by the whole structure.

Within the arm of the jetty, a group of 23 anchors was found resting on the original seabed, at a current depth of about 1.5 m. Associated with them were many of the locally produced pottery storage vessels (ten of which have been recorded so far) that had probably been lost during the time that the port was active. Their presence provides further confirmation that the jetty and the anchors were part of the same port operation as the encampments located not far from the coast, and the set of storage galleries excavated a further 5.5 km west. All the evidence ties together and points to the fact that this remote site is the earliest known open-sea port complex in the world (c. 2630 BC).

## The Red Sea ports and expeditions for raw materials

We now know of three ancient ports on Egypt's Red Sea coast, clearly demonstrating that the Egyptians were already able to conduct seaborne expeditions at a very early stage in their history. These facilities were in use only periodically, when major expeditions were organized and sent out by the pharaonic rulers, often several years apart, and are therefore now known as 'intermittent ports'. But what drove the Egyptians to go to so much effort to build these port facilities in remote places far across the desert from the main centres of population? The answer lies in their great need for raw materials, which were essential for the proper functioning of the state – particularly the copper needed for the tools crucial in the construction of monuments, especially the giant pyramids that were being built at that time. The main exploitable deposits of copper lay in a mining zone in the southwestern Sinai Peninsula, across the Red Sea from these ports. The boats to transport the workers to mine and collect the copper had first to be taken apart and transported in sections from the Nile Valley to the coast via tracks crossing the Eastern Desert, in what must have been long and arduous operations. In between the missions, the systems of galleries found at all three sites so far identified facilitated the on-site storage and safekeeping of the necessary equipment, including the boats themselves.

Sinai was indisputably the main target of these maritime expeditions, which regularly crossed the Gulf of Suez from at least the reign of Sneferu at the beginning of the 4th Dynasty. But it is also certain that boats setting out from the Red Sea ports had a greater range, and could have also voyaged to more remote destinations. The land of Punt – located somewhere at the southern end of the Red Sea and a place regarded by Egyptians as being on the edge of the known world – was probably initially one of the intended destinations for such expeditions. This is particularly evident in the case of Mersa Gawasis, where an abundance of written documentation explicitly refers to Punt. There is little doubt that it was also true for Ayn Sukhna, where – at a time when the port at Mersa Gawasis did not yet exist – we see the arrival of exotic products that clearly derive from southern sources (unworked obsidian and pottery characteristic of south Sudan or Ethiopia). Such a connection is also very likely to have existed at Wadi el-Jarf, from the beginning of the 4th Dynasty onwards, although the land of Punt is not yet identified in surviving textual sources from this period. However, the first Egyptian written references to incense (*senetjer*) and myrrh (*antiu*), two of the most characteristic products of the Puntite region, appear at precisely the time of the reigns of Sneferu and Khufu, when the Wadi el-Jarf site was in use, and this may not be a simple coincidence.

Another piece of evidence may be significant in this respect. Fragments of ebony were frequently identified in an archaeobotanical study conducted by Claire Newton during the 2019 Wadi el-Jarf excavation season. This prized wood was clearly sometimes used for the manufacture of artifacts, but we have also found unworked logs, perhaps raw materials transported from the southern extremes of the Red Sea. Ebony – its modern name actually derives from the Egyptian word *hbni* – is (along with obsidian, incense and exotic animal skins) one of the most representative products involved in Egyptian trade to the south with Africa and with the Indian Ocean. Such trade existed from the earliest periods of Egyptian history. The discovery of ebony at Wadi el-Jarf is the first known indication of possible contact with the Bab el-Mandab region, located at the southernmost tip of the Red Sea, where this type of valuable product may have been obtained via 'indirect exchange', as commercial roads connected people in this area.

All these discoveries of pharaonic remains along the Red Sea coast, primarily made within the last 20 years, now indicate that the Egyptians, rather than being inexperienced and reluctant sailors, seem to have acquired a high level of experience in maritime navigation. They must also have possessed great logistical skills in order to maintain these strategic coastal installations for more than a thousand years. Their most regular expeditions from the Gulf of Suez coast were to southern Sinai, which can in effect be described as 'shuttle journeys' from the ports at Ayn Sukhna and Wadi el-Jarf across the Red Sea. Their purpose was to efficiently supply the expeditionary troops and ensure they were supported and fed for periods of several months as they worked in the copper and turquoise mines. In addition, these same port facilities were no doubt occasionally used for the organization of much more adventurous operations, in search of exotic imports from the very fringes of the ancient Egyptian universe.

# WHY THE RED SEA AND THE PYRAMIDS ARE LINKED

# CHAPTER 3

# THE QUEST FOR COPPER
## The Crucial Mines in Sinai and their Role in Building the Pyramids

At the beginning of the 4th Dynasty, as in most other periods of pharaonic history, copper was the most strategic resource for Egypt. (Bronze, made from alloying tin with copper, only came into widespread use in Egypt from the 11th Dynasty onwards, i.e. from the Middle Kingdom.) Copper was essential both for weapons and for the tools employed in different areas of Egyptian craftwork. It was used, for instance, both for carpenters' blades and saws, especially for boatbuilding, and for the small picks and chisels with which blocks of stone were quarried for the monumental constructions of the time. In the period when the huge pyramids of Sneferu and Khufu were being built, there was even greater need for copper, for the small chisels with which masons dressed the vast areas of pyramid casing blocks and the saws used to guide the quartz sand that did the actual cutting of the hard stones that copper is too soft to work, as described at the end of this chapter.

The pharaonic state was therefore regularly obliged to organize major expeditions into the desert areas that surrounded Egypt in order to obtain sufficient quantities of this raw material. There are copper mines in the Egyptian Eastern Desert, and some deposits

The mine at Wadi Kharig (OPPOSITE) was one of the sources of copper in South Sinai exploited by the ancient Egyptians (see pp. 71–73).

The importance of copper to the Old Kingdom Egyptians is revealed in Papyrus K from Wadi el-Jarf (BELOW). This accounts document lists the delivery, seemingly to the site, of not only different foods – dates, wheat, fish and fowl – but also copper adzes, chisels and picks. These tools were no doubt used in aspects of shipbuilding at this harbour site on the Red Sea coast.

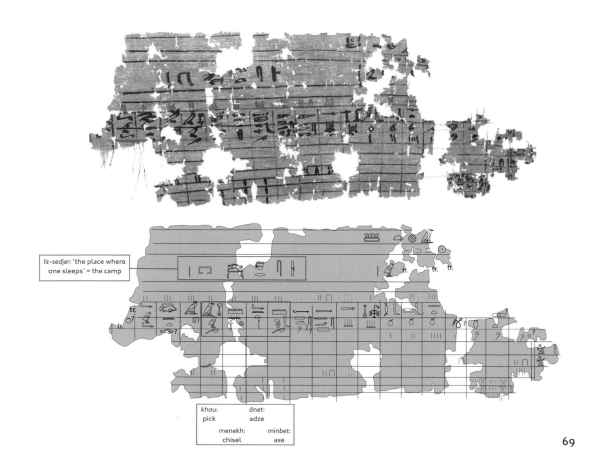

Is-sedjer: 'the place where one sleeps' = the camp

khau:
pick

ānet:
adze

menekh:
chisel

minbet:
axe

69

A miners' camp in Wadi Araba in Egypt's Eastern Desert, where deposits of copper were exploited during the 3rd and 4th Dynasties.

in particular were exploited in ancient times in the Wadi Araba, a natural route leading directly to Wadi el-Jarf. Archaeologists have known about extraction sites in this region, dating to much of the 3rd and 4th Dynasties, since the beginning of the 21st century. Remains of dry-stone shelters have been identified, sometimes with rooms arranged like the teeth of a comb (or 'comb-style') that are to some extent comparable with the buildings found at Wadi el-Jarf, as well as tools and pottery that date to the same periods. Exploitation of copper sources is even more significant in the southern part of the region, at sites such as Wadi Umm Balad and Wadi Dara, at around the same latitude as the modern town of Ras Gharib on the Red Sea coast. Both copper and gold were extracted in a very large area around the Wadi Hammamat, another major axis passing through the Eastern Desert, at the level of the ancient city of Coptos. Copper mining at all these sites generally coincided with the very beginning of Egyptian history, and the most important remains usually date to a period stretching from the Naqada III period through to the 4th Dynasty (*c.* 3200–2600 BC). In some cases, the mineral deposits had already been virtually worked out at this early stage of pharaonic history, a vivid sign of the Egyptian state's drastic need for copper at this time.

Undoubtedly, however, it was in the southwestern part of the Sinai Peninsula (to the east of the coastal towns of Abu Zenima and Abu Rodeis) that the most significant copper deposits were being exploited by the Egyptians. Their activities there meant that they had no need to resort to international trade in order to gain access to this crucial material. Although the commemorative texts set up in this region, especially at Wadi Maghara, mostly refer to turquoise – the precious stone that also could be mined in this area (and that provided the popular toponym for the region: 'Terraces of Turquoise') – it was undoubtedly copper that was the true raison d'être for these operations. It is not known for certain which were the main Sinai deposits being exploited by the Egyptians at the very beginning of their history, but some, such as the mines at Wadi Kharig and Bir Nasb, have been securely identified, especially from the 5th Dynasty onwards. It is likely, however, that most of the remains that might have revealed the early history of this exploitation are now lost. An immense area in the region of Gebel Umm Bogma, to the south of Bir Nasb, could well have been the epicentre of such mining activity, but it is in this very region that manganese – which occurs in exactly the same geological horizons as copper – has been intensively extracted since the beginning of the 20th century to such an extent that the actual landscape has been completely transformed. No archaeological survey can be realistically attempted in this region now, and so this crucial piece of our potential knowledge of the expeditions that might have been sent here at the beginning of Egyptian history has vanished. On the other hand, a survey undertaken by us (Pierre and Damien Laisney) in this region in the first decade of the 21st century revealed evidence, further to the north, of several places where the 'reduction' of malachite (a copper carbonate mineral) had taken place in ancient times. This is a chemical procedure that involved roasting the mineral to obtain the metallic copper. Indeed, this type of copper-ore processing seems to have occurred regularly throughout the Old Kingdom.

One particular set of archaeological remains we discovered in 2009 sheds light on the impressive scale of activities possibly existing when the major pyramids were being built in the early 4th Dynasty. At the site of Seh Nasb, located at the mouth of a large

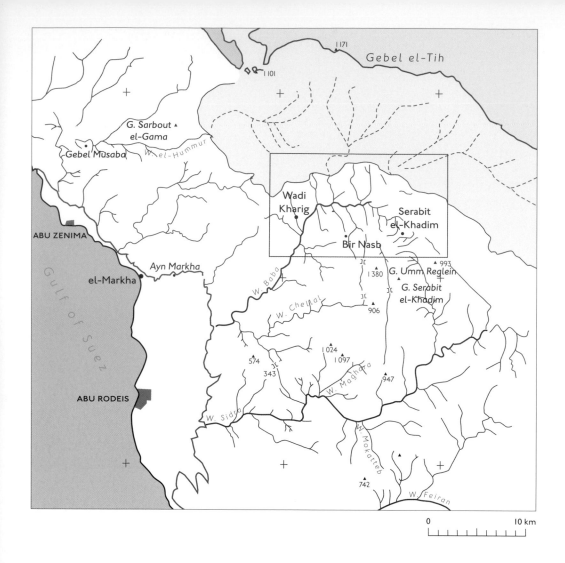

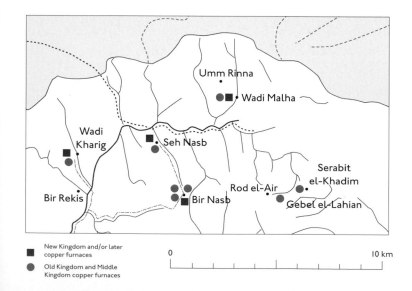

■ New Kingdom and/or later
copper furnaces

● Old Kingdom and Middle
Kingdom copper furnaces

Map of the mines of South
Sinai in the Old Kingdom.

A miner's pick, found at Wadi Kharig.

View of a mine at Wadi Kharig, where seams of copper ore are easily visible (RIGHT).

General view of the site of Seh Nasb from Gebel el-Lahian. What appear to be dry-stone walls are in fact furnaces, up to 80 m long, for the smelting of copper. We estimated the presence of at least 3,000 smelting units, indicating the working of copper ore on a vast scale.

wadi running from north to south through the ancient mining zone of South Sinai, an absolutely staggering number of furnaces created to smelt copper ore were uncovered. They were situated not in the immediate environs of the mines where the ore was being extracted but on a natural platform exposed to the changing prevailing winds, where the smelting operation could be carried out virtually continuously. Seh Nasb also sits at the junction of several transport axes, facilitating the supply of the raw materials needed for the smelting process.

The furnaces at the site are organized into large installations or batteries, sometimes comprising groups of several hundred. In each group, individual furnaces are arranged in a rough grid pattern, and oriented in different directions, mostly north–south or east–west, with smelting units systematically placed on both sides of each furnace. We counted a total of 28 of these groups of furnaces, the smallest of which extended for about 11 m while the most extensive

stretched for as much as 80 m. The total length of the entire set of furnace groups was around 1 km – a very considerable area. As part of our overall survey project we excavated some of the groups of furnaces, which turned out to be much better preserved than they had initially seemed from the visible surface remains. In each case an initial supporting wall was constructed, forming the centre of the group and also providing its orientation. On either side of this central core small dry-stone box-like structures were built, each measuring 30 × 30 cm and each supported at the back by a slab which served as the base of a hearth. They were separated from one another by uprights at right angles to the orientation of the group as a whole. Each furnace was around 60 cm in height. The natural wind action penetrating through a 20 × 20 cm square opening in the side of each furnace raised the temperature and drove the smelting process. A similar-sized square opening at the top of the furnace was used to fuel it. On average there were about 3.5 furnaces per linear metre, from which it can be calculated that at this site alone there was an exceptional concentration of more than 3,000 furnaces,

Closer view of a battery of furnaces at Seh Nasb.

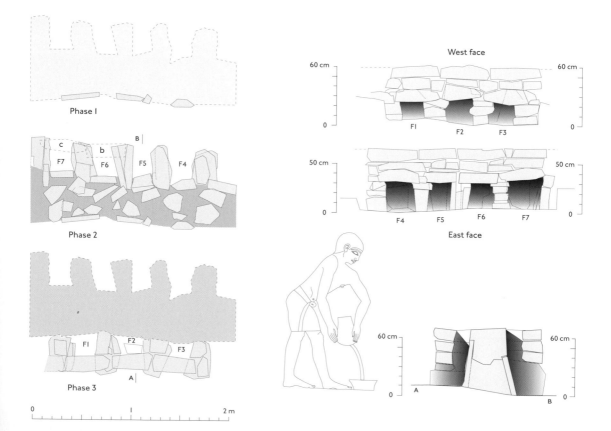

Phase I

Phase 2

B

c

b

F7    F6    F5    F4

Phase 3

F1    F2    F3

A

0        1        2 m

West face

60 cm

60 cm

F1    F2    F3

0    0

50 cm

50 cm

F4    F5    F6    F7

0    0

East face

60 cm

60 cm

A    B

0    0

which suggests an almost industrial scale of ancient exploitation of copper ore.

Many questions still remain. For instance, where would the combustible materials required to fuel such large-scale processing have been sourced? The smelting took place in Sinai itself, close to the actual mining areas, but wood was probably rare in the peninsula even at this early stage of Egyptian history. The timber needed was therefore probably brought by teams from the Nile Valley on the boats operating from the Red Sea ports. What quantities of copper were being processed in such huge areas of furnaces? The almost total absence of slag across the entire Seh Nasb site makes this aspect of the operations difficult to evaluate. A modern reconstruction of the furnaces, undertaken by Philippe Fluzin at the Ayn Sukhna archaeological site, has, however, demonstrated the great efficiency of these simple structures in terms of processing the ore. Using only natural ventilation, temperatures higher than 1200° C (2192° F) were easily achieved, and the furnaces performed well in terms of their metal product, with only a low level of slag observable in them at the end of the experimental smelting process. Although it has still not been possible to date the Seh Nasb installation more precisely within the Old Kingdom, its unusually ambitious size, organization and scale inevitably connect it closely with the immense achievements of early 4th-Dynasty Egypt. It was of course a period when the requirements of the major state construction projects meant the demand for copper reached completely new heights.

## The role of copper in building the pyramids

Indeed, the builders of the gigantic pyramids of the 4th Dynasty, from Sneferu (*c.* 2675–2633 BC) to Menkaure (*c.* 2572–2551 BC), must have amassed more copper at the sites of Meidum, Dahshur and Giza than was being accumulated anywhere else in the world during these generations. In excavations at Giza of the pyramid builders' settlement and infrastructure by AERA (Ancient Egypt Research Associates), led by one of us (Mark), copper objects, though not very numerous, are scattered throughout. At the Heit el-Ghurab site (also known as the 'Lost City of the Pyramids' or 'Workers' Town'), AERA team members have found about 60 copper objects, mostly small objects of everyday life – needles, weaving points, fish

Part of a battery of furnaces for copper smelting at Seh Nasb after excavation.

Plan (left) showing the construction phases of the furnaces: (1) the stone wall at the back of the furnaces, dividing the two rows; (2) the development of the west face; and (3) the final development of the east face. Reconstructions of the excavated battery of furnaces at Seh Nasb (right), showing the east and west faces along with a cross-section of a single furnace, with figure shown for scale.

hooks, two bracelets, a possible blade, beads and an arrowhead, with needles and points in the majority. A complex of galleries or 'comb-style' buildings, elongated structures arranged like the teeth of a comb, occupies the centre and the majority of the area of the Heit el-Ghurab site. We have interpreted these galleries as barracks, and the fact we find small items of copper throughout suggests that worker/boat crews of about 40 men, like the gangs in the Wadi el-Jarf Papyri, would have been provisioned with copper implements.

Copper also turned up in our excavations of another 'comb-building' – the set of galleries that stretch for 450 m west of the Khafre Pyramid, which Flinders Petrie called Workmen's Barracks, our Area C. The comb-buildings also have parallels at Wadi el-Jarf and distant quarry and mining sites. In the periphery of the Egyptian state, however, rather than at Giza, its core, these buildings are less formal. In the Area C galleries, which range between 2.5 and 3 m wide and are just under 30 m long, excavation revealed no internal domestic structures such as we find in the larger Heit el-Ghurab galleries, which are 4.6 to 4.7 m wide and 35 to 50 m long. Material culture from Area C suggests that people occupied mainly the entrances of this state-planned comb-building, where they carried out craftwork and hard-stone sculpture.

Pieces of copper occurred throughout the Area C excavation units: nondescript fragments and small copper 'nails' or pins and a needle. A particular concentration was found at the entrance end of gallery C11, at the southern end of the complex. Here 21 pieces appear to have been broken from a thin, flat strip. The scraps of copper, pieces of malachite, a piece of copper ore and a pottery sherd with 'slag' adhering to it made us wonder whether the occupants produced small copper objects in the open front areas of the galleries. But other tangible evidence of copper-working, such as crucibles, *tuyères* (blow pipes for increasing the heat in the smelter or furnace), moulds, waste, slag and other metalworking tools, is lacking.

Abd el-Aziz Saleh and his team from Cairo University also found possible traces of copper working in an industrial settlement on the southeast rim of the quarry southeast of the Menkaure Pyramid during excavations in the 1970s. House-like structures with ovens surround a wide, open court where builders left large pieces of raw alabaster. On the north side of the court Saleh found a row of 12 horseshoe-shaped hearths or ovens, suggestive of the kind of industrial processing of copper seen at Seh Nasb – although there

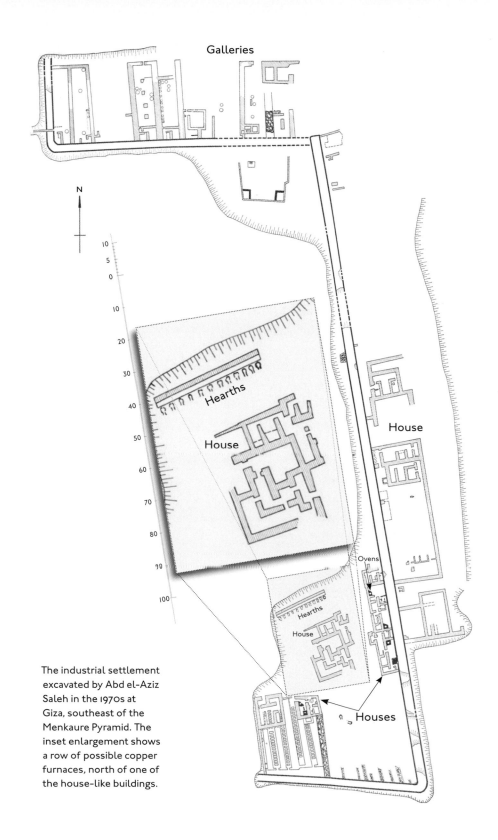

Galleries

N

Hearths

House

House

Ovens

Hearths

House

Houses

The industrial settlement
excavated by Abd el-Aziz
Saleh in the 1970s at
Giza, southeast of the
Menkaure Pyramid. The
inset enlargement shows
a row of possible copper
furnaces, north of one of
the house-like buildings.

the hearths are small box-like structures. Saleh interpreted the Giza hearths as being used for food production, though he also noted apparent copper ore – possibly malachite – in association with 'three shallow cavities of which one measures 75 × 65 × 15 cm and another 30 × 20 × 10 cm while the third is featureless'. Can these be compared to the Seh Nasb box hearths, each measuring 30 × 30 cm? Two big circular hearths were also found by Saleh nearby.

At Giza, we have found no evidence of the quasi-industrial smelting of copper ore on the scale of Seh Nasb because the pyramid-builders carried that processing out at the source, near mines in Sinai and other peripheral places. Instead, the royal house appears to have supplied workers at the site of construction with copper tools that were already processed – like the ready-ground cereal grain and prepared stone and flint tools that were also provided. The frequency overall at Giza of small copper objects and small-scale copper works tells us that copper was abundant, ubiquitous and widely distributed.

Copper was costly both to obtain and to process, and so it must have been conveyed by state teams recorded in the Wadi el-Jarf Papyri, like Merer's. Egyptologists, though, do not agree on precisely how rare and precious copper was. Model and real tools,

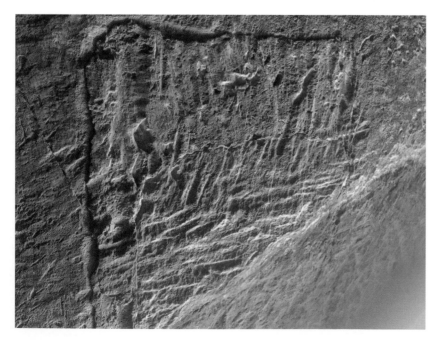

Marks made by copper chisels in the Grand Gallery of the Great Pyramid at Giza. Although costly to obtain and process, and therefore denoting high status when deposited in elite burials, copper was sufficiently ubiquitous to be found quite extensively in places such as the 'Workers' Town', Heit el-Ghurab, at Giza.

and vessels of copper, have turned up in Old Kingdom burials at Giza and elsewhere. Martin Odler and Veronika Dulíková of the Czech Institute of Egyptology, Charles University, have suggested in their study of model copper tools that the royal house restricted and controlled the copper that went into such sets of little model axes, adzes, chisels and saws placed in tombs for the afterlife. Because copper was costly, these items signified the high status of the deceased. Proprietors of large estates had households which included craftsmen who produced the model copper tools, and probably real ones also, as did the royal house, so both state and estate employed metallurgists. Did wealthy estate owners rely on the royal house for the raw copper? Documents from the Middle and New Kingdoms do show state control over copper and other metals. At the same time, people of more common status exchanged copper in markets, so it seems probable that copper trickled down, and we see this in the wide distribution of copper pieces in archaeological sites.

Ancient Egyptians expressed the comparative value of different materials and commodities in terms of the *deben*, a unit of weight. This was true for copper in the Old Kingdom, and later for bronze. In Deir el-Medina, the New Kingdom settlement of royal tomb-builders at Thebes, weights inscribed with the name of a worker and the copper tool assigned to him allowed authorities to check whether he had removed any copper before returning his tool. Monitoring and accounting for copper axes, adzes and chisels is also attested in papyrus accounts of a royal dockyard workshop at This in the Middle Kingdom reign of Senwosret I.

We should keep in mind the high value of copper when we examine the marks left at Giza by copper tools, which mostly took the form of pointed chisels and nearly flat, finger-width chisels. Such traces of the human hands that built the Giza pyramids can still be seen in many places where the builders did not sand the surface smooth. They used the pointed chisel to rough out surfaces, as visible, for example, in the striations left all over the unfinished walls of the Subterranean Chamber in the Great Pyramid, which were made by pounding a pointed chisel (most probably with a wooden mallet). There is a possibility some of these pointed chisels were made of flint, but most were probably copper.

With soft copper, it was hard to achieve a sharp cutting edge wider than a finger. Such finger-width chisel tracks are most often seen on the finer limestone, such as Merer and his team brought from the eastern quarries at Tura, as recorded in his logbook found at Wadi el-Jarf. In the Grand Gallery today, raking light from modern fluorescent lamps brings into relief waves of parallel chisel trails that arc laterally across the limestone walls like schools of fish. It is possible to see just where the masons chiselled short parallel tracks perpendicular to the joints, so as not to crack and break the corners.

Nick Fairplay, a master stone carver, suggested that runners must have taken copper chisels from the masons working the stone to a facility where they could be annealed and re-sharpened. In the same way, runners in the modern granite quarries of Aswan take steel chisels from those working granite blocks to a shed where the worn tools protrude, like the needles of a porcupine, from a pile of glowing embers. When the chisels are red hot, a metalworker pulls one out and pounds the cutting end to sharpen and harden it, then dips it, with a loud sizzle, in cold water.

Tracks of the finger-width copper chisels can be seen in many places at Giza: in the stress-relieving chambers above the King's Chamber inside Khufu's pyramid, on the casings of the queens' pyramids and mastaba tombs in the cemeteries, and even on some of the Great Pyramid core blocks. At the top of Khafre's pyramid, where casing blocks survive intact, the chisel marks on the joining faces and undersides are just 8 mm or less in width. It is hard to

Copper saw marks in basalt paving at the upper temple of the Great Pyramid site.

comprehend that Khufu's forces dressed 67,137 sq. m (6.9 ha) of the outer surface of his pyramid casing with copper chisels the width of an index finger.

Copper also left its traces in cuts made in hard stones. For instance, numerous saw marks can still be seen on the extremely hard, black basalt slabs of the court pavement in Khufu's upper pyramid temple, which masons cut and fitted together in jigsaw puzzle-like patterns. Copper itself cannot slice such hard stone. Quartz sand did the cutting, guided by toothless copper blades. Some blocks reveal parallel, deep 'plunge cuts' where masons pulled out what must have been a drag saw (or frame saw) and then made a new cut next to it. The cuts sometimes retain a dried mixture of quartz sand and gypsum tinted green by the copper blade. In 1880 Flinders Petrie pointed out saw marks on Khufu's red granite sarcophagus that still stands in the King's Chamber. Visitors today can see these striations in the raking light of their smartphones – fine lines a millimetre or less in thickness. To drill small cylindrical holes in granite, such as found in the door sockets of the Khafre valley temple, tubes of copper may have been used together with an abrasive.

What is remarkable, considering the high worth of copper as a standard of value and exchange (in *deben*), is the amount of copper lost from the blades used to cut these hard stones. Denys Stocks replicated ancient methods to demonstrate what is involved in casting a broad copper blade in separate small crucibles. He then used such blades to cut granite and found that he lost a centimetre of copper from the blade for every 1 to 4 cms' depth of cut. On average, therefore, for every 3 cm of cutting, Khufu's masons must have lost 1 cm of copper. We can only wonder at the order of magnitude of mining, smelting and casting involved to produce all the saws and chisels needed for building Khufu's Great Pyramid. The cost in copper of a granite sarcophagus, a basalt temple pavement and the fine limestone casing for a great pyramid like Khufu's must have been vast. When looked at in this way, the industrial-scale facilities for procuring copper in distant mining sites like Seh Nasb make eminent sense. And it helps us to understand the extraordinary infrastructure represented by Khufu's port at Wadi el-Jarf and the meticulously organized mindset reflected in the papyri found there.

# CHAPTER 4

# FROM SNEFERU TO KHUFU
## Great Kings and their Giant Pyramids

It is said that evolution, biological or cultural, even the evolution of Egyptian civilization, happens in bursts. Khufu's port at Wadi el-Jarf, the papyri found there and the Great Pyramid of Giza are all products of a building burst that spanned from the reign of Djoser (*c.* 2750–2720 BC), at the start of the 3rd Dynasty, to that of Menkaure (2572–2551 BC), the penultimate king of the 4th Dynasty, but reached its apogee under Sneferu (2675–2633 BC) and his son Khufu (2633–2605 BC). Building on such a scale required the marshalling and overseeing of the efficient supply of vast amounts of materials to the construction site, including stone and copper for tools, as well as manpower. The copper, as seen in the previous chapter, mostly had to be sourced and transported from Sinai, making a port on the Red Sea a crucial part of the pyramid-building infrastructure.

## Djoser's building burst and other early attempts

It was Djoser (Netjerykhet), and his legendary architect, Imhotep, who built the first pyramid. This was the famous Step Pyramid at Saqqara, constructed over the course of Djoser's reign. Rising in six steps to a height of 60 m, it stood in the middle of a large stone enclosure that also contains courts, shrines, chapels, finely carved columns, platforms, statues and a huge mastaba, the South Tomb. Deep below ground, workers quarried 5.7 km of shafts, chambers and magazines, including the king's burial chamber.

Following Djoser, King Sekhemkhet and an unnamed king both tried to build their own step-pyramid complexes, at Saqqara and at Zawiyet el-Aryan, but never completed them. Elsewhere, local builders raised miniature step pyramids in certain provinces; why is a mystery, as none contains a burial chamber. Spaced out along the provinces of Upper Egypt, the small provincial pyramids also mark the formal organization of the country into administrative districts, called nomes. Sneferu, first ruler of the 4th Dynasty, built three gigantic pyramids, making him the mightiest of all pyramid builders, surpassing in volume even the Great Pyramid of his son, Khufu. But before this, he also built the last and largest of the provincial step pyramids at Seila, on the eastern shore of the Faiyum.

OPPOSITE The Bent Pyramid at Dahshur, the second pyramid built by Sneferu, where the angle of the slope had to be altered as work progressed because of difficulties in construction (see pp. 92–102).

OVERLEAF Egypt's first pyramid, the Step Pyramid of Djoser (Netjerykhet), rises at Saqqara from the ruins of surrounding courts, shrines and chapels. View to the northwest.

## Sneferu's first pyramids

Sneferu's first pyramid at Seila rose a modest 23.4 m in four steps from a base 36 m to a side. So far as is known, it hides no passage or chamber. With two chapels, one on the north and one on the east, this pyramid represents a transition from Djoser's Step Pyramid, with its northern temple, to the eastern temple that became standard for almost all Old Kingdom pyramids. In the eastern chapel, workers left two round-topped stelae, one uninscribed while the other bore Sneferu's Horus name, Neb-Maat ('Lord of Truth'), and his King of Upper and Lower Egypt name, Sneferu. As a prototype causeway, builders banked the sides of a wadi that slopes to the eastern chapel and laid large limestone blocks in it. Subsequent eastern chapels would quickly evolve into elaborate stone upper temples, with causeways that stretched down to the Nile Valley floor.

No sooner had Sneferu completed his Seila pyramid than he moved to Meidum on the eastern edge of a peninsula of high desert that separates the Nile Valley from the Faiyum basin, where he suddenly scaled up, building bigger even than Djoser. On the valley floor, Sneferu may have built a 'pyramid town' named Djed Sneferu ('Sneferu Endures' or 'Sneferu is Stable'). This would have been the centre of royal administration while building activity continued on his pyramid. Meidum is advantageously positioned near one end of the Wadi Araba corridor (around the Gebel el-Galala el-Bahariya), which leads directly to Wadi el-Jarf.

Today, the pyramid at Meidum consists of a three-stepped tower rising out of a mound of debris, left by builders or stone robbers, but Sneferu's builders began it as a seven-step pyramid, now labelled E1. Each of the seven steps consisted of two accretions, layered against a central core tilted in by about 75°, with each accretion composed of a loose fill of irregular stones covered with well-set, regular courses of squared blocks. The builders then cased the steps with finer limestone from Tura – the same quarries from which the inspector Merer and his work-gang would later fetch stone for Giza – as was standard step-pyramid building practice. But for the burial chamber and access to it, they began something more innovative: a limestone chamber near ground level, accessed by a sloping passage quarried into the plateau surface.

As they raised the pyramid, they inserted a northern entrance passage sloping down through the masonry – a feature that would become standard in pyramids throughout the Old Kingdom. The

The Meidum Pyramid. View from the northwest to the northwest corner, where excavations in the 1980s exposed the casing of the pyramid in its final form, as a true pyramid with sides that sloped about 52°, like the later Great Pyramid of Khufu.

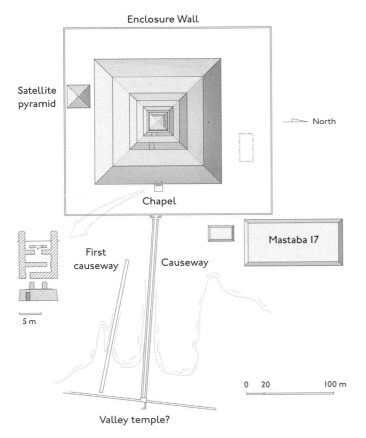

Enclosure Wall

Satellite pyramid

North

Chapel

First causeway

Causeway

Mastaba 17

5 m

Valley temple?

0   20          100 m

Plan of the Meidum Pyramid complex. Sneferu had his builders transform his initial step pyramid here into a true pyramid with a temple at the eastern base, a satellite pyramid, an enclosure wall, and a causeway running from the eastern base to the valley floor, elements transitional to Khufu's Great Pyramid at Giza. An unnamed prince was buried in the large Mastaba 17 off the northeast corner of the enclosure.

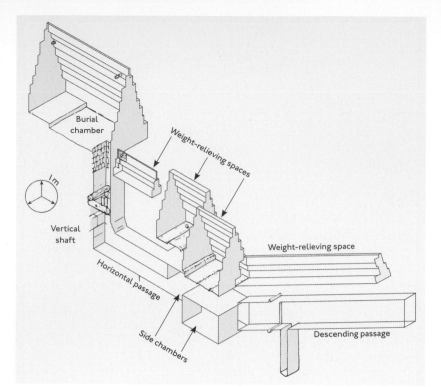

Burial chamber

Weight-relieving spaces

1 m

Vertical shaft

Weight-relieving space

Horizontal passage

Side chambers

Descending passage

passage would open high up in the face of the pyramid above the base, and at the bottom, a horizontal corridor led past two side chambers to a shaft rising vertically to the burial chamber. To roof this small chamber, builders used corbelling in stone for the first time. From just over a metre above the level of the floor, they brought each course inwards by 10–20 cm, until the two side walls were separated by 10 cm at a height of 5 m above the floor. The two side chambers that open off the horizontal section of the entrance passage were roofed with flat limestone lintels, but above them the builders also created corbelled stress-relieving spaces. Where the lower part of the sloping entrance passage enters the bedrock, the builders created another stress-relieving space, with a massive stone lintel laid perpendicular to the slope. Khufu's builders made the same arrangement over the descending passages of his pyramid and those of his queens at Giza.

Sneferu's masons would soon learn that when building gigantic pyramids, foundations are critical. They founded the E1 pyramid on bedrock rich in desert marl clay. After four or five steps, the builders were ordered to enlarge the pyramid (E2). Raising it by an additional step meant first starting at the bottom to add one more accretion

and then continuing to expand with accretions that lean in by 75°. Had pyramid E2 been finished, it would have risen in eight steps to a height of 85 m from a base length of 120.75 m.

While constructing E2, Sneferu's builders also began the first satellite pyramid, another feature that would become standard. What was the purpose of a companion pyramid, measuring only 50 cubits (26.25 m) to a side? Most likely it was to inter a statue that embodied the king's *ka*, his vital force. Scant remains of this pyramid were found by excavators in the early 20th century. Significantly, the blocks of the sides were set at an incline of 30° to the vertical, as opposed to step-pyramid courses, which incline 15° to achieve a 75° slope to the faces, meaning that the builders intended a true (un-stepped) pyramid that sloped 60°. A fragment of a royal stela found nearby still displayed the legs of a falcon. Sneferu probably set up two stelae bearing his *serekh*, the standard king's Horus name, written in a frame that represents a palace, topped by the falcon of Horus. Like that at Seila, this satellite pyramid, with 60° sloping flat faces, served as a conceptual model and trial run for the next step in Sneferu's pyramid experimentation.

ABOVE LEFT View down the descending passage of the Meidum Pyramid.

ABOVE RIGHT The Meidum Pyramid's burial chamber, showing the corbelled roof, and the pavement that remains over the bedrock floor.

## The move to Dahshur: the Bent Pyramid and the North Pyramid

In his 15th year, for reasons unknown, Sneferu began a new pyramid necropolis at South Dahshur, closer to Saqqara, and probably stopped work at Meidum. At Dahshur, Sneferu's builders attempted the first true pyramid on a gargantuan scale: a pyramid with a slope of 60°, like the Meidum satellite, but with a base length enlarged to close to 300 cubits (around 157 m). Evidence for their initial attempt is seen in the complex internal arrangements, with two entrance passages, one in the north face and one in the west, each leading to separate chambers. In both corridors, a seam shows where the face of the original 60° pyramid meets a mantle that had to be added later.

Sneferu's builders framed the lower part of the northern passage and chamber in an open pit below ground, similar to E1. The passage first slopes down from the entrance through the mantle, changing to a gentler angle where it meets the sloping face of the first pyramid. At the bottom is an antechamber, where five corbelled overhangs on the east and west sides narrow upward to a height of

Sneferu's Dahshur pyramids. Centre: the Bent Pyramid and its satellite pyramid. Left background: the North (Red) Pyramid.

12.6 m to a rounded vault. Traces of mortar and small stones on the walls show that masons filled the space and constructed a stairway to an opening into the North Chamber, the corbelled vault of which rises to 17.3 m in fifteen overhangs. At some point the builders also filled this chamber, to an unknown height, perhaps in response to ominous signs of cracks and ruptures in the walls. A short passage in the southern wall leads to the 'chimney' – a vertical shaft close to the pyramid's vertical axis, about a metre square and rising 15 m. Two cavities with their own corbelled roofs open off the chimney, which was perhaps a *serdab*, a blind chamber containing a statue that could 'look out' through a window that opens on to the lower North Chamber. Or, if the builders intended the cavities to hold portcullis blocks to close the chimney, it may have been a passage to a burial chamber that was never built. Their vacillations drove rapid pyramid evolution.

Next, they created the West Chamber, 3.2 m higher in the pyramid body, having buried the top of the North Chamber where it rose above ground level. As they raised the pyramid, they formed the western passage sloping down through the pyramid. Beyond a joint with the face of the inner pyramid, the walls are fractured and damaged. A metre further on, the ceiling cracked and sank by about 5 cm, while the floor stayed flush – it seems the inner pyramid sank.

The western passage meets a horizontal corridor that runs east for 20 m, with two slots in its side walls and ceiling for portcullis blocks intended to slide down and close the passage. The western block was engaged, but robbers punched through it; the second remains in the open position. With a turn to the left, the horizontal corridor arrives at the West Chamber, again roofed by corbelling.

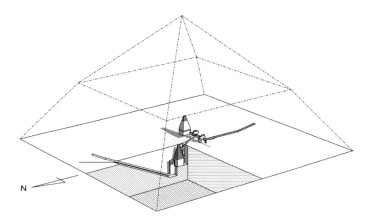

Cutaway view of the passages and chambers of the Bent Pyramid at Dahshur.

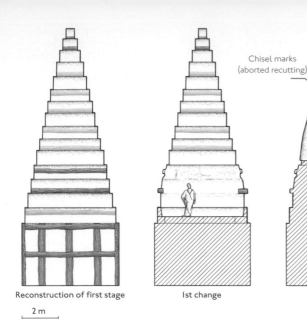

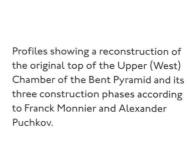

Chisel marks
(aborted recutting)

Profiles showing a reconstruction of
the original top of the Upper (West)
Chamber of the Bent Pyramid and its
three construction phases according
to Franck Monnier and Alexander
Puchkov.

Reconstruction of first stage

2 m

1st change

2nd change

The builders left in place a framework of roughly hewn cedar beams
which they used to support the walls as they raised them. As with
the North Chamber, they filled this chamber with small, rough
blocks, creating a crude stairway to the top of the loose masonry
built to elevate the king's burial platform. The higher floor was
paved with limestone slabs, and masons cut away the corners
of the corbelled overhangs to provide more space for the burial.
Before they finished, they raised the floor yet again, up to the fifth
overhang, cutting away more corbelled corners.

All the evidence points to a desperate attempt by the builders
to salvage and adapt the room to receive the king's burial in the
face of structural challenges. Ceiling blocks in the lower western
passage had started to sink, forcing masons to plug it with tightly
fitting blocks. Since they still planned the West Chamber for the
burial, they needed to access it via the northern passage, through the
antechamber and the lower North Chamber. This is why they filled
those chambers with stones and created stairways, and then cut a
gallery from the south wall of the North Chamber to the horizontal
corridor leading to the West Chamber – now the only way to gain
access for the increasingly perilous burial. But the interior stone
began to split and fall and they faced problems with the pyramid's
superstructure, with its steep 60° angle. To address this, they added
an external mantle, tilting the blocks inward in the old step-pyramid
style, changing the lower slope to 54–55°, which increased the side

The North (Red) Pyramid at Dahshur, built by Sneferu after his difficulties with the Bent Pyramid. It had a lower angle of slope and is the first true pyramid.

length to 187.43 m. Still the unstable foundation caused problems. In the northern passage, the mantle sank 23 cm and the walls cracked; the pyramid base pushed out 60 cm; enormous fissures appeared in the casing, which the masons patched with stones. At a height of 47.04 m, the builders reduced the slope to 43°, giving the Bent Pyramid its bend, even as they abandoned the West Chamber, and, eventually, the pyramid, as a burial place for the king.

Forced to start over yet again, after his fourth major change in plan, Sneferu finally completed a true pyramid at Dahshur North. Here, silicified sand offered a better foundation for a pyramid with a base length of 220 m and a reduced angle of 44°44′. Named 'Appearance of Sneferu', it reached a height of 105 m. Significantly, for the first time, Sneferu's builders laid both core and casing stones in horizontal courses, rather than tilted inward. For the core, workers brought the reddish-yellow limestone that lent this elegant pyramid its modern name, the Red Pyramid. Experience

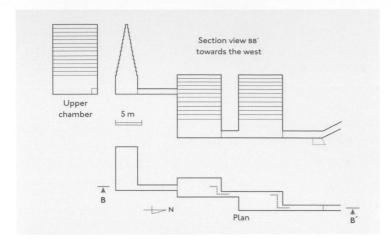

Section view BB′
towards the west

Upper
chamber

5 m

B

N

Plan

B′

Plan (bottom) and north–south profile (along line B–B′ as indicated on the plan) of the chambers and passages in the North (Red) Pyramid in its original condition. Upper left: east-west cross-section of the upper chamber.

Exquisite corbelling at the top of one of two antechambers in the Dahshur North (Red) Pyramid.

allowed the builders to plan and execute the North (Red) Pyramid in one phase, with efficient use of material and no major change in plan. Builders' graffiti mentioning dates found on different courses by archaeologist Rainer Stadelmann show that the builders were able to raise the pyramid 10–12 m – a fifth of its mass – in just two or three years.

As with its superstructure, the North Pyramid's internal structure has a greater clarity than that of the Bent Pyramid. A descending passage opens high above ground level in the northern face's outer casing (now missing) and slopes down for over 62 m to end at a horizontal passage. This runs into an antechamber which rises 12.31 m in a series of 11 corbels. Beyond this, the passage leads to a second antechamber, of similar size and also with corbelled east and west walls. The centre of this chamber is on the vertical central axis of the pyramid. In these antechambers the builders magnified and refined the corbelling, with no flat ceiling slabs at the top. A corridor opens in the south wall of the southern antechamber 7.8 m above floor level leading to the burial chamber, perhaps as a disguise and a deterrent – there are no portcullis or blocking stones. The oblong chamber rises to 13.68 m high in 13 corbels. There is no trace of a sarcophagus, but excavations retrieved remains thought to be from a single male skeleton showing signs of mummification – perhaps Sneferu himself.

Thanks to a simple internal structure and elegant outer form, Sneferu's builders finally completed a true pyramid as an eternal abode for the king, but they ran out of time to complete an equally elegant temple to perform his rituals. Close to the foot of the pyramid, Stadelmann observed thin walls of a pair of small chambers, possibly an offering hall and sacristy. A deep hole against the pyramid itself, filled with a piece of dark granite, could be the remains of a false door. A white plastered mud-brick wall enclosed an area around the pyramid, with a thin mud-brick wall round the temple itself. Towards the front, two rectangular limestone foundations once supported a pair of chapels with reliefs of the seated king wearing the crowns of Upper and Lower Egypt. At the end of the 19th century a decree of Pepi I turned up close to the cultivation edge near a rectangular limestone enclosure, which was entirely removed. Was this the North Pyramid's valley temple? In the decree, Pepi I exempted denizens of Sneferu's Dahshur (two?) pyramid towns from certain duties.

Remains of the chapel of the Bent Pyramid, with mud-brick walls, a stone canopy over an offering slab, and the stubs of two tall stelae that once bore Sneferu's Horus name in a *serekh* (a rectangle representing a stylized palace façade).

Ruins of the Bent Pyramid valley temple lie in the sandy bed at the western head of the central Dahshur wadi. The Bent Pyramid rises on the plateau to the southwest.

## Completing the Bent Pyramid

Sneferu and his builders did not forget the Bent Pyramid, but perhaps because the North Pyramid had become the priority, masons finished off the top of the earlier structure quickly, with a slap-dash casing in wavy, patchwork courses. On the ground, workers showed greater care for the old, problematic pyramid, continuing to add accoutrements as part of a larger landscaping project.

An enclosure wall, built with fine limestone casing on foundations of local stone, surrounded the pyramid. At the centre of the east side, the builders erected a chapel with two monolithic, round-topped stelae bearing the king's names, with a large alabaster offering slab between. To the north of the pyramid, they placed another offering table, but this time of limestone, near the pyramid's centre axis. A platform nearby may have supported a statue of the king, and miniature pottery vases attest to the homage paid to Sneferu here.

In a nearby wadi channel, Sneferu's builders constructed a ramp to haul limestone casing up to the pyramid. At the bottom of the ramp, the king's entourage originally celebrated his rule in a festival court and garden. They built a temple garden within an enclosure,

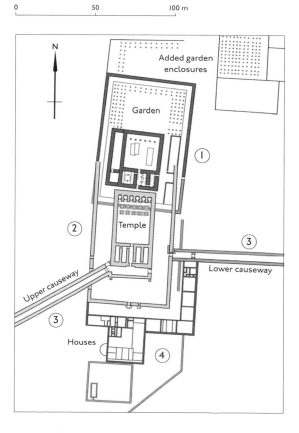

The evolution of Sneferu's wadi complex. 1) First, he built in mud brick an oblong garden pavilion with flower beds, hundreds of trees, a pathway and a mud-brick building, perhaps a royal rest house; 2) Next he added an oblong limestone temple to the south, leaving parts of the garden intact; 3) Then he added an upper causeway in limestone that ran from the Bent Pyramid enclosure to a court along the southern side of the temple, and a lower causeway in mud brick that led from the eastern entrance to the mouth of a canal basin that stretched east through the lower, central wadi to the floodplain; 4) Finally, Sneferu added enclosures and houses for priests, to the south of the temple.

Peter Collet traces female personifications of estates and villages who bring the hieroglyph for 'life' and offerings, symbolizing produce. A series of such figures, carved in relief, once graced the walls of the entryway to Sneferu's Bent Pyramid valley temple. The crossed circle on each of their heads is the hieroglyph for 'village' or 'town'.

The Bent Pyramid lower causeway excavated in 2012. View to the west with the Bent Pyramid on the high plateau.

with rows of palm, sycamore figs, conifers and cypress surrounded by flower beds around a central court. Within the court stood a mud-brick building, consisting of entrance rooms and a courtyard with a colonnade and a basin. But around Sneferu's 30th year on the throne, the southern parts of the garden were razed and builders laid out his valley temple of fine limestone. On the west wall of a corridor within, leading to an open court, craftsmen carved in relief a series of female offering bearers, personifications of estates in the south and the north. Each estate once bore a name compounded with 'Sneferu'.

The supply ramp was then repurposed as a foundation for an upper ceremonial causeway by adding fine limestone walls to make a 3-m wide corridor that ran 704 m to an opening in the valley temple's west enclosure wall. Before the southern wall, two limestone stelae showed Horus falcons atop the king's *serekh*. Here people worshipped Sneferu through the rest of the Old Kingdom down to the 12th Dynasty. Geophysical survey showed part of his 'pyramid town' lay buried north of the valley temple over a 350 × 200 m area. Excavation has revealed large houses for royal family members who supervised Sneferu's building programme.

Like the festival garden that preceded it, the valley temple sits halfway between the Bent Pyramid and the alluvial plain. A lower mud-brick causeway ran east from the valley temple. It, too, first served as a supply ramp for limestone deliveries, but was transformed into a ceremonial causeway, 2.58 m (5 cubits) wide. It slopes down to an opening in the western wall of a harbour basin. Prefiguring Khufu's later grand works, quarrymen had dredged a wadi that ran east to the floodplain into a deep channel basin for delivering building supplies. It measures 95 m wide and almost 10 m deep, and stretched 1 km through the wadi to the floodplain. Because it served initially to bring stone to the foot of the ramp, Merer, had he lived a generation earlier, would have brought stone into this basin, instead of the 'Lake of Khufu' (She Khufu).

The ultimate irony is that the Bent Pyramid – the one that shook, cracked and sank – survived antiquity as the best preserved of all the gigantic pyramids, with so much of its casing intact. This became the pyramid complex where Egyptians most celebrated Sneferu and his long reign in feasts and jubilees before and after his death. One last Bent Pyramid accoutrement, the satellite pyramid, was, like the Seila pyramid and the satellite at Meidum, a harbinger of things to come, this time in the Great Pyramid of Khufu.

South of the Bent Pyramid, on its north–south axis, Sneferu built a small satellite pyramid, with faces sloping up 44°30′ from a base length of 52.8 m (100 cubits) to a height of 25.55 m. Here, we see techniques that Khufu's masons brought to perfection, for instance in the way the casing blocks were laid and cut. Internally, from an entrance in the north face on the centre axis a descending passage slopes down at an angle before levelling out. The passage then ascends once more, with a section where the ceiling rises to 2.3 m high for a length of 9.2 m. Here, the details of both internal structure and blocking system provide a prototype for the Great Pyramid's Grand Gallery.

At a point just over 3 m up the ascending corridor, the masons cut two parallel grooves in the floor of the passage, and a pair of holes in the walls above them to receive the ends of a wooden 'brake log'. This held back as many as four plugging blocks in the ascending passage. When the time came to seal the pyramid, they set wooden braces with one end into the grooves and the other against the face of the lowest block. Down below, workers could haul on ropes tied around the braces to pull them away, allowing the blocks to slide down. While two went missing in ancient times, the upper two plug blocks remain, having slid a short way and become stuck.

At the top of the ascending passage, a chamber is accessed by climbing over a vertical step (not unlike the step at the top of the Grand Gallery). The chamber's upper walls step in by eight corbels to reach a total height of almost 7 m. Above the door a monolith serves as an architrave that spans the width of the chamber.

East of the satellite, excavators found portions of two round-topped stelae that once stood on the east–west centre axis of the pyramid, with a mud-brick altar in between. The upper part of one was missing, but the other bore Sneferu's *serekh* and Horus name, 'Lord of Maat (Truth)', and his other names: 'King of Upper and Lower Egypt, the Two Ladies, Lord of Maat, Horus of Gold, Sneferu'.

## Return to Meidum and the development of the standard pyramid complex

In the last 15 years of his reign, Sneferu returned to his first giant pyramid at Meidum to transform the unfinished step pyramid into a true pyramid (E3) with an angle of 51°51′, nearing that of Khufu's pyramid at Giza. Meidum thus represents the beginning and end of Sneferu's giant pyramid-building programme.

Sneferu's builders added a mantle, giving E3 a new base length of 144.3 m and an intended height of around 92 m. They laid casing stones in horizontal courses, so not at the inward tilt of the old accretion layers, and filled out the steps of the old E2 pyramid with local grey limestone, yellow clayey backing stones and a fine white limestone casing. Although they built E1 and E2 on limestone bedrock, they laid the casing of the E3 mantle on two or three courses of foundation slabs in a sand layer above bedrock.

The pyramid itself – the superstructure of the royal tomb – became the central element in what Egyptologists call the 'pyramid complex', a standard east–west axial layout consisting of an upper temple at the eastern base of the pyramid and a causeway leading down to a valley temple. At Meidum, Sneferu's forces created the first such layout in simple form, although they also seem to have intended an eastern axial alignment at his Dahshur North Pyramid. They surrounded the pyramid with an outer enclosure wall pierced on the east side by the entrance to the causeway. This ran unroofed east–southeast with respect to the pyramid for 210 m, and from the lower end, mud-brick walls that took off at right angles north and south might have demarcated some kind of valley temple or perhaps the pyramid town, Djed Sneferu. Given the incipient forms of the other elements of the pyramid complex at Meidum, the causeway may end at a simple enclosure and landing platform.

On the east side of the pyramid's base, almost on its central axis, the builders added a stone chapel. Like the Bent Pyramid eastern chapel, it is small in comparison to the size of the pyramid, about 9 m square. The masons came close to completing it but did not finish dressing the lower courses, and at the rear two stately, round-topped limestone stelae, again with an offering slab between them, are uninscribed. It is hard to imagine that Sneferu's workforce would have left them uninscribed intentionally. Similarly, the strained masons never finished the final polish on the E3 casing. All this points to the conclusion that Sneferu's final building phase at Meidum stopped suddenly. Given the hurriedly finished mortuary temple of the North (Red) Pyramid at Dahshur, it seems likely that Sneferu's long and troubled development of pyramids came to an abrupt end when the king died (c. 2633 BC), and an ambitious young son, Khufu, ascended the throne.

## Khufu's Great Pyramid

The new king must have quickly withdrawn the work crews from both Dahshur and Meidum, and, perhaps learning from his father's building misfortunes, looked to found a new royal necropolis with the right conditions to construct his own pyramid. Khufu's Overseer of Works found the perfect place on the Giza Plateau, where an embankment of the limestone Moqattam Formation rises on the north-northwest and slopes gently to the south-southeast, forming a natural, easy ramp up on to the plateau. Khufu's quarrymen could cut large stone blocks from a sequence of thin, clayey limestone layers interspersed with thicker, hard layers. The harder bedrock at the top of the embankment provided a foundation for a pyramid larger than any of Sneferu's. The port at Wadi el-Jarf on the Red Sea continued in operation throughout Khufu's reign to supply his pyramid construction, although it was much less conveniently sited for Giza than for Sneferu's pyramids to the south.

A broad wadi between the Moqattam embankment and the southern Maadi Formation knoll, the Gebel el-Qibli, provided a conduit to deliver materials up to the construction site. With boundless ambition, Khufu dredged a deep canal basin from the wadi mouth to a nearby Nile branch for delivering materials, including the Tura limestone brought from the river's opposite bank by Merer and his men as detailed in the Wadi el-Jarf Papyri. From the wadi mouth, a wharf-like peninsula of low desert stretched east into the floodplain. As Khufu's workers dredged the harbour basin, they raised and extended this wharf on which they could build their harbour-side infrastructure. The harbour-basin was the bottleneck for all men and material, what the Wadi el-Jarf Papyri call the Ro-She Khufu, the 'Entrance to the Lake (or basin) of Khufu', a kind of port authority at the perfect checkpoint to monitor flow.

## Based in bedrock: platform, core and casing

Khufu's surveyors laid out the square for his pyramid base at the northeastern edge of the Moqattam Formation, only 70 m from the edge of the escarpment where it abruptly drops 40 m. Into a bedrock surface that sloped 6° from northwest to southeast, quarrymen sculpted a square, 260 m to a side, that would take in the pyramid base itself (an average of 230.36 m to a side), as well as the court surrounding the pyramid and the width of its enclosure wall. In the pyramid core they left much of the bedrock sticking up 2 to 7 m. Sculpting over 6 ha of hard rock surface was an operation an order of magnitude greater than the foundation and levelling work of Sneferu's pyramid builders.

Masons carried out the finest levelling for the baseline of the pyramid casing on a platform of fine Tura limestone. A single course sufficed because it lay upon hard, levelled bedrock. They custom-cut one slab to fit against another, with joins at various angles too fine for the proverbial razor blade to fit between. The bedrock left protruding in the core meant masons could not lay the platform under the whole pyramid base, only around the perimeter, and they could not control the squareness of the platform by measuring equal diagonals across it. Nonetheless they laid the platform in a near-perfect square, a perimeter 924.8 m long, with a maximum difference in level of 4.7 cm and a negligible average deviation from the cardinal directions.

The Great Pyramid of Khufu at Giza, west side, looking over the Western Cemetery of officials and retainers.

PART II    Why the Red Sea and the Pyramids are Linked

Khufu's masons clad the outer facing of the whole pyramid with 8.5 ha of stone hauled from the Tura quarries by teams like Merer's. Because so much is now missing, we must extrapolate the original dimensions and slope from only 54 m of the original casing baseline that survives. Casing blocks of the first course are 1.5 m tall and weigh 13.5–15.5 tonnes, with joins that average 0.5 mm in width. The greatest difference in the length of the sides is 18.3 cm, but within a 95 per cent confidence window it is possible that it was less than 5 mm – almost perfection. Petrie calculated the mean angle of the finished cased pyramid as 51°51′, plus or minus 2′, and from a mean side length of 230.5 m he calculated a height of 147.7 m, although 146.59 m is now more commonly accepted.

Long ago people removed most of the outer casing, so when looking at the Great Pyramid today we see the outermost core or 'backing stones' that made the fit between inner core and casing. A gash that Howard Vyse blasted out of the southern face in 1837 exposes the composition of the deeper core – wedge-shaped, oval and trapezoidal pieces, smaller stone fragments of variable shapes and sizes, and mortar and rubble are jammed into wide crevices. Although the builders used finer limestone near the corners and for the uppermost courses in order to stitch together a tighter fabric as they reached the apex, this jagged reality is far from the common notion that the pyramid is composed of uniform, squared, well-fitted blocks.

While it may represent the classic Egyptian pyramid in popular imagination, the Great Pyramid is, in fact, the most anomalous. Never before, and never again, would any pyramid builder attempt Khufu's boldness in inserting chambers so low beneath and so high up in the masonry of a pyramid. The anomalies begin at the entrance.

Because the casing, backing and core stones have been removed, the Descending Passage now opens in the nineteenth course of masonry. Above a narrow entrance, only 1.05 m wide, two pairs of huge, gabled rafters (chevron stones), weighing around 25 tonnes, rest one on top of the other and slope down to large blocks set at an angle to receive them. It is possible that originally there were seven pairs of such stone rafters in a lower layer, with four pairs resting above them. The chevrons sit above a very large lintel slab set on edge; five more such lintels may once have leaned against it in the space where backing stones and casing are now missing.

The northern side of the Great Pyramid showing the gabled entrance above and to the left of the forced hole purportedly made under the orders of Caliph al-Mamun in c. AD 820, nearly on the north–south centre axis of the pyramid. The actual entrance is displaced 7.2 m to the east of the axis.

Why did Khufu's builders so 'over-engineer' the entrance? Was it because of the sliding and settling that their predecessors experienced in building at Dahshur? Only the builders would know of this arrangement, concealed as it was in the finished pyramid. So could Khufu's designers have intended the chevron stones to have a symbolic or magical effect, like the gabled, star-studded ceilings over later burial pyramid chambers? Still, it seems easiest to accept that Khufu's Overseer of Works was motivated to build this great vault above the entrance for a more straightforward reason – hard-earned caution. In 2016, the ScanPyramids consortium detected a void just behind the chevrons in the shape of a corridor running at a horizontal or upward slope into the pyramid. While they believe the chevrons were intended to protect this hidden passage, the more likely explanation is that the void is another weight-relieving space above the Descending Passage, like the weight-relieving spaces above the passages in the Meidum pyramid, although here magnified.

## The Great Pyramid passage system

All the passages in the Great Pyramid fall on one line, running east of and parallel to the north–south centre axis of the pyramid. At the passage system's highest point, a turn to the west by the King's Chamber puts Khufu's sarcophagus directly on this axis.

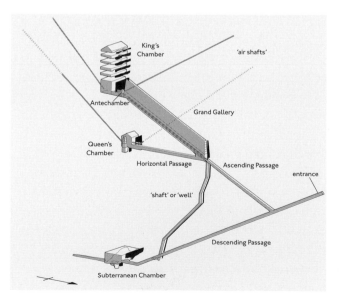

The internal passages and chambers of the Great Pyramid, also showing the 'air shafts' oriented to the circumpolar and other stars.

The Descending Passage, 105.34 m long, slopes down first through the pyramid masonry and then through the natural bedrock without deviating more than a centimetre in angle or orientation. It points to the circumpolar stars, 'The Imperishable Ones', that neither rise nor set, an image of eternity and a destination of the king in the Afterlife.

At its bottom end, workers then cut a horizontal passage to the Subterranean Chamber. Here, 30 m below the surface, quarrymen using hammerstones and copper chisels half-hollowed out a chamber from bedrock before downing their tools. They left behind squarish humps of rock assigned to single quarrymen to remove, and heaps of limestone fragments and chips from their work, leaving a frozen moment in the construction process. It was once thought that this was the original intended burial chamber before those in charge decided to abandon it and instead designate the middle chamber, the Queen's Chamber, as the resting place of the royal mummy, but then changed their minds again, deciding on the King's Chamber. There is evidence, however, that all three chambers were planned from the beginning, based on a long tradition, before and after Khufu, of royal tombs having three chambers. If so, what, then was the purpose of the Subterranean Chamber? Some Egyptologists suggest that its rough, unfinished state may indicate a link to the chthonic aspect of the Afterlife, making it an earthly symbolic representation of the Underworld cavern.

The Ascending Passage, which opens off the Descending Passage, together with the Grand Gallery it widens into, were designed by Khufu's architects to house the system to close the pyramid and seal the King's Chamber. An earlier version, and the original concept behind this primitive 'machine', was created in the small satellite of the Bent Pyramid.

At the point where the Ascending Passage joins the roof of the Descending Passage, a granite block still 'hangs' in the ceiling, plugging the end of the upper passage. Notches cut into the walls on either side once received a wooden brake log that is long missing, and the huge granite plug is held only by a slight narrowing of the lower end of the Ascending Passage. It is the lowest of three such granite plugs, placed end to end.

Khufu's builders formed most of the Ascending Passage from Tura-quality slabs set with wall joints at right angles to the slope of the passage, or parallel to it. But at certain points they cut the passage straight through single larger slabs, or a pair of slabs. These 'girdle stones', set on edge, are a metre thick and over 2 m tall. By making these blocks larger than the passage and then cutting through them, the builders anchored the passage in the core masonry. After their fathers' experience of slippage and sinking at Dahshur, Khufu's builders worried about the pyramid mass pressing down on the junction of the Ascending and Descending Passages. Higher up the passage, they spaced the girdle stones further apart, because the thrust lessened, but they still framed the girdle stones between two extra-large wall blocks – here again over-engineering for the risks they took in placing passages and chambers so high up in the pyramid.

After a stretch of almost 40 m, the cramped Ascending Passage suddenly opens out into the Grand Gallery, 2.10 m wide and 8.6 m high. At the point where the two passages join, the floor of the Grand Gallery opens to the Horizontal Passage leading to the Queen's Chamber. The sloping floor of the Ascending Passage continues on the same plane after the gap and is the same width as the floor of the central channel of the Grand Gallery, which is formed between two banks running up the side walls. This channel was designed to store the granite plug blocks that would seal the pyramid, before they were slid down to close the Ascending Passage. For this device to succeed, the builders had to install a movable false floor, supported on wooden beams set into holes on either side, in order to span the gap created by the opening to the Horizontal Passage.

Architects had worked out corbelling to near perfection in Sneferu's North Pyramid, and using this experience they raised the Grand Gallery walls in seven corbels. They set the first course of wall blocks on the benches running along the side walls of the gallery, followed by seven more courses, bringing each forward by one palm measure (7.5 cm), narrowing the walls to within 2 cubits (1.05 m) of each other. Ceiling slabs were fixed into saw-tooth notches cut into the tops of the walls, at a downward angle, so that each slab did not put pressure on its neighbour, alleviating the weight on the lower, northern portion of the Gallery. Khufu's builders were innovating continuously. They tilted the Gallery up at the angle of more than 26° for a length of 47.84 m – their forebears had raised impressive corbelled vaults, twice as high as this, but none set at such an angle.

The Grand Gallery and Ascending Passage together form the container for one of the world's first machines of movable parts.

The Ascending Passage in the Great Pyramid remains blocked by a granite plugging stone (above) almost at the point where it meets the Descending Passage (below). Two further plugging stones lie behind the one visible here.

Khufu's masons cut a series of niches, notches and grooves in the benches and lower walls of the Gallery – the cogs in this machine. At regular intervals they cut slots in the tops of the benches, and in the wall at the back of each slot, a series of niches, bevelled as if to slide something in. Then, however, they closed the niches with tightly fitting stone slabs, as though to erase them. Although no one has a satisfactory idea as to their purpose, brake logs come to mind, their ends inserted into the niches, to hold the granite plugs. But the spacing of the niches would only leave room for blocks that are smaller than the three plugs still lodged at the bottom of the Ascending Passage (1.75, 1.6 and 1.65 m long). Builders experimented with the basics of this system in the satellite pyramid of the Bent Pyramid, where the plug blocks remained stuck in the waiting position, and failed to close the passage. Perhaps Khufu's architects conceived the wider Grand Gallery, with its benches, niches and notches, as a way to avoid repeating a system that did not work. In the end, they gave up anyway, filling in the niches and doing away with the brake logs. They left the notches in the bench tops open, possibly as sockets for vertical wooden uprights of a wooden frame that may have ensured the stability of the Grand Gallery as they were building it – similar in purpose, if finer in execution, to the wooden frame still in place in the upper West Chamber of Sneferu's Bent Pyramid. In order to pass the ropes between the frame's uprights and the wall, the masons cut the shallow trapezoidal cuttings across the faces of the niche patches.

Now, they planned to seal the King's Chamber entrance with portcullis slabs lowered from above, a defence against robbers previously used in tomb passages of the Early Dynastic Period and under Sneferu at Meidum and Dahshur.

## The inner chambers: the Antechamber and King's Chamber

At the top of the Grand Gallery a large limestone block known as the Great Step rises just under a metre to the highest floor level inside the pyramid, at 43 m above the outside platform. From this landing, a passage leads to the small Antechamber, walled in red granite and limestone. Three large portcullis slabs were suspended in the ceiling of the Antechamber, held aloft by wooden chocks and ropes until the king's burial was completed. From the space above the portcullises

The King's Chamber of the Great Pyramid looking west to the granite sarcophagus, which is aligned on the north-south centre axis of the pyramid.

and from outside the chamber, workers gradually released the brake ropes and lowered the three slabs, one after another. Although it is likely that those who closed the King's Chamber filled the spaces above with limestone blocks, robbers removed this blocking and made their way into the king's final resting place over the portcullis slabs.

The King's Chamber housed Khufu's mummy in a sarcophagus cut from a single piece of granite that remains in place in the western end of the chamber. Granite was also used for the walls of the chamber, which stands intact, 10 cubits (5.24 m) wide and 20 cubits (10.48 m) long. In the north and south walls, Khufu's builders cut

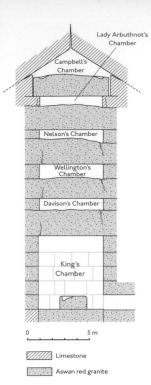

The King's Chamber was roofed with massive granite beams, each weighing 35–55 tonnes, above which the architects stacked another four granite-roofed chambers and a fifth chamber roofed with limestone chevrons. Although conventionally interpreted as structures to relieve weight over the King's Chamber, the chevron beams above the topmost chamber may symbolize the double doors of the sky-gate opening for the king's ascent.

**Legend:**

Limestone

Aswan red granite

small openings (18–21 cm wide and 14 cm high) to the so-called 'air shafts', narrow pipes of limestone that slope up through the pyramid to emerge on the outside of the pyramid high above the ground. Through them, Khufu's spirit could ascend on one side north to Alpha Draconis, the pole star in his time, and 'the Imperishable Ones', the circumpolar stars, and on the south side to Orion, identified with Osiris, god of the Netherworld, and to Sirius, 'the companion of Orion'. Was Khufu's aim in his pyramid building to embody tradition, or was he making it up as he built? Another set of 'air shafts' – or soul shafts – was cut in the Queen's Chamber, but in no other pyramid. Considering the amount of effort involved, someone truly believed in their efficacy, but while such a belief or idea may have continued, air channels did not.

At exactly one-third of the pyramid's height of 146.59 m, Khufu's builders roofed the King's Chamber with nine massive granite beams, estimated to weigh between 35 and 55 tonnes each. In another case of possible over-engineering, they then stacked above this roof four more granite ceilings, spaced between 60 cm to 1 m apart. The granite beams forming the ceiling of each chamber make up the 'pavement' of the chamber above. At the top, they built a fifth chamber, crowned with huge, chevron beams. The usual interpretation of this system, and the architect's intention behind it, was to relieve the weight above the King's Chamber, and so these spaces are commonly called 'Relieving Chambers'.

But did Khufu and his architect see the chevrons above the fifth chamber as charged with magical power – as symbols of the double doors of the sky-gate opening for the king's ascent? Hidden deep within the pyramid core, the chevrons must have played some special role, because builders could have achieved the same result as the stack of chambers with the kind of corbelling their fathers perfected at North Dahshur. To obtain the magical efficacy of the chevrons, they needed to raise them high and away from the Grand Gallery, and to avoid collapse, they needed to fit gigantic granite struts to resist lateral pressure and protect the Grand Gallery.

In 2017–19, the ScanPyramids Project used muon tomography to detect a 'Big Void' about 5 m above the Grand Gallery, with a minimum length of 30–40 m and a cross-section similar to that of the Grand Gallery below. ScanPyramids has not yet been able to determine the exact shape or slope of the void, so the ScanPyramids team illustrates it as a blurred, sloping cloud of points running parallel to the gallery. If it were simply a corbelled vault running along the gallery roof, they would not have detected it as so separate and distinct. If the upper, southern end of the void is just above that end of the gallery, it would come to within several metres of the ends of the granite beams of the Relieving Chambers, which should exert a force on the void, especially if it does have the same volume as the gallery. And with a volume of that size, this additional space would likely need its own vault. Most probably, the void is space that the builders framed in to protect the Grand Gallery against superincumbent weight.

## The Queen's Chamber

The Ascending Passage, Grand Gallery, Antechamber, King's Chamber and Relieving Chambers form one continuous system, planned together. With walls and gabled roof of fine limestone, the Queen's Chamber is an appendix to this system, at the end of the Horizontal Passage leading from the lower end of the Grand Gallery. The chamber is misnamed – no queen was interred here. The most noteworthy attribute of the Queen's Chamber is a corbelled niche sunk into the eastern wall, which could have held a larger-than-life-sized statue of Khufu. Petrie found that the mid-line of the gabled roof lies exactly on the east–west centre axis of the pyramid.

The builders sealed off the Horizontal Passage and Queen's Chamber by blocking access to it when they laid in the false floor from the bottom of the Grand Gallery channel to the Ascending Passage. In the Queen's Chamber north and south walls the builders formed two 'air shafts' like those from the King's Chamber. But unlike those, they did not cut openings at the lower ends into the room, leaving them masked, in effect sealing off the Queen's Chamber a second time. The shafts were only revealed in 1872 when Waynman Dixon cut through the walls to open them, having detected their position by tapping on the walls. Even more curiously, Khufu's builders plugged the upper ends of these 'air shafts', in both cases at a distance of around 63.6 m from the chamber, with limestone blocks, each featuring two copper pins that droop down against the face of the block. Using a series of miniature robots equipped with video cameras, teams have discovered that the pins project through the stone plugs and curve back on themselves in small loops, too small for rope or string to be threaded through to lower the blocking stones into place.

What did these blocked 'air shafts' mean? Pyramid Texts speak of drawing back bolts to open the double door of the horizon (*akhet*), and repeat the recitation that 'the sky's doors have been opened'. In carefully equipping the Queen's Chamber with its own miniature soul-passages, yet leaving them blocked, the builders created a blind chamber for installing a statue of the deceased, like the *serdab* in mastaba tombs. In this interpretation, Khufu's body was eventually laid to rest in the sarcophagus in the King's Chamber, and his statue, a substitute body, stood in the niche in the Queen's Chamber. As the upper shafts provided magical conduits for the king's soul to ascend from his mummy, so too the lower shafts provided conduits for his vital force, his *ka*, to ascend from his statue and complete Khufu's transformation and union with the imperishable stars in the northern sky and the constellation Orion and the star Sirius in the southern sky. Khufu's masons never planned to cut the channels through the Queen's Chamber walls, and they always intended to block the upper ends, leaving magical metal pins as 'bolts of the sky' doors. Like false doors in tombs, these were token, miniature, magical and hidden. The copper pins are not bolts to keep something locked shut, but symbolic 'pulls' to be unlatched.

## Khufu's pyramid complex

Like Sneferu's Bent Pyramid, Khufu's Great Pyramid formed one part of a large landscaping project, with accoutrements added by his builders after they had largely finished the pyramid itself. The Tura limestone that Merer and his men delivered in the last years of Khufu's reign likely went into his valley temple, causeway, court pavement around the pyramid, enclosure wall, satellite pyramid and upper temple.

For the first time since Djoser's temple north of his Step Pyramid, Khufu's builders created a large upper temple of stone. The small chapels of the Bent Pyramid and final Meidum Pyramid (E3) are cenotaphs, and do not qualify as links in the development of the pyramid funerary temples, so Khufu's is a critical step in architectural history. We know it extended more than 53.35 m from the pyramid and stretched 52.5 m (100 cubits) wide north–south. Remains show that it had a cloistered court, paved with basalt, and a long, narrow hall sanctuary. At some later point someone excavated a shaft in the middle of the sanctuary, which prevents

The cedarwood barque of Khufu, almost 44 m long, one of two funerary ships buried in rectangular pits cut into bedrock along the southern side of the Great Pyramid. This boat is from the eastern pit, excavated in 1954. Master conservator Hag Ahmed Youssef reassembled the barque from more than 1,200 pieces. It was placed in a museum at the pyramid site. A new home for the vessel is being created at the Grand Egyptian Museum.

us from knowing whether it housed niches for statues, a false door or a stela. Connected to the temple, Khufu's builders raised a tall enclosure wall of Tura limestone around the entire pyramid, surrounding a paved court inside.

A fleet of boats was moored around the pyramid. Parallel to the pyramid's base on its eastern side, quarrymen carved out two pits shaped like boats and large enough to hold fully assembled vessels, one on either side of the upper temple. A third boat-shaped pit lies on the north side of the upper end of the causeway, and two smaller pits lie between the queens' pyramids. All these pits had been opened in the past and were found empty. On the southern side of the pyramid were two large rectangular pits in which those who tended to Khufu's funeral placed the disassembled parts of two ships of cedar in correct relative positions. They then closed the pits with massive Tura limestone slabs set onto a ledge. The names of both Khufu and his successor, Djedefre, have been found inscribed in paint on these slabs. As the Wadi el-Jarf Papyri date to the final or penultimate year of Khufu's reign, Merer's deliveries could have included some of these slabs.

Restorers painstakingly reassembled over many months the more than 1,200 pieces of the boat found in the eastern pit on the pyramid's south side. The result is a full-sized vessel, built mostly from planks of cedarwood, almost 44 m long – considerably longer than the estimated 14–15 m of the disassembled boats discovered at Ayn Sukhna. A cabin stood in the middle of the deck and the six pairs of oars found in the pit may have been used in steering or for propulsion, though the ship could also have been towed along by other craft. Egyptologists cannot agree in fact if Khufu's southern barques were actually used, or what their function was. The fact that both were so systematically dismantled suggests they functioned once to bring the king's mortal remains for burial in the pyramid. The Egyptians would never have taken them apart if they had been meant for a ritual purpose: to carry the king's spirit to join the sun god in a daily journey across the sky.

Near the southeastern corner of the Great Pyramid, Khufu's builders added a satellite pyramid with sides 21.75 m long. Although most of it has now disappeared, some of the fine limestone blocks from the casing and foundation remain. The substructure, cut by the builders into the bedrock, consists of a T-shaped sloping passage and chamber, an arrangement that would become standard for later satellite pyramids.

Khufu's causeway ran 825 m from the upper temple down to his valley temple. To accommodate the difference in height between the upper and valley temples a foundation 45 m high was constructed in order to bridge the escarpment. In 1990, engineers digging along the Mansouriyah Canal for a sewage project encountered basalt blocks, comparable to those used in the upper temple. They must mark the location of the valley temple. The engineers' cutting, and the archaeologists' trenches that followed, found traces of a temple about 100 cubits (52.5 m) wide – as broad as the upper temple. The causeway was attached to the back, west wall of the valley temple, and would have formed the main entrance to the entire pyramid complex. Several bores drilled to the south of the valley temple hit traces of settlement at around 14.8 m asl, the remains of Ankhu Khufu, the city named in the Wadi el-Jarf Papyri. This was where the royal administration was based while Khufu's pyramid was under construction, with the valley temple and a palace as its centre.

In the floodplain beyond, Khufu installed a system of water transport infrastructure of even greater magnitude than Sneferu's kilometre-long harbour basin in the wadi leading to the Bent Pyramid valley temple. Much of the materials and manpower for building the giant pyramid would have poured in through this infrastructure. The contours of the modern valley show a large depression in front of the valley temple, and in 1993 excavation for the foundation of a modern building hit a basalt wall built on a limestone foundation – the same materials as Khufu's upper and valley temples and at the same elevation as the basalt slabs of the valley temple. Fragments of similar walls running east–west were spotted in engineering trenches to the north and south. From these walls, we can extrapolate the original basin to have measured 400 m north–south by 450 m east–west. This was the She Akhet Khufu, the 'Lake', *she*, 'of the Horizon of Khufu', the name of Khufu's pyramid.

The valley temple was perched on the western bank of the basin, in line with the western Nile channel on which Merer sailed to Giza when coming from Tura South. During the Nile inundation, water would have lapped up against the foot of the temple. But the 'Lake of the Horizon of Khufu', Khufu's own marina, was only one part of a much vaster water infrastructure. A larger central basin, most probably the She Khufu, the 'Lake of Khufu', of the Wadi el-Jarf Papyri, extended west from a gateway formed between two mounds of higher ground, the Ro-She Khufu, the entrance to Khufu's lake. As one small part of the giant construction project, Merer and his men would have sailed through the entrance, off-loaded their delivery of stone and then perhaps spent the night in the bustling settlement centred around the palace and valley temple, getting some rest before their next day's labours.

# CHAPTER 5

# FROM KHUFU TO KHAFRE
## Wadi el-Jarf to Ayn Sukhna

Papyrus of the royal official Neferiru. This
small papyrus is complete; it was found at
the entrance of gallery GII at Wadi el-Jarf, in a
stratigraphic context which indicates a period
before the final closing of the magazines.
This document, giving only the name and titles
of its owner, may have granted Neferiru safe
conduct on the desert tracks.

The site of Wadi el-Jarf has several advantages that make it suitable as the location for an 'intermittent port' on the Red Sea coast, at a time when the Egyptians were clearly conducting their first experiments with this kind of installation. For the port to operate most efficiently, it was essential that there was access to a supply of good drinking water, which was probably provided by a spring at what is now St Paul's Monastery, 10 km from the site. Another requirement was that the coastal landscape should be favourable for the anchorage and safekeeping of the boats. At Wadi el-Jarf there was a large natural opening in the reefs offshore, and the foothills of the mountains inland provided a suitable rock face for carving out the necessary galleries to store most of the expeditionary equipment and supplies for the mining missions. Finally, it was important that the port was connected with an administrative centre that was able to control all the operations from the Nile Valley. A supply chain would therefore have had to be maintained in order to ensure the continuous provision of supplies during periods when the Egyptians were active at Wadi el-Jarf. This would have involved constant movement of people along the desert tracks, comprising convoys, troops and messengers carrying orders, as well as officials involved in the operations, over a period of several months.

One such official is represented at Wadi el-Jarf by a papyrus found at the entrance of gallery GII in 2015, in a stratigraphic context which indicates a date before the final closing of the magazines. The document simply gives the name and titles of 'the great one of the carrying chair, the controller of the dwarves of the department of the clothes of linen of the first quality, the controller of the necklace makers and royal administrator Neferiru'. Similar titles were later held by the dwarf Seneb, well known from the statue group of him and his family. This papyrus was not rolled, but folded, and was probably worn around the neck in a pendant by its owner. It could be the most ancient 'ID-card' so far known in the world, allowing the official Neferiru – probably linked to turquoise production – to travel freely through the tracks of the desert.

## The origin and development of the port
This requirement for good links to the centre of royal administration at the time is perfectly illustrated at the point the site was first established as a port. Our excavations have yielded several

PAGE 121 An ostracon, or inscribed stone fragment, from Wadi el-Jarf, mentioning a work-gang associated with King Sneferu (see pp. 124–25).

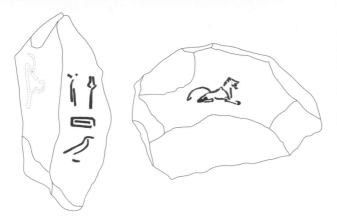

Ostracon naming the work-gang 'The Lion' and 'The controller of the *aper*-gang' Shaa, probably associated with Sneferu, and found in the earliest occupation levels of the 'intermediate building'. Many of the storage galleries at Wadi el-Jarf may have been created during this king's reign.

Gallery G5

Gallery G6

Gallery G14

Control marks found in the closing system of various galleries, naming the gang of 'the followers of the Lion', probably the same team that appears in Sneferu's levels in the 'intermediate building'.

Commemorative inscription and drawing of 'Idu, the scribe of the Faiyum' (literally the 'scribe of the Southern Lake' – She Resi). It was left on the wall at the entrance of gallery G3 by an official who came from this region, probably during the reign of Sneferu, at the time the expeditions to Sinai were most probably organized from an administrative centre in Meidum. A very cursive column of text to the right of the standing man could be a 'biographical' inscription explaining that this scribe came here, like his father before him, from the place of Atfih, at the entrance to the Wadi Araba, the natural corridor linking the Nile Valley to the Red Sea and giving access to the Wadi el-Jarf harbour.

seal impressions bearing the name of Sneferu, founder of the 4th Dynasty, and there is a well-preserved occupation level dating to this king's reign in the area around the so-called 'intermediate building'. It was in this context that we found an ostracon mentioning a work-gang named 'The Lion'. Given that the system by which the storage galleries were sealed up is associated with control marks relating to this team, this perhaps allows us to suggest that a significant proportion of the galleries at the site date to Sneferu's reign.

As described in the previous chapter, King Sneferu had three gigantic pyramids constructed successively, after an initial, smaller step pyramid at Seila. The first was at Meidum, on the edge of the Faiyum region, exactly opposite the Wadi Araba corridor linking the Nile Valley with the Red Sea which terminates at Wadi el-Jarf. At the time when the royal work-gangs were involved in the construction of this huge monument at Meidum, it is easy to imagine that the most important administrative centre in the country must have been established in the immediate vicinity of this building site.

This was the situation not only at the very beginning of Sneferu's reign, when his pyramid was built in the 'step pyramid' style characteristic of 3rd-Dynasty tradition, but also in the final decade of his reign. He returned to Meidum then to transform his monument into a geometrically 'true' pyramid, on the basis of the experience his builders had subsequently gained at two further pyramids at Dahshur (40 km to the north). Thus, during these two phases of Sneferu's reign, the site of Wadi el-Jarf was particularly well positioned, directly in line with the most important administrative centre in the country.

During Khufu's reign the situation changed. With his decision to construct his royal funerary complex at the site of Giza, 80 km to the north of Meidum, the port of Wadi el-Jarf suddenly became more marginal and would clearly have lost much of its attraction. Other disadvantages of the port's location might then have been more acutely felt: water was available, but its source was somewhat distant, obliging the teams based at the site to organize a complex set of logistics in order to both acquire and store it. Additionally, the fact that the first mountainous spurs were located more than 5 km from the shoreline of Wadi el-Jarf meant that the different elements of the site as a whole (camps, storage areas and the port itself) were spread over a wide area, creating communication problems

The last level of occupation of the 'intermediate building' (at the time this structure was completely sanded up by the wind) is characterized by small walls – at a very high level – dividing the long rooms (the 'galleries') into smaller cells, probably to shelter occupants from the wind for a short period. This phase may date to the reign of Khafre, to judge from seal impressions.

between the individual components. It is therefore likely that the main purpose of the 'intermediate building', located in the centre of the site overall, was to control the entire system. Nevertheless, the papyri discovered at Wadi el-Jarf demonstrate that the royal work-gangs – whether by pure habit or because of a lack of desire for change – continued to use the site for their expeditions to Sinai throughout Khufu's reign.

### The port after Khufu

The site has yielded no traces of activity from the relatively short reign of Djedefre, Khufu's successor. On the other hand, there are remains from the reign of Khafre, the fourth ruler in this 4th-Dynasty lineage, who ascended the throne after Djedefre. Seals including his name have been found in the latest occupation levels of the 'intermediate building', though this seems to have been a relatively ephemeral phase of activity. It is attested virtually everywhere in the building and came after a lengthy period of abandonment, during which the structure was almost entirely backfilled with wind-blown sand. The expedition occupying the building at that time had sought to protect themselves from the wind by dividing its large elongated cells into smaller units, using stone walls placed high up on top of the sand. In the same way, the area around the port itself was re-occupied. Small housing areas were scattered across the part of the site where the main camps had been located in the time of Khufu, close to the jetty. These new residential areas reused stones from the construction of the geometrically planned, comb-style buildings of the previous era.

What was the purpose of this final Egyptian presence at Wadi el-Jarf? The evidence available so far providing possible answers to this question relates to the section of housing nearest the sea (the 'intermediate building' and the port area). Perhaps only the coastal part of the site was used in Khafre's reign, taking the form of a simple staging-post on the journey to the Sinai mines – the area exploited by the Egyptians for copper ore is located directly opposite the point on the coast where the jetty was built. Or could it simply be the case that an expedition mission had specifically been dispatched to Wadi el-Jarf to recover material that could still be salvaged, at a time when it had already been officially decided to abandon the site? The fact remains that the reign of Khafre clearly represented a watershed; indeed, it was around this time that the site of Ayn Sukhna was probably provided with its own system of rock-cut storage galleries, similar to those at Wadi el-Jarf, but on a smaller scale.

## The move to Ayn Sukhna

Seal impressions referring to Khafre, the first ruler to be mentioned at Ayn Sukhna, have been recovered in the excavations of the storage galleries found there amid material indicating that subsequently the site was regularly occupied up to the end of the Old Kingdom. The names of most of the rulers of the 5th and 6th Dynasties have been identified there, in fact. For a royal administration that was based permanently in the vicinity of Giza, close to the construction sites of the pyramids of Khafre and Menkaure, the decision to establish a port near the northern end of the Gulf of Suez would have been

The presence of royal expeditions at Ayn Sukhna during Khafre's reign is known from several seal impressions. From its style, the most ancient commemorative rock inscription at the site probably dates back to the same period. It was carved on the mountain above the gallery system, and is dedicated to an official named 'The inspector of recruits Dag'. His representation is followed by a female character carrying a basket on her head, very similar to the 'funeral domains' that appear in the reliefs of royal and private chapels from the 4th Dynasty onwards, which symbolically feed the cult of the deceased. The texts also wish him a good burial in the West, and suggest that bread and beer would be delivered to him every day.

completely logical. Not only did the site of Ayn Sukhna have the advantage of being very close to a natural source of water, but it also offered easy access to the coastline, as well as incorporating a mountainous spur reaching down almost to the sea. It was therefore easy to create the rock-cut storage galleries needed to store nautical equipment that allowed expeditions to two different destinations to sail the Red Sea. However, these galleries were much poorer in quality than those at Wadi el-Jarf: they were cut into a friable sandstone and were continually collapsing throughout the pharaonic period, forcing the teams that used them to take measures to reinforce their entrances.

Nevertheless, the decision taken during the reign of Khafre to use Ayn Sukhna as the principal port seems to have been vindicated, given the fact that it was then occupied at regular intervals for nearly a millennium by Egyptian expeditions setting out for Sinai and Punt. Although the site of the main port for these missions was moved from one location to another, it retained the same toponym, Bat (literally 'The Bushy Land'). This name was clearly transferred from Wadi el-Jarf to Ayn Sukhna, where it is found twice in official inscriptions of Djedkare-Isesi inscribed on the walls of some of its storage galleries.

If the purpose of the activity at Wadi el-Jarf in the reign of Khafre was to salvage anything that might still be useful for maritime expeditions, whoever was responsible for this work left behind something of much greater value to us today – the Wadi el-Jarf Papyri.

Commemorative inscription of the 5th-Dynasty king Djedkare-Isesi at Ayn Sukhna. It was left on the wall of gallery G6, and gives an account of an expedition sent to Sinai. We learn that the team was transported by *kebenet*-boats (literally boats of the 'Byblos style') and that they were departing for a place named Bat (literally 'The Bushy Land' in the district of 'Inet'). The same place name also appears on tiny fragments of Papyrus E in Wadi el-Jarf, suggesting that it was previously the name of this first harbour.

*kebenet*-boats
(Byblos-type boats)

... from the place of Bat ('The Bushy Land') in the district of Inet

# PART III

# THE WORLD'S
# OLDEST WRITTEN
# DOCUMENTS

# CHAPTER 6

# FINDING THE PAPYRI

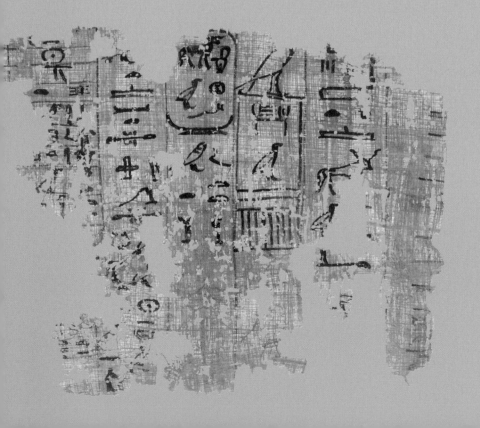

The 31 rock-cut storage galleries we rediscovered at the Wadi el-Jarf site had mostly been re-opened in antiquity, and in some cases had been largely stripped of their original contents. It is likely that systematic removal of everything the Egyptians considered to be of value was organized during the final visit to the site, probably in the mid-4th Dynasty. The ending of operations at Wadi el-Jarf may have occurred during the reign of Khafre, since he is both the last 4th-Dynasty king attested in texts at the site (in the abandonment levels) and also the first to appear in texts at Ayn Sukhna, which clearly then took over as the main Red Sea port for the rest of the 4th Dynasty.

When shutting down the Wadi el-Jarf facilities, it seems that particular attention was given to removing the pieces of cedarwood that made up the shells of the boats stored in the galleries. The material found during our investigation of these storerooms generally consisted of numerous broken pieces of lower-quality wood fitted with tenons to enable them to be assembled into boats, as well as fragments of rope. In short, the Egyptians removed everything that could be easily recycled or reused. The items recovered so far are somewhat disappointing, therefore, in that they provide little information on the nature of the boats operating at the site. More usefully, some carpenters' marks and red ink annotations that were originally intended to assist in the assembly and dismantling of the boats do survive. There is one discovery, however, that may tell us a little more: at the entrance to gallery G5 we found a very large piece of boat frame, comprising part of a hull. Although this had unfortunately largely disintegrated, its diameter of 2.75 m may point to the use of relatively large boats at that time, perhaps as much as 15–20 m in length. In comparison, the disassembled solar boat found buried in a pit next to Khufu's pyramid measured 43.6 m in length when its mainly cedarwood elements were pieced back together.

Analysis of material from the most recent phases of investigation of the G18–G28 galleries may, in future years, shed new light on Egyptian boatbuilding. The systematic excavation of the entrances to this second group of artificial caves has revealed an exceptional concentration of well-preserved organic artifacts including cordage, wood and textiles. This suggests that, surprisingly, some of these stores still contained much of the material that had

Papyrus G, an accounts text, discovered in the entrance to gallery G2 at Wadi el-Jarf (see pp. 142–43).

133

Part of a boat found at
Wadi el-Jarf and a fragment
of rope from the site.
(Not to the same scale.)

Fragments of wood and ropes found at the entrance of gallery G26. These well-preserved remains, and others similar to them, seem to indicate that a substantial amount of seafaring gear was left behind at Wadi el-Jarf when it was abandoned early in Khafre's reign.

A large section of wooden boat frame from the bottom of a ship, discarded and thrown in the closing system of gallery G5 at Wadi el-Jarf. We can deduce that the complete vessel may have been as much as 15–20 m in length.

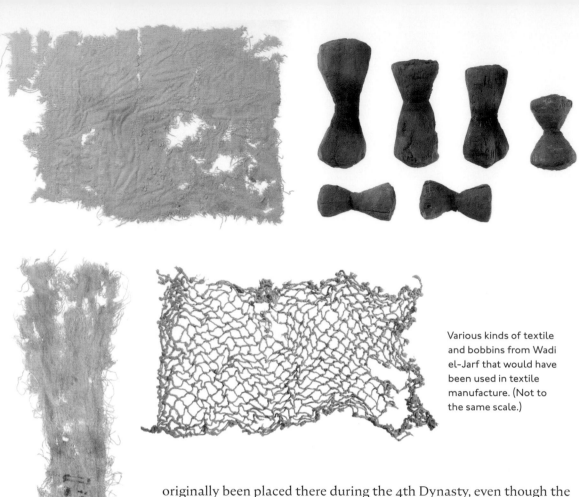

Various kinds of textile and bobbins from Wadi el-Jarf that would have been used in textile manufacture. (Not to the same scale.)

originally been placed there during the 4th Dynasty, even though the deposits had all clearly been looted. Moreover, the frequent presence of textiles impregnated with a resinous substance may indicate that the practice of caulking boats was already known at this time, although this will only be confirmed by thorough examination of the material. The continuation of the fieldwork should in any case provide a wealth of information for those studying pharaonic boatbuilding.

This material relating to seafaring was not the only evidence to emerge from the excavation of the stores. They have also yielded an abundance of domestic artifacts – objects made of stone (flint blades, weights and stone pounders), copper chisels, wooden tools (mallets and weaving shuttles), and a large quantity of textiles, some of which may have been bags originally used to store materials. A number of imprints of cylinder-seals, impressed into special clay for this purpose, have also been found in some of the excavated galleries. These seals were clearly used to control access to the contents of

CLOCKWISE FROM TOP LEFT A variety of items found at Wadi el-Jarf: a so-called 'pillow stone' – in fact used for grinding items, or as an anvil – inscribed with the marks of a phyle or work-group; a stone pick; a wooden mallet; copper tools; and a seal impression from the time of Khufu. (Not to the same scale.)

chests or bags storing equipment and supplies for the royal work-groups, and they preserve the titles of various officials involved in the supply process.

There are also traces that people left behind of a more personal nature. The walls of some storage galleries bear commemorative inscriptions, celebrating the fact that a specific expedition or individual passed through the port. For instance, a painted image in the entrance of gallery G3 depicts a small standing figure, wearing a wig and a loincloth and holding a staff; he is identified by a hieroglyphic caption above his head as 'Idu, the scribe of the Southern Lake'. Since the toponym 'southern lake' usually refers to the lake dominating the Faiyum region in northern Egypt, Idu is probably one of the leaders of an expedition sent to Wadi el-Jarf from the Faiyum. Troops travelling to Sinai would have regularly had to pass through the area of the Faiyum before leaving the Nile Valley and following the natural desert corridor of the Wadi Araba to the Red Sea coast.

## Water in the desert

Among the most impressive items excavated from these galleries were huge groups of large pottery storage jars, which would have played a key role in the overall life of the port. They were clearly made at the site itself, as shown by a set of basins used to work the clay identified in front of the G8–G11 galleries, and numerous potter's wheels discovered at several places during the excavations. The potters probably fashioned the vessels at the entrances to the galleries, so that they had enough light to work by but were shaded from direct sunlight. It also seems that they dried the vessels here before stacking them in the kilns to be fired. Kilns were located at the edge of the cluster of storage galleries, in well-ventilated sites that were also somewhat set away from the living areas.

A remarkable freshwater spring that currently rises within the perimeter of the Christian monastery of St Paul, and which can produce 4 cu. m of water per day, must have provided the essential water for the pharaonic work-gangs when the port of Wadi el-Jarf was in operation and been intensively exploited by them. The spring is situated about 10 km from the port, so presumably processions of donkeys loaded with water-skins would have trekked back and forth almost continuously. Once delivered to the galleries area of the site, the water was then stored in the large pottery jars, each with a standard capacity of 30 litres. In this way an abundant supply of water was provided for the members of the expeditions – probably numbering several hundred at a time – who lived at the site for lengthy periods. These large storage jars were therefore a fundamental part of the operation of the port of Wadi el-Jarf, without which it could not have functioned.

Over the course of the main period of use of the port, several batches of these jars were clearly manufactured at the site. When each new batch of vessels was made, the work-gang responsible for it systematically marked its name on the containers before they were fired. Galleries G15a, G15b, G22 and G23 were specifically used to store this type of jar, which were sometimes found by the hundreds (gallery G22 alone still contained nearly 350 of them at the time of its excavation in the 2017–18 season). The detailed study of the successive batches of storage jars produced at Wadi el-Jarf – at least three of which are well attested in the documentation from all parts of the site – now allows us (alongside other evidence) to propose a relative chronology for the period of occupation of the site as a whole. The first batch probably dates to the reign of Sneferu, the founder of the 4th Dynasty, and the others are spread throughout the reign of his successor, Khufu. From this it can be estimated that the port was active for about 70 years, corresponding to the reigns of Sneferu and Khufu, before it was abandoned and maritime activities moved to Ayn Sukhna.

A kiln for making pottery, one of several located at the edge of the Wadi el-Jarf storage gallery area and set apart from the living quarters.

Gallery G22: a magazine for the storage of hundreds of pottery jars belonging to 'The Escort Team of "The Uraeus of Khufu is its Prow"' (probably Merer's team).

## The work-gangs and their names

Who were the work-gangs who frequented the site during the 4th Dynasty and allowed it to function? Who first carved out the galleries from the rock and created the monumental-style system for sealing up their entrances, who made the storage jars, and who assembled and disassembled the boats used in the Red Sea? Two distinct groups of texts found in the excavations have yielded the names of at least six of the expeditionary teams, who were clearly present at different moments in the use of the site. The first set of texts was those written on the storage jars, and the second the large-scale control marks, painted in red ink on the large blocks of limestone that make up the system of closing the gallery entrances.

The names given to individual work-gangs usually obey the same basic logic: each team (*aper* in ancient Egyptian) was named either by a form of words referring to the king who ruled at that time, or by a phrase associating the gang closely with a specific named boat, which was itself equipped with individual royal insignia. One example of the first type (i.e. phrases naming the king in power at the time) is *rekhu bikui-nebu*, which appeared on dozens of jars in gallery G15a in particular, but also turned up throughout the site. It may be translated as 'Those who are Known to the Double Golden Horus' and is explicitly linked to one of the five names of King Khufu. Egyptian kings generally had fives names or epithets that made up their royal titulary, and Khufu's Golden Horus name was 'The Double Golden Horus'. In this way the name emphasizes just how closely the team seems to have worked with the king, a proximity that is also confirmed by information provided in Papyrus D, which will be discussed later.

The second type of team name is represented by at least three examples. One, *aper shemsu wer mai-es*, which may be understood as 'The Escort Team of "Great is his Lion"', is well attested in both control marks and jar-labels. Another team bears the name *aper shemsu Khnem-khuef-wi in wadjti-es*, literally 'The Escort Team of "Khufu Confers on it his Two Uraei"'. These two phrases may at first glance seem to be quite obscure, and we might wonder to whom Khufu conferred his uraei, and for whom was the lion great. A solution, however, was provided by a third team name based on this same method, which was found on hundreds of storage jars as well as on the papyri at the site. This name, *aper shemsu ma wereret Khnem-khuef-wi*, may be translated as 'The Escort Team of "The

A general view from the inside of gallery G22, showing the huge number of pottery jars found there.

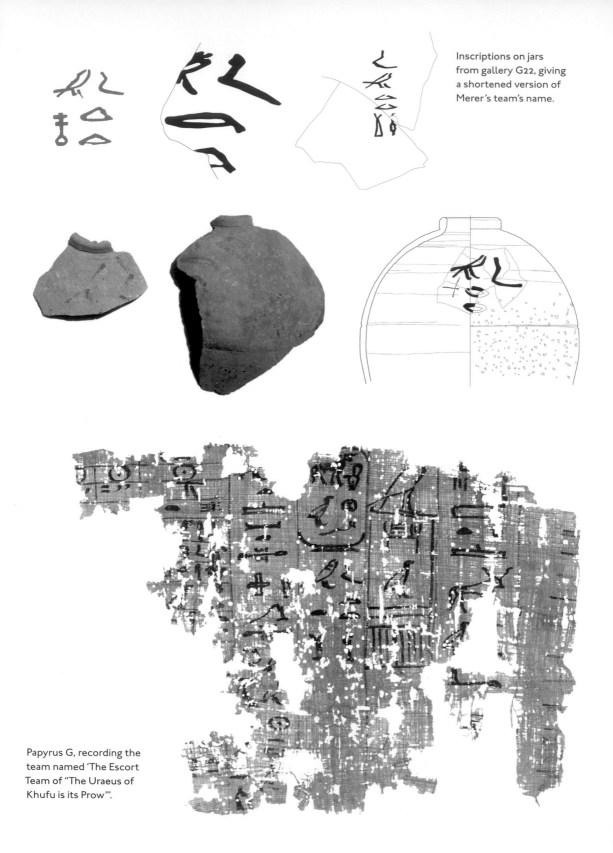

Inscriptions on jars from gallery G22, giving a shortened version of Merer's team's name.

Papyrus G, recording the team named 'The Escort Team of "The Uraeus of Khufu is its Prow"'.

Uraeus of Khufu is its Prow'", which shows that the teams were named after the boat to which they were probably attached. The vessels were honoured by having their bows equipped with a royal emblem, which evidently might be a uraeus-snake or a lion. It was this last work-gang that certainly left their archives at the site, a set of papyri probably abandoned at the time of the last important mission that operated at Wadi el-Jarf.

## A lucky discovery: the papyri

Fragments of papyri were found in many parts of the site, particularly in the area around galleries G1–G17, but the main concentration was essentially in a restricted area in front of galleries G1 and G2, oriented towards the south. Small fragments were initially collected just a few centimetres below modern ground level in front of gallery G2. These consisted of some meagre fragments of spreadsheet accountancy texts, but also fragile pieces of logbooks that mention Akhet Khufu ('Horizon of Khufu'), the pyramid complex of Khufu at Giza. They occurred fairly consistently, but in varying densities, throughout the entire excavation of the zone around the entrance of gallery G2 and the area between galleries G1 and G2. Then, on 24 March 2013, a more substantial collection was unearthed 5 m from the entrance of G2. This 'bundle' included an accounts text with a precise date from the reign of Khufu (Papyrus G); a small slip mentioning deliveries of food and various other supplies, including copper tools, to the work-teams (Papyrus K); and a large fragment of a logbook (part of Papyrus C).

Papyrus B, Inspector Merer's logbook, as discovered at the G1 entrance.

Papyrus H, an accounts document, as discovered also at the G1 entrance.

Finally, beginning four days later, the clearance of a pit between two large blocks closing the entrance of the G1 gallery produced the largest and most significant discovery – hundreds of fragments of papyrus rolls, including documents now identified as logbooks (Papyri A, B, C, D, E, F and AA) and accounts texts (Papyri G, H, I, J and U).

Joins subsequently made between fragments of Papyrus C that had been found on the surface, in front of galleries G1 and G2, and the greatest part of this document later found in the pit, seem to demonstrate that all the material derived from a single deposit. Originally the documents had been buried between these two large blocks at the time the storage gallery was sealed up. However, the cache had subsequently been disturbed and the documents contained within were scattered, some being thrown outside. Although superficially it might seem a pity that the papyri were damaged by this ancient plundering, it appears in fact that it paradoxically facilitated better preservation of some of the documents. Those that remained at the bottom of the pit where they had originally been placed had almost entirely decomposed as a result of the effect of the stagnant water that collected there. It was the papyrus rolls that were trapped in the main thickness of the sediment that withstood the environmental conditions most successfully, since rainwater generally drained away before reaching them: Papyri A, B and H were therefore the best preserved.

This was an astonishing and completely unexpected discovery, and the survival of these ancient documents for us to find over four thousand years later depended on two pieces of luck. The first is that the archives were left behind at the site at all, since we would usually have expected them to be taken back to the administrative headquarters for checking and archiving at the end of the mission. Secondly, the deposit was disturbed, perhaps due to an attempt to reopen the adjacent gallery soon after it had been closed. These two chance events resulted in better preservation of at least some of the papyri.

Papyrus G gives the most useful and precise information relating to this batch of archives. Most of the document, comprising the actual accounts data, is lost, but its initial section has survived, specifying the date on which it was written, and mentioning the name of the beneficiary of the goods with which the accounts are concerned. The first two columns, written in hieroglyphs that are both large and very detailed, run as follows: 'the year after the 13th census of large and small cattle / the Horus Medjedu'. The latter is Khufu's 'Horus name', the royal name most regularly found on official documents from his reign, particularly the seal impressions. In this early phase of Egyptian history the method used for dating events was based on the censuses of livestock and wealth throughout the country that seem to have taken place once every two years, although the precise ways in which this calendar operated are still much debated among historians.

In this specific case, if the first census had coincided with the first year of Khufu's reign, Papyrus G would date to year 26 of his reign, but if it took place only in the second year of his reign, then the date indicated by the document would be year 27. In any case, the date seems to be close to the end of Khufu's reign, since the same year ('after the 13th census') of Khufu has also been recorded in the Western Desert, at a mining site discovered in 2001 by a German expedition, where dated rock inscriptions of Khufu are linked closely with mention of his successor, Djedefre. According to an unpublished control mark in one of the boat pits associated with the Great Pyramid at Giza, the king's reign may have ended shortly after the 'year of the 14th census'.

All the papyri from the archives discovered at Wadi el-Jarf can be dated between the beginning of this 'year after the 13th census' (i.e. regnal year 26 or 27) and the first four months of the following year. In addition to this key chronological indication, the third column of Papyrus G also supplies us with the identity of the owner of this batch of documents: a work-gang named 'The Escort Team of <the ship named> "The Uraeus of Khufu is its Prow"'. This evidence is crucial, since a shorter version of the name of this same team has been found hundreds of times on storage jars at the site; these jars were probably marked with the name of their owner at the time they were made. Of the group of about 350 storage vessels of this type excavated from storage gallery G22, half bore painted hieroglyphic signs comprising parts of this work-gang name. Several other fragments of papyrus also include references to the same date and work-gang, suggesting that what we have is a coherent set of documents essentially relating to this one team of workers over a period of slightly more than a year, at the very end of the reign of Khufu, the second king of the 4th Dynasty. It seems this was the last group of workers and sailors based at Wadi el-Jarf before its final abandonment, and the link between the archives of this work-gang and the port is firmly established by the references made to them in Papyrus G.

Overall, the contents of the archive are quite varied, mostly comprising accounts describing the delivery of various foodstuffs or equipment to this team of royal workers, but it also includes the remains of a dozen logbooks in which the daily activities of the team are succinctly reported, and this is indisputably the most important part of the archive.

The major question raised by the discovery of this important documentary archive is how and why the deposit of papyri came about in this way. As the main cache of papyri discovered in the entrance to gallery G1 was in the middle of the sediment, concentrated in several strata, it has been assumed that they were simply thrown in when the storeroom was sealed up and the site abandoned. The clear secondary disturbance of the deposit, a large part of which then ended up scattered over the terrace in front of the G1 and G2 galleries, may be misleading in this regard. It is possible, in fact, that the documents were originally kept in cloth bags, since hundreds of pieces of textile were found in the same area. In addition, some of the documents discovered in the pit, despite being completely decomposed, were still partially held together by thin cordage, intended to keep them rolled up. This may imply that there was at least some kind of deliberate organization to the storage of the papyri, however minimal. In any case, the fact that these detailed documents were abandoned, and not carried back by their owners to the Nile Valley to be officially archived, no doubt suggests that they were regarded as no longer of any use, but why? There is no question about their immense value to us. It was fortunate that they were then completely forgotten and overlooked in this remote desert location – until our excavations brought them back into the light.

# CHAPTER 7

# TRANSLATING THE PAPYRI

The use of papyrus as a medium for written archives probably developed at quite an early date in Egypt. Perhaps surprisingly, the ancient Egyptians did not opt to use unbaked clay tablets impressed with a reed pen to write administrative documents, as had been the method employed since the origins of writing in Mesopotamia. On one occasion, however, Egypt does seem to have experimented with the medium of the clay tablet. Hundreds of tablets (including letters, accounts and lists of staff), incised with hieratic, were found in the archives of a 6th-Dynasty provincial palace at Balat, in the Dakhla Oasis (*c.* 2300 BC). In this instance, it was perhaps the remoteness of the oasis from the Nile Valley, the principal source of papyrus, that lay behind the decision. In all other times and places, it was this aquatic plant (*Cyperus papyrus*), abundantly available in the marshy margins of the Nile Valley, that was always preferred as a formal writing medium (sherds of pottery and stone – ostraca – could be used for more informal notes and letters).

The sheets of papyrus were manufactured by first extracting the fibres from papyrus stems, which were soaked and beaten. The resulting strips were placed in layers at right angles to each other, compressed and finally dried, to produce the writing surface. Individual sheets could be joined together to make long rolls. The earliest currently known fragments of papyrus as a writing medium were found at Saqqara in the tomb of the chancellor Hemaka, an elite administrative official who held office in the reign of Den (the fifth ruler of the 1st Dynasty, *c.* 2950 BC). No inscription was visible on these fragments when they were discovered, either because they had been left blank or because the ink had long since faded. Papyrus is a fragile medium and does not survive well in a humid environment, so finds dating back to the earliest periods in Egyptian history are extremely rare. Virtually all the papyrus archives of the Old Kingdom seem to have been lost, even though study of the documents found at Wadi el-Jarf suggests that they would have existed in large numbers. Sadly, most of the information that would undoubtedly have allowed modern historians to gain a better understanding of the organization of the pharaonic state in the early days of its existence has therefore also been lost.

Until the Wadi el-Jarf discovery, the most important papyrological archive for this period was a set of documents discovered at the site of Abusir, between Giza and Saqqara. The Abusir Papyri relate to the funerary complexes belonging to two kings who ruled in the first half of the 5th Dynasty (Neferirkare-Kakai and Raneferef), as well as that of a queen named Khentkawes (wife of the former and mother of the latter). These documents mostly consist of accounts of activities relating to the temples where the deceased rulers received daily worship. Lists in the form of tables record deliveries of foodstuffs for these institutions, as well as inventories of the equipment supplied to them. Roster schedules log the tasks assigned to the staff dedicated to the royal duties in the temples. The papyri have been dated almost exclusively to the reign of Djedkare-Isesi, the penultimate king of the 5th Dynasty (*c.* 2468–2432 BC), and they provide extremely valuable insights into the functioning of the state at a period when the Old Kingdom was well advanced.

Other, more exceptional one-off discoveries, which generally also date towards the end of the Old Kingdom (either late 5th Dynasty or 6th Dynasty), have been made at Saqqara, Elephantine (in Upper Egypt) and Sharuna (in Middle Egypt). The documentary archive that is probably most comparable to the one found at Wadi el-Jarf is a set of six complete papyrus scrolls discovered at Gebelein, in Upper Egypt, in a wooden box deposited in a grave. This archive, which mostly comprises tabulated accounts, has been published by Paule Posener-Kriéger, who has argued that they may be dated earlier, either mid-4th Dynasty or the beginning of the 5th Dynasty. On the basis of the palaeography of the papyri she has suggested an even more precise date, placing them in the reign of Menkaure, close to the end of the 4th Dynasty. One of the documents includes a date of 'the year after the 11th census', which may refer to any one of a number of 4th-Dynasty rulers, including Sneferu and Khufu, who reigned for a sufficient length of time to reach this census, and it is not really possible to be any more certain. The style of the hieroglyphs in the documents certainly seems to be very similar to the writing on the documents more recently discovered at Wadi el-Jarf.

## How the papyri are organized

All the chronological information relating to them indicates that the Wadi el-Jarf Papyri fragments are the oldest known explicitly dated Egyptian documents. More than a thousand pieces have been recovered, probably originally deriving from at least 30 rolls all belonging to this specific group (i.e., not counting the one-off discoveries of papyri made elsewhere on the site). In terms of the sheer quantity of papyri, this collection is second only to the Abusir archive, which it pre-dates by about one-and-a-half centuries. The Wadi el-Jarf Papyri are also much more varied in content than other previously studied papyrus archives from the Old Kingdom.

Among the papyri there are accounts texts relating to different foodstuffs delivered by the administration to the team of workers whose activities are recorded in the documents, using a tabular method very similar to the format employed in the Abusir archives (see above). Fragments of letters, staff lists and even identity papers, as well as perhaps a few bits and pieces of an ancient map, have also been found. But the most unprecedented texts are undoubtedly the major series of more than 400 'logbook' fragments, which originally derived from at least seven specific documents of this type. This kind of text is well known throughout Egyptian history, specifically in the case of teams of workers permanently employed by the pharaonic state. Registers of this kind were kept on a daily basis, logging the activities of the work-gangs and verifying that they were fully occupied with the tasks allotted to them by the administration. A much later parallel is the famous 'Necropolis Journal' from the Deir el-Medina New Kingdom tomb-workers' village. Written by a scribe to record the important events affecting the community, the journal always indicates whether the team was working on specific days or not. It is therefore a true 'time and motion' log, kept by the administration in exactly the same way as for other state assets. The practice of writing logbooks in this way must have been prevalent since the Old Kingdom, and at least three such documents were already known before the Wadi el-Jarf discovery. One is a 6th-Dynasty papyrus from Saqqara and the other two are tablets from among the Balat archive mentioned above. The sheer quantity of information recorded in the documents discovered at Wadi el-Jarf, however, has hugely improved our ability to understand how these administrative records were organized.

Papyrus A, one sheet of which is particularly well preserved, provides a good example of the way in which all the data were assembled. The upper part of the papyrus comprises one long line of text, including a reference to the month during which the recorded activities of one team took place: the first month of the 'inundation' season (Akhet), which corresponds to the month of July, in the reign of Khufu. Several indications reveal that each of these administrative documents was able to record at least two months of work. Further down the page, a second line is subdivided into boxes, each containing a day of the month, from 1 to 30. The first is *wepet* ('that which opens') and the last is *arket* ('that of the end'). All the others are simply noted as numbers: day 7, day 8, day 9 etc; the hieroglyphic sign for *herw* (which represents the sun and means 'day') is in each case accompanied by a numerical notation. Below each day-box are usually two columns of hieratic text (the cursive version of the hieroglyphic script) reporting the events of that day.

The writer of this particular text seems mostly to have been the middle-ranking inspector called Merer, who was in charge of part of a work-gang. As discussed later, he indicates on what task the team 'spent the day' (*weresh*), before specifying the place where they 'spent the night' (*sedjer*), in this way following the movements of the team and recording what duties they were involved in. A line framing each column of text is generally in black ink, while red ink is used for the lines framing each tenth day. On the basis of this, it seems that a ten-day sequence (or 'decan') was probably the basic unit of how work was organized. The writing is usually very neat; the daily reports are written in black, but some sections of text are written in red, as a means of emphasizing their relative importance. The red sections are mostly indications of items and events that were provided for the team, such as the arrival of monthly rations, the giving of textiles as payment, and festivals celebrated by the team. Finally, the scribe was able to use the bottom section of each document to note down certain other pieces of information, perhaps acting as his aide memoire before writing the daily report itself. In content, the logbooks are quite repetitive, but thanks to the sheer number of documents that have survived, the great length of some of them, and the fact that they report on such a variety of expeditions, we ultimately gain considerable information both on the activities of this one specific team of workers and on the more general issue of the organization of the Egyptian administration at this point in history.

The great significance and interest of these documents were obvious from the first moment they began to be uncovered at the site. And even when we were simply finding the first few fragments of inscribed papyrus – before the really key hoard of texts emerged – we were intrigued to notice examples that seemed to be inscribed with dense columns of hieratic script in which the cartouche of Khufu was constantly repeated. However, we had to wait until the final week of the 2013 excavation season, and the discovery of the first large fragments of Papyri A and B, to fully appreciate the nature of these texts and the internal rationale of the archive, before piecing them together for study and publication.

## Conserving the papyri

While we were still in the field at Wadi el-Jarf, the pressing issue – before we even thought about studying the documents – was essentially to ensure the conservation of the fragments as soon as each one was excavated from the pit. This was a huge task, given that several dozen pieces of papyrus were being transferred every day from the excavation site to our study-rooms, which were housed in Portakabins at our camp. The protocol that we followed in dealing with the conservation of the papyrus had been suggested by a colleague who had worked at the Bibliothèque nationale, the national library of France, on the restoration of this type of material. First, we did our best to remove all the particles of earth or sand still attached to the papyrus fibres – this was a delicate task, carried out on a clean work surface with very fine brushes. The next step was to re-humidify the papyrus, in order to restore its flexibility and allow us to flatten it out. For this, we used what the archaeologists at the

Fragments of the Wadi el-Jarf Papyri at the time of their discovery. Papyrus is a fragile medium, not surviving well in humid environments. Nearly all the Old Kingdom archives have been lost: the Wadi el-Jarf documents indicate that they would have been extensive.

French Institute in Cairo call 'Fournettes', named after the Hellenist Jean-Luc Fournet, who developed this technique while working at Tebtunis (in the Faiyum region, in 1992–96) in order to treat the huge quantity of Greco-Roman papyri excavated at this site. These Fournettes take the form of a glass or plastic box, the base of which is moist. The papyrus is placed on a grid or mesh in the upper part of the box, exposing it to the moisture below while protecting it from direct contact with the water. After a few hours, the moisture permeates the document, which can then be manipulated without risk of tearing the fibres.

Once the document has been prepared in this way, the most delicate stage can be undertaken: the papyrus is unrolled and flattened on a sheet of blotting paper, specially chosen both for its lack of acidity and the fact that it can be kept moist throughout the operation. Then it is a question of straightening the papyrus fibres as much as possible, using pliers and soft brushes, as well as dental tools selected for their precision. Straightening the fibres successfully in this way can maximize the legibility of the documents, since it sometimes improves the chances of seeing certain hieroglyphic signs inscribed on the most worn or twisted sections of the papyrus. By this means connections can sometimes be made between several fragments of the same sheet. The papyrus is then dried under a press consisting of several layers of de-acidified blotting paper placed under a heavy weight. Books from our small field library could be used as weights for this purpose, if needed. Patience is required for the next stage – waiting for several days until the papyrus is completely dry before removing it from the press, then placing it between two glass plates to keep it safe.

At the end of our 2013 field season, we were able to hand over to the Egyptian Ministry of Antiquities more than 50 of these glass plates of various sizes, some containing almost complete documents, others simply fragments. The Ministry could then transfer them to stores in the Suez Museum. This conservation work continued in the 2014 and 2015 seasons, dealing with the tinier fragments that we had run out of time to treat at the end of the 2013 season. About a hundred glass plates, containing more than a thousand fragments of papyrus varying greatly in size, are still being studied and published.

Our initial conservation work was essentially an emergency operation, carried out in the field in order to facilitate the conservation and transfer of these precious fragments of papyri

First restoration of Papyrus
G, an accounts text.

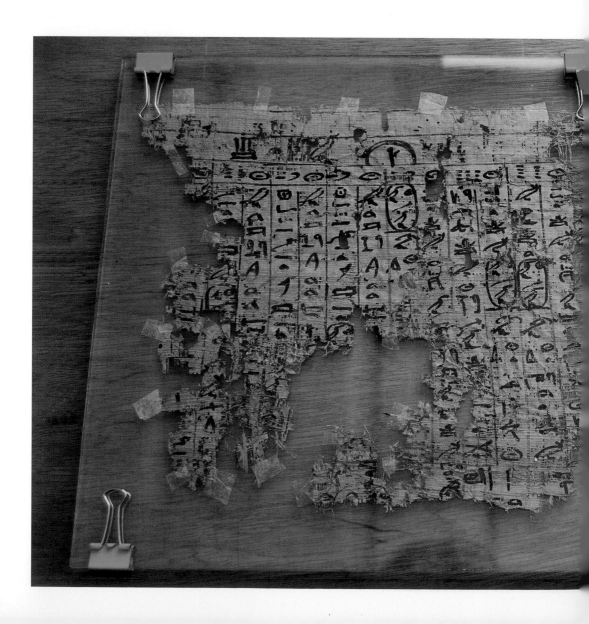

At the Wadi el-Jarf excavation campsite, Pierre Tallet works on the restoration of documents.

Conservator Eve Menei working on the final restoration of a papyrus in the Suez Museum.

Papyrus A, one of the logbooks kept by Inspector Merer, framed between sheets of glass after its unrolling.

Fragment of Papyrus B, a logbook kept by Inspector Merer, before (ABOVE) and after (BELOW) final restoration.

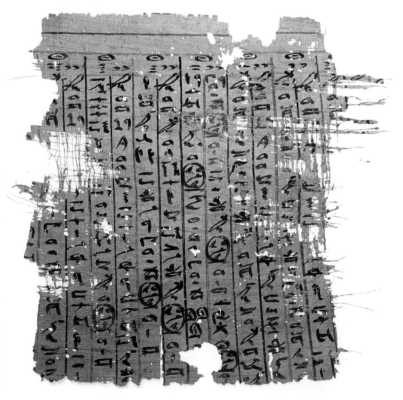

PART III    The World's Oldest Written Documents

in the best possible conditions under the circumstances. However, if these papyri were to be put on permanent display in museums in Egypt, it was clear the intervention of a real specialist in this area would be needed, to ensure the optimal revitalization of the fibres in the documents. This would then improve our ability to make more precise connections between different parts of the same document, especially those that had been found completely separately. An additional process of restoration has therefore been launched – and is currently still under way – both at the Suez Museum and in the laboratories of the Egyptian Museum in Cairo. This is being led by Eve Menei, a recognized specialist in papyrus conservation, and its aim is both to complete the presentation of the documents and to make new connections between the hundreds of fragments of papyrus rolls, especially the accounts texts, which make up more than half the archive.

## Deciphering the logbooks

The process of deciphering the best-preserved logbooks has been relatively straightforward. The hieratic script the texts are written in is particularly neat and regular, showing that scribal practices had become fairly standardized even at this early stage in Egyptian history. Also, the language used is relatively simple, a narrative style based mostly on the use of verbs in the infinitive – a practice found throughout pharaonic history, especially in military reports. The daily reports are fairly repetitive in each of the documents found so far, which actually helps to attribute different fragments to very specific papyri. Peculiarities in the layout of the different logbooks also facilitated our initial sorting of the documents, particularly in terms of the presentation of the daily information relating to date, as well as the presumed original height of the columns, which varies from one papyrus to another. All this information has allowed us to propose a theoretical reconstruction of the original arrangement of the seven logbooks that we have identified in this batch of archives, sometimes also gaining a sense of the documents' full original lengths (see Table 1).

When daily dates are preserved in individual documents, they allow certain fragments to be put back in order. The writers of each of the documents systematically drew a red vertical line both at the end of each set of 10 working days (i.e. after every 20 columns of text), and also at the end of each month. This is an enormous help in our reconstructions, since it makes it easier to place some of the surviving fragments in their correct locations on a theoretical grid. Papyri A and B were the largest of the surviving fragments, sometimes with as many as 15 daily reports preserved one after the other, which meant we were able to decipher their texts in a continuous sequence almost as soon as they were placed between the sheets of glass at the end of the 2013 excavation season. Our only real difficulty was the identification of some of the hieratic signs used, since these texts are the first examples of this cursive script at such an early date. Some of the ways in which certain hieroglyphic signs were transcribed changed in subsequent systems of writing them, so much so that the earlier signs cannot always be immediately read. Nevertheless, increasing familiarity with these texts as we studied them further has easily overcome such problems.

A number of other challenges are, of course, encountered in deciphering the logbooks that are least well preserved. The fragmentary nature of these documents, with the frequent loss of the daily dates accompanying the reports, tends to be the most common reason for the inability to reconstruct the original rationale of the information they record. In addition, because of the condition of the fragments, some signs and words are only partially preserved, making them hard to identify. Thus we have only a general overview of the activities recorded in Papyri C and E, with no real chance of reconstructing the chronological sequence of these fragments. Papyrus D, on the other hand, is a long document that originally corresponded to two months of activity by the work-gang. Over a hundred fragments have survived, enabling it to be put back together in general terms, even though this represents barely 15 per cent of its original extent. The success in reconstructing this papyrus is due to the fact that most of the adjoining fragments were still associated with one another at the time of their discovery. This meant that fragments of several successive sections of the text were preserved together in stratigraphic layers. Important sequences of fragments could then be established during the process of placing them between sheets of glass, since we always kept the fragments in the order we had found them.

From observations made during our work on the whole group of documents – particularly the best-preserved documents such as Papyrus H (an accounts text that survived almost intact) – we can see that each papyrus was rolled up from the left-hand side, with the inscribed surface facing upwards. This is shown by the fact that a large section at the right-hand end of the roll of Papyrus H was left blank, which would have protected the inscribed section by keeping it completely rolled up inside. Similarly, the title of the Papyrus H accounts text is written on the back of the papyrus, at the right-hand side, so it would be visible from the outside when the document was rolled up. From this, bearing in mind that all the documents were written from right to left (since this is the direction of hieratic script), and the contents were in chronological order, it follows that the earliest reports were written at the edge of the roll, and the most recent ones – sometimes also the best preserved – were in the innermost part of the roll. If a complete cross-section were to be cut vertically through the original roll, we would find that fragments were organized in the reverse order of the chronology

## TABLE I  Dimensions of the logbook papyri

| Papyrus | A | B | C | D | E(a) | F | AA |
|---|---|---|---|---|---|---|---|
| Minimum length of known continuous text | 63 cm | 96 cm (B I–IV) 150 cm (B I–IV + B X + B Y) | No continuous text | 168 cm (D I–VI) | 26.5 cm | 36 cm | No continuous text |
| Total known length (achieved by adding together the known columns) | 81 cm | 265 cm | 85 cm | 130 cm | Unknown | 66 cm | 16 cm |
| Length of text corresponding to two months | 180 cm | 180 cm | 204 cm | 168 cm | 204 cm | 90 cm | 60 cm |
| Width of columns | 1.5 cm | 1.5 cm | 1.7 cm | 1.4 cm | 1.4 cm | 1.5 cm | 1 cm |
| Total height | 19.5 cm | 22 cm | 15.5 cm | 20.5 cm | Unknown | 16.5 cm | 15 cm (min.) |
| Height of the top margin | 4 cm | 4 cm | 3.5 cm | 3.5 cm? | 3.5 cm | 3.5 cm | 4.8 cm |
| Height of the bottom margin | 2 cm | No bottom margin | No bottom margin | 3 cm | Unknown | No bottom margin | No known margin |
| Height of the columns containing the report | 13.5 cm | 18 cm | 12 cm? | 14 cm | Unknown | 13 cm | 15 cm (min.) |
| Notation of days | Line | Column | Line | Line | Line | Column | Column |

of information contained in the document (that is, day 1, the earliest, to day 10, the most recent), so from the centre of the roll outwards the order would be from the most recent to the earliest (from day 10 to day 1).

For this reason, if we systematically pull apart a bundle of excavated fragments with the inscribed side facing upwards, the most recent parts of the text (i.e. those that include the latest dates) will be encountered first, and the earliest will be at the back of the bundle. To achieve the greatest accuracy in reconstructing these fragments, the best approach is to place each of them on a theoretical grid, moving from left to right. Hypothetically, by placing different groups of fragments (at least six distinct bundles of excavated pieces) in the correct relationships with each other, taking into account such factors as impossible spatial connections, the logic of the text itself and aspects of the daily dates that have been preserved, the overall spread of information on the roll can largely be restored to its original appearance, as set out in the next chapter.

Full publication of the entire set of papyri is therefore a distinctly long-term undertaking, with the difficulties lying not so much in pure translation as in the process of first physically reconstructing the documents and interpreting the data that they contain. We have now completed publication of all seven logbooks that we have been able to identify, but the same work now needs to be undertaken for the remainder of the documents, primarily consisting of accounts texts. This type of papyri repeatedly presents us with a different type of problem. Several words recorded in these texts give the names of categories of material or foodstuffs which have no parallels in the entire known corpus of Egyptian texts. This is due not only to the very early date of the Wadi el-Jarf Papyri but also to the nature of the texts themselves. They are known to historians as 'practical texts', since they are entirely geared towards daily life, and their perspective differs profoundly from that of the official inscriptions that constitute the bulk of our sources for this period of Egyptian history (such as funerary scenes and individual 'biographies'). For the identifications of different foodstuffs, the process of interpreting these papyri will have to rely very much on archaeological data, and particularly the study of artifacts and zoological and palaeobotanical remains found at sites that were occupied during the same period, the early Old Kingdom.

It was also precisely at this time that the ancient Egyptians were engaged in building the largest of all the pyramids, including the Great Pyramid. The accounts and logbooks from Wadi el-Jarf when deciphered tell a unique and direct story of the daily lives of a team of workers in the reign of Khufu, thus providing unprecedented information that can provide us with a better understanding of this key period in Egypt's history. But how did they end up at this site and what exactly do they say?

# CHAPTER 8

# WHAT THE PAPYRI
# TELL US

Piecing together the excavated archaeological evidence and the information found in the documents, it is clear that the papyri excavated at Wadi el-Jarf constitute the archives of a single work-gang, numbering in total 160 men, named 'The Escort Team of "The Uraeus of Khufu is its Prow"'. The records cover a period that corresponds to slightly more than a calendar year, probably between the end of the year of the 13th census (years 26–27 of the reign of Khufu), and the very beginning of the year of the 14th census (years 28–29), during which the king may have died. Most of the information would therefore relate to the year after the 13th census, when this work-gang was mobilized to undertake at least five different tasks, recorded respectively by Papyri A, B, C, D and E, all of which are logbooks. The whole group of 160 men seems to have been divided into four 'phyles' (or sections, from the Greek for tribe), probably comprising about 40 men each. Each phyle, *za* in Egyptian, had its own name: 'Great' (*weret*), 'Asiatic' (*setjet*), 'Prosperous' (*wadjet*) and 'Small' (*nedjeset*). In at least one text (Papyrus D) we can see that these different groups are entrusted with parallel tasks, probably at about the same time, but in very different locations.

The logbooks discovered at Wadi el-Jarf are in fact of two different types: some – Papyri A, B and probably C – were probably kept by the 'Great' (*weret*) phyle, led by a middle-ranking official, an inspector named Merer. Many of the daily reports in these three papyri begin with the same formula: 'Day x, the inspector Merer spends the day with his phyle (*za*) in ...'. It is possible that documents of the same type were kept in parallel by each of the four separate phyles, a suggestion perhaps confirmed by one fragment in the batch of papyri on which three successive columns of text begin with the phrase 'the inspector Mesu spent the day'. In the same way, several other fragments give the names of at least two other officials (Nykaunesut and Sekher[...]) who may have served as heads of other phyles and kept their own logbooks. Since the most studied papyri tend to record two months of activity, a set of 24 papyrus rolls of this type would have been required to record the activities of all four phyles of the entire work-gang over the course of a year. However, it is not known for certain whether all the phyles did in fact generate this kind of report. Since Merer is head of the 'Great' phyle, which seems to have been the most important and highly rated of the four, this may explain the care he took in his logbook to record its

Part of Papyrus C found at Wadi el-Jarf, referring to activity in the Nile Delta (see pp. 168–69).

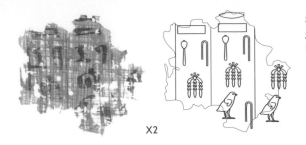

Small fragment of a lost logbook giving the name of an inspector Mesu (fragment X2).

X2

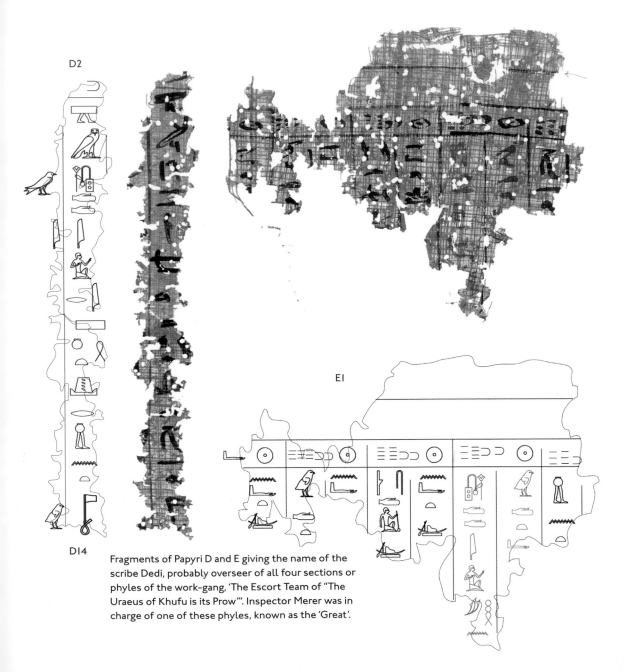

D2

E1

D14

Fragments of Papyri D and E giving the name of the scribe Dedi, probably overseer of all four sections or phyles of the work-gang, 'The Escort Team of "The Uraeus of Khufu is its Prow"'. Inspector Merer was in charge of one of these phyles, known as the 'Great'.

activities. Nor is it certain that the logbooks were actually designed to cover the whole year. None of the documents found seems to mention the period from December to March, so perhaps, for part of the year at least, individual teams were free to return home and join their families.

Other reports – the D and F papyri – are of a different type. They take a more general view of the four sections of the work-gang that are mentioned throughout the documents. In this instance, the author of the report is a scribe named Dedi, who seems to represent the central royal administration as overseer of the entire work-gang, rather than an inspector of an individual phyle. The 'Great' phyle, directed by Merer, appears regularly, but here it alternates with the 'Asiatic' (*setjet*) and 'Small' (*nedjeset*) phyles. The fourth phyle, 'Prosperous' (*wadjet*), is mentioned only once. It is possible, therefore, that six additional documents in the name of the scribe Dedi were originally produced, transcribing information recorded higher up the bureaucratic chain. But was this type of report in fact produced all year round, or only during the part of the year when the work-gang was based at Giza, in the centre of the Egyptian administration? And did Dedi accompany the workers even when they were sent somewhere as remote as the port at Wadi el-Jarf? The different ways in which the original complete documentary archive might be reconstructed vary enormously depending on the possible answers to these questions. In theory, if we extrapolate from the data collected so far, this single group of workers could have generated up to 30 logbooks at the end of each full year of work. The loss of information would therefore be potentially absolutely huge, even if we restrict ourselves to documents that might have existed in the archive at Wadi el-Jarf.

We have been able to formally identify seven separate logbooks, but some additional, unrelated fragments point to the possibility that originally a dozen logbooks were left behind in the archaeological deposit we excavated. So, given the length of a reign like that of Khufu, what if every single team of 40 people – out of the several thousand workers involved in the construction of the king's pyramid – had produced one journal like Merer's, every two months, over a period of thirty years? Table 2 on the following page shows the distribution through the year of mentions of the various phyles in the logbooks we found, arranged according to the bureaucratic level of information recorded in them.

**TABLE 2**  Timetable of references to the work-gang recorded in the logbook papyri

| Team | The scribe **Dedi** (overall supervision) | 'The Escort Team of "The Uraeus of Khufu is its Prow"' | | | |
|---|---|---|---|---|---|
| Section (phyle) | | Great (1) | Asiatic (2) | Prosperous (3) | Small (4) |
| Supervisor | | Inspector **Merer** | — Inspector **Mesu** <br> — Inspector **Sekher**[...] <br> — [...] **[Ny]kaunesut** ʃ(?) | | |
| IV Shemu (June) | Papyrus D <br> 1 (X7), 2 (X1), 3 (X1) | | Fragment X2 <br> Fragment X125 <br> Two of the three other sections (phyles)? <br> Unknown missions | | |
| I Akhet (July) | Papyrus D <br> 1 (X4), 2 (X4), 4 (X2) | Papyrus A | | | |
| II Akhet (August) | Papyrus F? | Papyrus A or B | | | |
| III Akhet (September) | | Papyrus B | | | |
| IV Akhet (October) | | Papyrus B | | | |
| I Peret (November) | | Papyrus B | | | |
| II Peret (December) | | Papyrus C | | | |
| III Peret (January) | Period of inactivity, or a major gap in the surviving documents | | | | |
| IV Peret (February) | | | | | |
| I Shemu (March) | | | | | |
| II Shemu (April) | Papyrus E(a) | | | | |
| III Shemu (May) and later | | Papyrus E(b) – probably the report of a phyle (possible, but conjectural, attribution to Merer's phyle) | | | |

## Organization of the activities of Khufu's work-gang

From the details given in the logbooks it is possible to piece together a picture of the various activities that the work-gang (*aper*), and its different sections (phyles), undertook through the year. In the period covered, the work-gang was initially operating in the Giza region, from the last month of year 26, i.e. the year of the 13th census of Khufu (fourth month of the Shemu season – probably June) until November of the following year (first month of the Peret season). At that time it was responsible for the transportation of the labour force, the maintenance of a system of canals and artificial lakes created at the foot of the Giza Plateau, and the process of filling up the latter with water when the annual Nile flood took place (as described in Papyrus A).

Following this, the team was then occupied for a considerable period carrying limestone blocks from the quarries at Tura on the opposite bank of the Nile from Giza to the site of the pyramid (as described in Papyrus B). The gang was working at two different stone quarries (Tura North and Tura South), with an average of three round trips (Tura–Giza–Tura) within the space of ten working days. Each of these round trips appears to have been undertaken only by specific parts of the work-gang, probably the *weret* ('Great') phyle, likely to have been led by Merer, and the *setjet* ('Asiatic') phyle, which is also known to have been involved in boat journeys, according to at least one section of Papyrus B. At the same time, according to the information from Papyrus D, these phyles were also responsible for various tasks (provisioning and management of the stores) in connection with several institutions operating in the Giza region. One of these was known as Ankhu Khufu ('Khufu Lives!'), which probably refers to Khufu's valley temple (the pyramid complex as a whole was called Akhet Khufu or 'Horizon of Khufu'). Allusions are also made both to the (Royal) Residence (*khenu*) and the Granary (*shenut*), which, according to Papyrus D, seem to be located in the same area, suggesting that the royal palace was at this time situated near the pyramid construction site. This conclusion seems all the more logical given that construction of the royal funerary monument would have continued throughout the king's reign and must have absorbed all the wealth and agricultural surplus of the country. An immense and far-reaching network of levies stretching across the entire nation, of which the site of Wadi el-Jarf was one of the most remote elements, fed this system, operated by men like Merer's gang. The focal point for delivery of the material was probably concentrated at the foot of the Giza Plateau, in the immediate vicinity of the valley temple of Khufu. It would have been a bustling area, full of activity, and occupied by a large cluster of cultural remains comparable with those being excavated by Mark at Heit el-Ghurab dating from the reigns of Khafre and Menkaure, discussed in Chapter 11.

After this initial phase of work, at least two more, rather different, missions were allocated to the same work-gang, underlining how adaptable the teams were. The events reported in Papyrus C probably took place immediately after the work carried out in the Tura limestone quarries, that is to say in December of that year (i.e. the second month of Peret), a time when the level of the Nile waters would have been dropping, making the transport of heavy loads from one bank to the other across the floodplain impractical. This timing is suggested by a fragmentary date contained in one of the accounts texts (Papyrus G), which seems to correspond to the same phase of work. The main theatre of operations for the work-gang has now clearly moved to the centre of the Delta region, and specifically a marshy area probably at that stage in Egyptian history bordering the sea. Here, the work-gang was responsible for the construction – the Egyptian verb *khus* is used, literally 'tamping, compacting' – of a building called a 'double *djadja*', or 'second *djadja*'. It was situated close to two towns that are frequently named: Ro-Wer Idehu ('The Great River-Mouth in the Marshes') and Ro-Maa ('The True River-Mouth'). Luckily, thanks to corroboration from other Egyptological textual sources, both these settlements can be precisely located in the region of Tjeb-netjeret, the 12th Lower Egyptian nome (or province), and probably just a short distance from the Mediterranean coast. It is also very likely that these two place-names refer to the 'mouths' of one or more of the Delta branches of the Nile, at the point where they open into the Mediterranean.

Other place-names also seem to be associated with this construction site, such as Hut-Tepet ('The Foremost Foundation'), and all the operations in this area seem to have been controlled by a nearby place founded by Khufu, Hut Khufu, which not only provided the workers with their food but also supplied building materials for their tasks. The text does not indicate the exact layout of these places, but the use of the word *djadja*, which usually means a platform, esplanade or pier, suggests that the workers may well have been involved in the construction of a breakwater or double jetty, perhaps resembling the jetty that is still visible at Wadi el-Jarf. The rulers of the 4th Dynasty clearly embarked on a policy of major shipbuilding, attested from the reign of Sneferu onwards, enabling them to develop trading contacts with the eastern Mediterranean and specifically the Levantine port of Byblos. An investment in port facilities, furthering the opening up of Egypt along its coastal borders, both the Mediterranean and the Red Sea, therefore would seem an entirely coherent and logical step.

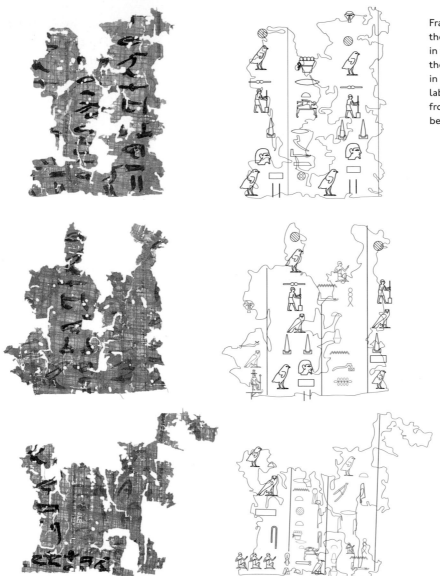

Fragments of Papyrus C, the account of a mission in the central part of the Nile Delta, probably in December, after the labour of carrying stones from Tura to Giza had been completed that year.

After this Delta mission, the documents remain silent on what the work-gang might have been engaged in for a long period – in fact there is no indication in the entire archive of any activity taking place in winter (January–March). This could of course be due to the loss of a large part of the archives – many documents, especially those at the bottom of the pit in which they had been deposited, had obviously not survived their long immersion in stagnant water. One possibility is therefore that logbooks that

| Document | Expeditions | Proposed length | Proposed time of year |
|---|---|---|---|
| Papyrus D | Work at the Portal of the Institution(?) of Ankhu Khufu | 2 months | Between Shemu IV (year of the 13th census) and Akhet I (year after the 13th census) |
| Papyrus A | Transportation of the labour force and opening up of the seasonal canals | 2 months | Akhet I–Akhet II (July–August); date of Akhet I given by the document |
| Papyrus B | Transportation of stone blocks from Tura to Giza | 3 months? | Akhet III–Peret I (September–November) |
| Papyrus C | Construction of harbour facilities in the Delta (in the 12th Lower Egyptian nome) | 1 month plus a short time further | End of Peret I–Peret II (November–December); date partially given by Papyrus G |
| Papyri E(a) and E(b) | Work on the Red Sea coast | 2 months each? | Between Shemu II (year after the 13th census) and Akhet IV (year of the 14th census) |

might have contained reports of these missing months have simply been completely lost. It is also conceivable, however, that this apparent gap in the records was a time of leisure for members of the work-gang. They were perhaps allowed a few months off to be with their families, particularly if this was not the busiest time of the year for transporting materials to royal construction sites.

Whatever the case, the fact remains that for the last mission we are able to identify, the work-gang were on the coast of the Gulf of Suez, probably as part of an operation from the port of Wadi el-Jarf. This is a plausible end point for the teams, given that this is the very place where the documents were ultimately deposited. A small group of Wadi el-Jarf papyrus fragments feature recurrent references to the toponym Bat (literally 'The Bushy Land'), which usually appears in relation to the Gulf of Suez region. It seems probable therefore that at least one of the logbooks found at Wadi el-Jarf was a record of this final mission, which immediately preceded the abandonment of the archives. Egyptian documents, whether ancient or medieval, show that sailing on the Red Sea took place only between April and the end of summer, no doubt because climatic conditions made it difficult at other times. All the known Red Sea expeditions during the pharaonic period – based on information from Sinai and the port of Ayn Sukhna – occurred in the period between the end of March and August.

It therefore seems likely that an expedition was sent by Khufu to Sinai between the second month of the season of Shemu (a date found on one Wadi el-Jarf accounts text fragment) and the third or fourth month of the season of Akhet (which follows immediately after Shemu), as indicated by Papyrus H, in the year after the 13th cattle-count of his reign. The small amount of information provided by the fragments relating to this final mission (Papyrus E) seems to suggest that a fortress was established at about this time on the Sinai coast, at the point where mining expeditions usually reached shore, which appears to be called Ineb Khufu ('Walls of Khufu'). It seems seaborne expeditions also took place, and perhaps rock-cut galleries were created, like those that served as stores at Wadi el-Jarf. The details provided by the various documents about the order and dating of the expeditions of this one work-gang can be arranged into a timeline, as shown in Table 3 opposite.

Taken together, the information contained in the set of logbooks demonstrates the great versatility of the work-gangs, who were capable of numerous tasks – not only handling the transport of heavy materials, but also maintaining a network of artificial canals, building harbour facilities and making voyages across the Red Sea. On a day-to-day basis, it is also possible that they served as stevedores/porters and overseers for the various royal institutions mentioned in the texts.

## Translation of Papyri A and B

Only two logbooks really provide continuous translated text: Papyrus A, two ten-day sections of which (A I and A II) are almost complete, and Papyrus B, which survives as a virtually continuous text covering forty days (sections B I–IV), together with two other sections covering ten days each (B X and B Y), which are not only less well preserved but also not able to be linked directly to the rest of the papyrus. Both documents report on the work of Merer's phyle, which is almost always mentioned at the beginning of each daily report. Papyrus A is explicitly dated to the first month of Akhet (the 'inundation' season), which, in this instance, appears to correspond to July, when the Nile flood would have been actually on the rise (because of the way the calendar was organized, Egyptian seasons, though named after the actual agricultural seasons, gradually slipped out of harmony with them).[1]

Papyrus B undoubtedly follows on immediately after Papyrus A: it relates the journeys made back and forth by Merer's phyle between the Tura quarries and the pyramid site at Giza, transporting blocks of fine limestone for use on Khufu's gigantic pyramid-building project. Depending on the precise chronology of the papyri in relation to the sequence of construction, these blocks were perhaps used in the outer casing of the pyramid, which was originally covered in this brilliant white stone, or for other elements of the royal funerary complex (such as the mortuary temple, areas of pavement, or the valley temple). Below are translations of these texts, which will be analysed in more detailed commentary in the next chapter.

## Papyrus A

### SECTION A I

First day <of the month>: [...] spend the day [...] in [...]. Day 2: [...] spend the day [...]. in? [...]. Day 3: Cast off from? [... sail] ing [upriver] towards Tura, spend the night there. Day [4]: Cast off from Tura, morning sail downriver towards Akhet Khufu, spend the night. [Day] 5: Cast off from Tura in the afternoon, sail towards Akhet Khufu. Day 6: Cast off from Akhet Khufu and sail upriver towards Tura [...]. [Day 7] Cast off in the morning from [...]. Day 8: Cast off in the morning from Tura, sail to Akhet Khufu, spend the night there. Day 9: Cast off in the morning from Akhet Khufu, sail upriver; spend the night. Day 10: Cast off from Tura, moor in Akhet Khufu. Coming of [lost title and name of an official] with instructions concerning the elite (*setep za*) and the *aper*-teams.

### SECTION A II

Day 11: Inspector Merer spends the day with [his phyle in] carrying out works related to the dyke of [Ro-She] Khuf[u ...]. Day 12:

....................................................................................................................

I   The ancient Egyptian calendar consisted of three seasons (Akhet, Peret and Shemu), each divided into four months of 30 days, which produced a year of 360 days. They added to it 5 epagomenal days – recorded for the first time in Wadi el-Jarf Papyrus H – which extended the whole year to 365 days. However, this calendar failed to keep in line with the tropical year, which lasts for 365.24 days, and therefore slipped by one day every four years.

Inspector Merer spends the day with [his phyle carrying out] works related to the dyke of Ro-She Khufu [...]. Day 13: Inspector Merer spends the day with [his phyle? ...] the dyke which is in Ro-She Khufu by means of 15 phyles of *aper*-teams. Day [14]: [Inspector] Merer spends the day [with his phyle] on the dyke [in / of Ro-She] Khu[fu ...]. [Day] 15 [...] in Ro-She Khufu [...]. Day 16: Inspector Merer spends the day [...] in Ro-She Khufu with the noble? [...]. Day 17: Inspector Merer spends the day [...] lifting the piles of the dy[ke ...]. Day 18: Inspector Merer spends the day [...] Day 19 [...] Day 20 [...] for the rudder? [...] the *aper*-teams.

## Papyrus B

### SECTION B I
[Day 25] [Inspector Merer spends the day with his phyle [h]au[ling] st[ones in Tura South]; spends the night at Tura South. [Day 26]: Inspector Merer casts off with his file from Tura [South], loaded with stone, for Akhet Khufu; spends the night at She Khufu; Day 27: Sets sail from She Khufu, sails towards Akhet Khufu, loaded with stone, spends the night at Akhet Khufu. Day 28: Casts off from Akhet Khufu in the morning; sails upriver <towards> Tura South. Day 29: Inspector Merer spends the day with his phyle hauling stones in Tura South; spends the night in Tura South. Day 30: Inspector Merer spends the day with his phyle hauling stones in Tura South, spends the night in Tura South.

### SECTION B II
[First day <of the month>] the director of 6 Idjer[u] casts off for Heliopolis in a *iuat* transport-boat to bring us food from Heliopolis while the elite (*setep za*) is in Tura. Day 2: Inspector Merer spends the day with his phyle hauling stones in Tura North; spends the night at Tura North. Day 3: Inspector Merer casts off from Tura North, sails towards Akhet Khufu loaded with stone. [Day 4 ...] the director of 6 [Idjer]u [comes back] from Heliopolis with 40 *khar*-sacks and a large *hekat*-measure of *beset*-bread while the elite haul stones in Tura North. Day 5: Inspector Merer spends the day with his phyle loading stones onto the *hau*-boats of the elite in Tura North, spends the night at Tura. Day 6: Inspector Merer sets sail with a boat of the naval section (*ges-depet*) of <the phyle of> Ta-wer, going downriver towards Akhet Khufu. Spends the night at Ro-She

Khufu. Day 7: Sets sail towards Akhet Khufu, sails towing <the boats> towards Tura North, spends the night at [...] Day 8: Sets sail from Ro-She Khufu, sails towards Tura North. Inspector Merer spends the day [with a boat?] of Ta-wer? [...]. Day 9: Sets sail from [...] of Khufu [...]. Day 10: [...]

## SECTION B III

[Day 13 ...] She [Khufu] [... spends the night at Tur]a South. [Day 14: ... hauling] stones [... spends the night in] Tura South. [Day 15:] Inspector Merer [spends the day] with his [phyle] hauling stones [in Tura] South, spends the night in Tura South. [Day 16: Inspector Merer spends the day with] his phyle loading the *imu*-boat(?) with stone [sails ...] downriver, spends the night at She Khufu. [Day 17: Casts off from She Khufu] in the morning, sails towards Akhet Khufu; [sails ... from] Akhet Khufu, spends the night at She Khufu. [Day 18] [...] sails [...] spends the night at Tura <South>. [Day 19]: [Inspector Merer] spends the day [with his phyle] hauling stones in Tura [South?]. Day 20: [Inspector] Mer[er] spends the day with [his phyle] hauling stones in Tura South (?), loads five craft, spends the night at Tura.

## SECTION B IV

Day 21: [Inspector] Merer spends the day with his [phyle] loading a transport-ship at Tura North, sets sail from Tura in the afternoon. Day 22: Spends the night at Ro-She Khufu. In the morning, sets sail from Ro-She Khufu; sails towards Akhet Khufu; spends the night at the granaries? of Ro-She Khufu. Day 23: The director of ten, Hesi, spends the day with his naval section in Ro-She Khufu, spends the night at Ro-She Khufu. Day 24: Inspector Merer spends the day with his phyle hauling (crafts?) with those who are on the register of the elite, the *aper*-teams and the noble Ankh-haf, director of the Ro-She Khufu. Day 25: Inspector Merer spends the day with his team hauling stones in Tura, spends the night at Tura North. [Day 26 ...] sails towards [...]

## SECTION B X

Day x + 1: [sails] downriver [...] the bank of the point of She Khufu. Day x + 2: [...] sails? from Akhet Khufu [...] Ro-She Khufu. Day x + 3: [... loads?] [... Tura] North. Day x + 4: [...] loaded with stone [...] Ro-She [Khufu]. Day x + 5: [...] Ro-She Khufu [...] sails from Akhet

Khufu; spends the night. Day x + 6: [... sails ...] Tura. Day x + 7: [... hauling?] Stones [Tura North, spends the night at Tura North. Day x + 8: [Inspector Merer] spends the day with his phyle [hauling] stones in Tura North; spends the night in Tura North. Day x + 9: [...] stones [... Tura] North. Day x + 10: [...] stones [Tu]ra North; Day x + 11: [casts off?] In the afternoon [...] sails? [...]

### SECTION B Y

x + 1 [... Tura] North [...] spends the night there. x + 2: [...] sails [...] Tura North, spends the night at Tura North. x + 3 [... loads, hauls] stones [...]. x + 4 [...] spends the night there. x + 5 [...] with his phyle loading [...] a craft. x + 6 [...] sails [... Ro-She?] Khufu [...] x + 7 [...] with his phyle sails [...] sleeps at [Ro]-She Khufu. x + 8 [...]

In spite of their repetitive nature, which admittedly may not make for fascinating reading at first glance, these two documents nevertheless provide a great deal of unprecedented information on the organization of work at the royal construction site at Giza (Akhet Khufu) at the end of Khufu's reign. What makes these dry, factual daily reports so extraordinary is that they are actually written by someone who witnessed the construction of the royal funerary complex first hand. Merer, the likely author of the journal, was primarily involved in overseeing his team and ensuring their duties were successfully and efficiently carried out, and so gives no information about logistics such as the methods of lifting the stone blocks to the top of the pyramid or the type of ramp used. Presumably such things were obvious to him, and were not the main focus of his reports. But he does provide a clear insight into the topography of the area of the construction site at Giza during this period, especially the network of canals and artificial ponds that had been developed to facilitate delivery of consignments of massive amounts of materials brought by boat. His terse records also help us to understand the way in which the work-gang operated, giving us an idea of the size of the workforce, the means by which they were provisioned, the supervisors who organized the workers, and the kinds of tasks that were entrusted to them. So exactly what tasks did Merer and his team perform at Giza, and what was daily life like for them? Fortunately, even the terse evidence from the papyri, when combined with evidence from the ground uncovered by archaeology, can provide an illuminating picture of the experience of a worker involved in building the Great Pyramid.

Papyrus A (together with transcription), the logbook recording the work of Inspector Merer's phyle or team in July and August, transporting the labour force on the Nile at the start of the flood season.

Two main fragments of Papyrus B (together with transcription), the logbook of Merer's phyle or team probably from September to November, when they were ferrying stone from Tura to Giza.

# PART IV

# THE STORY
# OF INSPECTOR
# MERER

# CHAPTER 9

# HOW MERER AND HIS MEN TRANSPORTED STONE TO GIZA

Day 12: Inspector Merer spends the day with [his phyle carrying out] works related to the dyke of Ro-She Khufu [...]. Day 13: Inspector Merer spends the day with [his phyle? ...] the dyke which is in Ro-She Khufu by means of 15 phyles of *aper*-teams. ... Day 16: Inspector Merer spends the day [...] in Ro-She Khufu with the noble? [...]. Day 17: Inspector Merer spends the day [...] lifting the piles of the dy[ke ...]

PAPYRUS A II

Papyri A and B were clearly written by an administrative official, Merer, who was not disposed to go into too much detail, and their contents only sketch the bare outlines of the activities of the team that he was directing. His reports are lacking in certain specifics, evidently because this information was well known both to the writer himself and to those for whom the report was intended, that is the officials who were ultimately responsible for controlling the workers' timetable. Merer only seems to expand the scope of his reports when, for one reason or another, the team departs from the standard 'routine' of work. This happens, for example, in Papyrus B, when Merer does not return at the expected time to deliver a load of stones from Tura, the reason being that in the meantime he had obviously been requisitioned to undertake a task elsewhere (at Ro-She Khufu) that had not previously been planned. Consequently, he finds it necessary to report the delay. It is therefore essential to understand the raw information that underlies the texts in order to fully understand them and ensure all the possible evidence is extracted from them about this crucial period in Egyptian history.

The first thing to note is that these reports in the form of logbooks give little in the way of quantified data, unlike the numerous accounts texts deriving from the same archives. One critical piece of information is missing from the outset – the actual size of the team or phyle (*za* in ancient Egyptian) that Inspector Merer was in charge of. This single fact – something that was no doubt obvious to everyone at the time of Khufu – is actually never mentioned. Estimates by modern historians of the make-up and hierarchy of these work-groups in the Old Kingdom have varied enormously, from groups of a few hundred men to teams of several thousand. Analysis of all the contemporary documentation has now provided us with a fairly clear idea of the organization of work at the royal construction sites. The most significant group of labourers

Detail of a relief from the pyramid complex of the 5th-Dynasty King Unas at Saqqara, showing granite columns being transported along the Nile (see pp. 193–95).

was the work-gang (*aper*), which was subdivided into four tribes, or phyles, with each phyle having their own specific name: the 'Great', 'Asiatic', 'Prosperous' and 'Small'. These groups were undoubtedly organized on a naval basis, and modelled specifically on the concept of tours of duty on a ship, with each phyle taking its turn to oversee the ship's navigation. The phyles were themselves further subdivided into four sections, the size of which can be reliably estimated at 10 men, according to a 4th-Dynasty ostracon discovered at Giza. Despite being relatively thin on the ground, the textual sources therefore show that a phyle was made up of 40 men, and that a complete work-gang comprised 160 men.

This conclusion has been recently confirmed not only by the Wadi el-Jarf Papyri but also by archaeology. Mark's work at Giza has revealed an area devoted to workmen's housing at the site of Heit el-Ghurab, near the foot of the pyramid of Khafre (see Chapter 11). Here the excavations have identified barracks used to house the workforce, galleries consisting of large, elongated rooms that appear to have had sufficient capacity to accommodate about 40 men. The living spaces therefore seem to have been exactly calculated to house a phyle such as Merer's. Detailed information contained in the Wadi el-Jarf Papyri has also tied in with the Heit el-Ghurab data. In Papyrus B, on the first day of the second month reported in the document, a *iuat*-boat piloted by a minor naval officer named Idjeru was sent to Heliopolis to supply the work-gang's food rations. He returned three days later with a cargo of 40 *khar*-sacks of *beset*-bread – this was a large quantity of very dense loaves, which can be compared with the so-called 'sea-biscuits' supplied in the 17th to 19th centuries to European ship crews on long voyages. Idjeru's cargo has a volume of nearly 2 cu. m, probably corresponding to about a metric tonne (1,000 kg) of this bread.

The average ancient Egyptian daily bread ration was of the order of 0.80 kg per day, a statistic frequently attested by various historical sources such as the early Middle Kingdom Hekanakhte papyri, and accounts from 12th-Dynasty fortresses in Nubia. The bread ration was considered to be the bare essential of the Egyptian diet, and had to be supplemented by other foods supplied by other means. Idjeru's monthly delivery of bread was therefore perfectly calculated for the maintenance of a troop of 40 men: if the total of 1,000 kg of bread is divided first by the number of days in a month (30), and then by the number of workers (40), a figure of exactly

0.83 kg is reached, which is in perfect agreement with the bread rations known from other Egyptian documents. It is also possible that the *khar*-sack of bread (each with a volume of 48 litres) was originally the precise measure calculated to correspond to a single individual's monthly ration in the Old Kingdom. Merer's team is therefore likely to have been a relatively small group, comprising 40 men, possibly suitable for manning a large-scale boat. In certain circumstances, as seen in the papyri, his team would work alongside others if the specific allocated task required it.

## Analysis of Papyrus A

Two sections of Papyrus A have survived almost perfectly and provide a good illustration of a phenomenon regularly encountered in the documents: the strict division of labour into ten-day (decan) work periods. The tasks assigned to the team changed completely between the first of these ten-day periods and the second. For the first ten days – during which Inspector Merer is not mentioned – the papyrus recounts the timing of trips back and forth between the quarries of Tura (Ro-Au) and Khufu's pyramid complex at Giza (Akhet Khufu). These journeys are carried out at a speed that might appear surprising: the reports for the first three days of the ten-day work period have not survived, but from day 4 to 10, five trips are recorded:

1. Departure from Tura on the morning of day 4, arrival in Giza the same day, and start of return; halt en route; day 5, return to Tura in the morning.

2. Departure from Tura on the afternoon of day 5, arrival at Giza in the evening, or the next day; departure from Giza on day 6 and return to Tura, where the team spends the night.

3. Departure from Tura on the morning of day 7 (probably heading for Giza), returning the same day to Tura.

4. Departure from Tura on the morning of day 8, heading for Giza; the team spends the night at Giza and sets off from there on the morning of day 9, returning to Tura.

5. Departure from Tura on day 10, and final mooring at Giza.

This routine progresses at a steady pace, with each trip taking place at either one-day or one-and-a-half-day intervals, covering the distance from Tura to Giza, a round trip of about 40 km. Papyrus B indicates a very different speed, with boats laden with cargo taking on average two or three days to make the same trip. In addition, there is no mention in the first report of operations involving the hauling of stone blocks and the process of loading them on board a boat, all of which takes at least two days between each trip. It appears therefore that Papyrus A cannot be describing the transportation of heavy loads. What, then, was the reason for these trips? The most logical solution is actually suggested by the next section of the document, which states that a troop of 15 phyles – i.e. a total of 600 men – is gathered at a place called Ro-She Khufu, literally 'Entrance to the Lake of Khufu', which is first mentioned in this papyrus. This large group greatly exceeds the team of 40 men who were probably under Merer's supervision. So it seems these particular trips between the Tura quarries and Giza were simply to carry a workforce periodically required for specific tasks. If each boat carried 120 men, five trips would have been sufficient to ensure their transfer. Significantly, a man described as a supervisor of *aper*-teams arrives on day 10, immediately after the workforce has been moved, presumably to give them their instructions about the operations they were required to carry out.

But what were these operations? Once again, the text is too laconic and oblique to provide any direct answer. During the second ten-day period covered in the report, there are regular mentions of 'works relating to the dyke of Ro-She Khufu', without specifying the nature of the task. However, the mention of this place is interesting in itself, since it introduces the whole arena of the hydraulic infrastructure that had clearly been created at the foot of the Giza Plateau to facilitate the supply of materials to the pyramid construction site, described more fully in Chapter 11. References to the 'Lake of Khufu' (She Khufu) and its access route (Ro-She Khufu) confirm that the Giza site was directly accessible from the Nile as a result of a huge artificial lake dug by the pyramid-builders. The existence of these lakes and waterways has been revealed in recent years through Mark's work in this area. He has not only analysed all the archaeological data from the Giza region, including evidence from excavation sites, but has also systematically used information from a set of 72 core drillings dug throughout the region by the

Anglo-American company AMBRIC in the 1980s, when they were contracted to study the area in advance of the installation of a sewage system for modern urban Giza (the Greater Cairo Wastewater Project). From these various investigations it has been possible to obtain a precise picture of the topography of the Giza area in the 4th Dynasty, when the main river channel was undoubtedly closer to the plateau on which the pyramids were built than it is today.

A large basin (or lake) was found to be aligned with the valley temple of Khufu's pyramid complex – the outlines of which, with edges made from basalt and limestone, were also uncovered by the Egyptian archaeologist Zahi Hawass when he undertook rescue excavations at Giza. Another area of artificial landscaping is located immediately to the east of the causeway of Khafre's pyramid. This part of the plateau is naturally sloping, and building materials had probably been transported via this route to the construction site of Khufu's pyramid – an operation made more difficult by the pronounced drop in the level of the terrain at the base of the king's pyramid. The basin opens out into a channel running between two mounds now occupied by the modern villages of Nazlet el-Batran, to the south, and Nazlet el-Sissi, to the north. Merer's papyrus, indicating the presence of canals and ponds in the area, therefore confirms the results of these archaeological studies.

However, the contents of the second section of Papyrus A are undoubtedly even more exceptional and unprecedented. After having accomplished an unspecified task (of which we know nothing apart from the fact that it was carried out at 'the dam of the entrance of Khufu's Lake'), on day 17 of the month the team proceeded to 'lift the piles of the dyke' in the presence of a high official of the princely class, perhaps the 'Director' (whom we will meet again later, and the beginning of whose titulature may have appeared just before a gap in the text of the day 16 report). It is the date of the document that is significant and provides the best idea as to the precise nature of the operation involving 'the piles of the dyke'. This was the first month of the Akhet (or 'inundation') season, which traditionally corresponds to the arrival of the annual Nile flood in Egypt, in the month of July. Perhaps this, then, is the earliest evidence for a hydraulic practice that is well known in later Egyptian history, but had not previously been attested for the pharaonic period: the opening of temporary 'seasonal canals', usually at precisely this time of the year. The practice is particularly well documented for

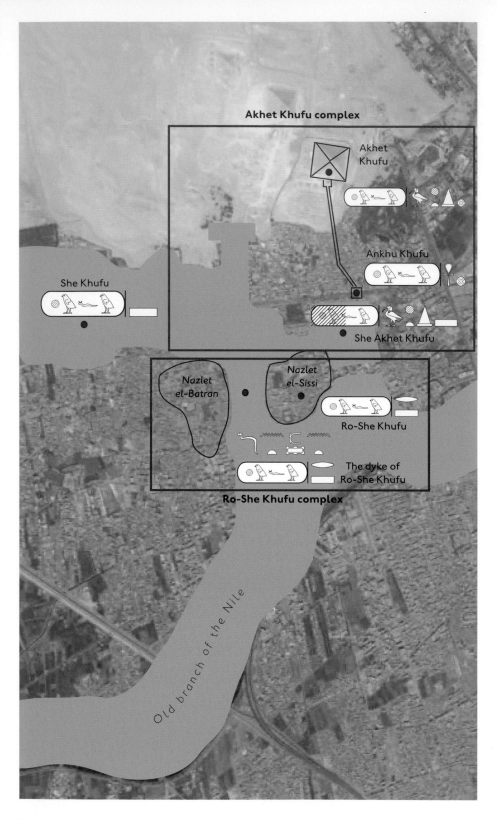

The waterways, lakes and channels in the Giza area at the time
of Khufu, over a satellite image, from the data of Papyri A
and B and Mark Lehner's archaeological research.

the medieval period, when many strategic transportation routes located along the edges of the river course were only used during the inundation period (particularly in the case of routes linking the Alexandria area to Cairo, or the Delta to the Red Sea). When the Nile level dropped significantly around November, these waterways were dammed up, retaining whatever water was left, to allow boats to continue sailing for longer, even during the winter months. This hydraulic system has been particularly well studied by John P. Cooper in a fundamental book, *The Medieval Nile: Route, Navigation, and Landscape in Islamic Egypt*. He focuses particularly on an account provided by the 18th-century British consul in Egypt, Abraham Parsons, describing the closing and reopening of the 'Cairo canal', one of the most important of these seasonal conduits:

> A barrier of planks was built from bank to bank of the canal, about eight to ten yards (7.3 to 9.1 metres) in from the canal mouth, and buttressed with poles bedded in the walls and floor of the empty canal. Earth was then banked up on the upstream side of this barrier, until it ran in line with the bank of the Nile itself, masking the mouth of the canal from view from the river. When the dam had been built to about half its final height, a series of small brick-lined culverts were laid across the thickness of the dam from its river face to the planks at the rear. The entrances to these channels were then sealed at their river end with sluice gates. When the time came, six months later, to open the canal, a system of pulleys and ropes was set up. At the signal of a cannon during the opening ceremony, these were used to open the sluices and pull away the buttresses supporting the wooden retaining wall. The result was a torrent of water rushing through each canal [that is, culvert], the building of planks immediately falls in, and is swept away with the incumbent earth.

The procedure was known as 'cutting the Nile' and it seems to us that the report provided in Papyrus A corresponds perfectly with the kind of system described by Parsons. Since access to the Giza Plateau would certainly have been one of the most crucial routes to fill to capacity, like the Cairo canal it would have been dammed during low Nile in order to hold back the water in the western Nile channel until the flood reached its peak. Only then was the dam cut and the water released, so that the force of its release would adequately fill the waterways and basins as far west as the desert plateau. Then, delivery and offloading of supplies could begin. The heaviest, bulkiest building materials, such as limestone from Tura, basalt from the northern edge of the Faiyum and granite from Aswan, far to the south, were probably only supplied during the period of the Nile inundation (between July and October/November), when an average water-level rise of around 7 m would have made the transport of heavy loads much easier. Even so, the difficulties involved should not be underestimated.

The most logical place to locate the 'dyke' to hold back the waters would have been precisely in the channel that passes between the points of higher ground now occupied by Nazlet el-Batran and Nazlet el-Sissi, which allows access into the entire system. If our interpretation is correct, Papyrus A provides a clear record of the operation that marked the beginning of the important annual phase of the site, with the 'lifting of the piles of the dykes' to flood the channel controlling the whole area below the plateau. Papyrus B, on the other hand, provides us with regular snapshots of the use of the waterway over the following months by the boatmen responsible for transferring cargoes.

## Analysis of Papyrus B

Papyrus B is the longest surviving document – it reports almost continuously on the activities of Merer's team over the course of three ten-day periods, from day 25 in the first month of the report up to day 25 of the following month. In addition, significant parts of two other ten-day sections survive, and a series of about fifty fragments. It seems likely that at least two months of activity, perhaps three in total, were recorded on the papyrus as a whole. The contents of the document are highly repetitive, essentially describing regular operations to transport limestone blocks from the Tura quarries to Giza. During this lengthy period of time in one specific year, only two other types of activity are mentioned in the main surviving section: first, the provision of monthly supplies to the work-gang (mentioned at the beginning of section B II), which involved the receipt of 40 *khar*-sacks of baked bread, as discussed above; and secondly, the participation of Merer and his team in a rescue mission to facilitate the departure of a sea-borne expedition (in the middle of section B IV). Just as with Papyrus A, however, a close study of all the

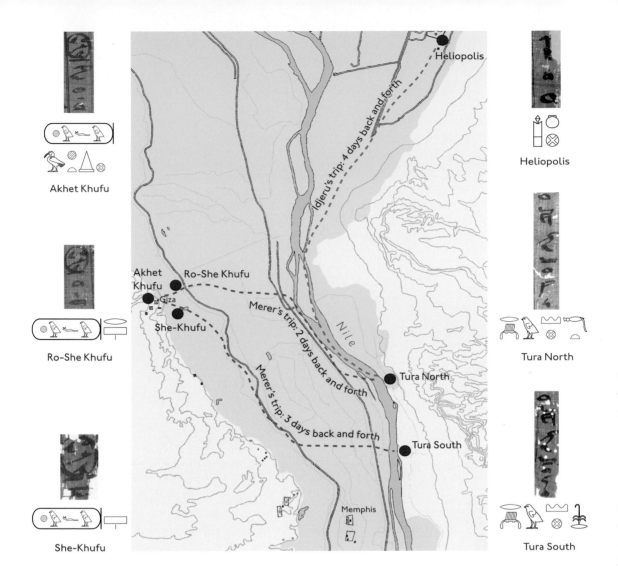

**Akhet Khufu**

**Ro-She Khufu**

**She-Khufu**

**Heliopolis**

**Tura North**

**Tura South**

data found in the papyri can undoubtedly provide us with a better understanding of the working conditions of the ancient Egyptians.

The Tura quarries, situated on the east bank of the Nile and a short distance south of modern Cairo, were being worked from at least the beginning of the Old Kingdom onwards. They were the source of high-quality brilliant white limestone that was considered particularly suitable for the outer casing blocks of the colossal pyramids erected at this time. According to studies made by Dietrich and Rosemarie Klemm, a geologist and an Egyptologist, the total area where these high-quality limestone blocks were extracted extends for more than 7 km, from the Maasara quarries in the south to those

The journeys of Inspector Merer from Tura North and South to Giza, and of Idjeru to and from Heliopolis, from the data of Papyrus B, plotted on a map of the region.

Map of the ancient quarries of Tura and Maasara, showing the local geology.

at Tura in the north. The stone blocks used for the outer casing of the pyramids built by Sneferu, founder of the 4th Dynasty, at Dahshur, seem to derive from Maasara, while those used for the pyramid of his successor, Khufu, seem to come from Tura. However, it is difficult to identify the exact locations of the quarries that were used for a particular monument both because of the continued exploitation of this stone throughout pharaonic history, and because there are at least 50 possible sites of ancient rock extraction. In modern times, the whole of this region was also used by the Egyptian army, making its scientific exploration by archaeologists difficult.

The text of Papyrus B does give an indication of the rotating importance of specific quarries, mentioning two distinct extraction zones at the end of Khufu's reign – 'Tura North' and 'Tura South' (Ro-Au Mehi and Ro-Au Resi respectively). These two quarries were exploited on alternate work shifts, with Merer's team spending one ten-day period loading stone in Tura North, then the next ten days undertaking the same task in Tura South. An extra day's sailing time was required when transporting the stone blocks from Tura South, probably because of the greater distance between the quarry and the final destination. It is thus likely that different sets of workers were employed in extracting stone simultaneously from both Maasara and Tura. Such a system of working highlights yet again the perfect logistical organization of the pharaonic work-gangs. By alternating transportation from Maasara and Tura over successive ten-day periods, whenever Merer's team of boatmen was not loading stone from one or the other of these quarries, the workers who were permanently engaged in actually quarrying the blocks could be stockpiling stone blocks near the riverbank, thereby increasing the speed and efficiency of the process of loading the blocks onto the boats.

This same efficiency can be observed in the general rhythm of the journeys between Tura and Giza. They take more time than those mentioned in Papyrus A, and are also interspersed with preparatory periods that usually last for two or three days, for hauling the blocks onto sledges and loading them onto the boat. It is clearly specified that the boat is laden with stone when sailing, which slows down its progress. Section B I reveals that it takes two full days for Merer to cover the distance of 20 km from Tura South to Giza (specifically days 27 and 28), while the return journey – with no cargo – takes only one day (day 29). There are still many questions concerning the actual pace of the work. On average, in every ten-day shift, Merer's team was able to achieve slightly more than two round trips between the quarries and the pyramid. If we extrapolate from this across the entire inundation season, which is the time of year when the transportation of heavy loads of stone was actually feasible (a period of about four months, from mid-July to the end of October and the beginning of November), the workforce would have made about 25 journeys over this period as a whole. There are, however, other factors for which no data are available to allow an evaluation of the full scope and scale of these operations. For example, do Merer and his team use more than one boat, and what was the maximum load that a boat could carry along the Nile at this date?

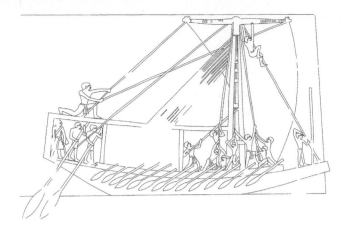

A boat shown in the tomb of Nefer at Saqqara.

Papyrus B seems to indicate that Merer's team most frequently operated with a single craft – perhaps a large *imu*-boat, which would have required a crew of exactly 40 men to manoeuvre it. Björn Landström's book, *Ships of the Pharaohs*, includes estimates of the actual sizes of Old Kingdom boats, based on representations found in the wall-paintings of tombs from this date. He suggests that the boats usually measured 25–30 m in length, and could therefore have been crewed by 35–50 sailors. To take just one example which may not be far removed from the conditions in which Merer and his men were operating, a boat depicted in the Saqqara tomb of Nefer, a 5th-Dynasty official, appears to have been crewed by a group of 42 sailors, comprising 28 rowers, 2 officers, 4 helmsmen, and 8 men dealing with the sails. Landström's estimate of the length of the boat is based on the minimum distance necessary between each row of oars (the so-called *interscalmium*) such that the boat can still be manoeuvred under good conditions. Landström sets the *interscalmium* at 105 cm, thus giving Nefer's boat a total length of 25 m. Although most of the time it is likely that a single boat sailed back and forth between the quarries and Giza, Papyrus B does also indicate that larger transport operations may have occasionally taken place, one of which (mentioned in section B II) seems to have simultaneously involved five cargo boats (described as *hau*-craft).

## Logistics

It is also possible to speculate about the kinds of loads that these boats were capable of carrying. Pictorial references from the Old Kingdom generally imply that boats could transport very large and heavy objects. Another 5th-Dynasty image is undoubtedly the most eloquent on this subject: among the reliefs decorating the causeway of the pyramid complex of Unas at Saqqara is a scene showing a boat carrying two palmiform granite columns intended for the royal funerary monument, each of which is said to be 20 cubits long (just over 10 m). Actual examples of columns of this size are known from this period, and, on the basis of the density of granite, the weight of each column can be estimated as about 38 tonnes (38,000 kg). It therefore seems that the total load transported by the boat depicted in the Unas causeway relief is probably 70–80 tonnes.

If we assume that Merer was in charge of a boat of this type, then one of his Tura–Giza journeys could have involved the transport of an average load of 30 limestone blocks, given that the average weight of the stones used in Khufu's pyramid is estimated at 2.5 tonnes (though there is great variation). Over the course of four months, he could therefore have delivered around 750 blocks of stone to the pyramid construction site, and a total of nearly 20,000 blocks (with a total weight of 50,000 tonnes) could have been transported by Merer's team during the entire 28-year reign of Khufu if this transportation of stone had carried on at the same rate throughout this time. Since the total number of Tura blocks forming the outer casing of the Great Pyramid is estimated at about 67,000 (representing a weight of 168,000 tonnes, assuming an average of 2.5 tonnes per block), it is possible to imagine that four phyles such as Merer's might have been sufficient to accomplish this particular task in just over two decades. Tura limestone was also used in other elements of Khufu's pyramid complex, including the pavement of the pyramid court, the satellite pyramid, the causeway and the valley temple, and the blocks Merer and his team delivered could possibly have been used in these.

Though this is all speculative, despite the relative lack of specific numerical data, the Wadi el-Jarf Papyri do enable us to take a fresh look at the construction of huge monuments such as Khufu's pyramid, which were long thought to have been built by vast work-gangs, ruthlessly exploited by some oppressive, cruel despot. In reality, however, the success of these gigantic constructions depended above all on flawless logistical organization, the employment of a highly skilled, well-rewarded workforce, and, in particular, the very high reliability with which the various tasks were carried out. The Wadi el-Jarf Papyri not only demonstrate that

Boats carrying palmiform granite columns, depicted on the causeway of the pyramid complex of Unas at Saqqara (5th Dynasty).

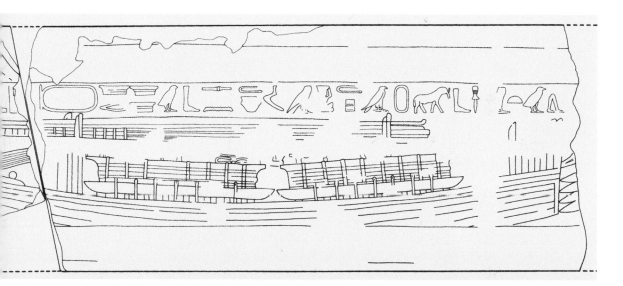

these three conditions were perfectly met, but also suggest that the monuments were constructed by far fewer teams of workers, operating with much greater proficiency and competence, than previously thought.

In addition, many other kinds of information are provided by Papyri A and B throughout their texts, especially the detailed vocabulary relating to the requirements of sailing on the River Nile. The direction of navigation is always clear, whether boats are heading north, with the current (*em-khed*), or going upriver to the south (*em-khesefut*, literally 'backwards'), using the north wind. Sailing on the Nile for Merer was probably not as straightforward as it might seem at first sight. At times the wind can drop, making it necessary to haul the ship along in order to make progress (*em-iteh*). In section IV of Papyrus B, Merer and his team are transferred to the Ro-She Khufu site to haul vessels commanded by a naval officer named Hesi who has been ordered to sail but cannot do so, perhaps because the boats are stranded by the seasonal fall in the Nile water level.

Papyrus B also highlights the role played by the facilities at Ro-She Khufu – the 'Entrance to the Lake of Khufu' – which were mentioned in Papyrus A. This was probably the main access point for the entire system of waterways and basins serving the Giza Plateau, which was closed off by a dyke during the winter period (when the level of the Nile would have sunk). During the time of year when these lakes were being used, this location seems to be regularly used as a staging post for the boats heading towards Khufu's pyramid complex. Merer usually stops there before going on to deliver his load of stone blocks to the pyramid, and the naval officer Hesi also moors there when stranded with his crew of sailors before being rescued by Merer. It is undoubtedly also a place for offloading, featuring warehouses or granaries, and there is additional evidence for an administrative sector dealing with control of building works for the royal funerary complex.

In section IV of Papyrus B the 'Director of Ro-She Khufu', a highly important role in charge of this centre of operations, is specifically named as Ankh-haf. Generally regarded as a son of Sneferu by a minor wife, and therefore the half-brother of Khufu, Ankh-haf is well known from his tomb at Giza and a striking statue now in the Museum of Fine Arts, Boston. His titles included Vizier and Overseer of the King's Works and he was probably the main individual in charge of the pyramid construction site at the end of Khufu's reign, as discussed in more detail in Chapter 12. That this important prince had his headquarters there identifies this place perhaps as the lynchpin for the entire system of facilities set up for the construction of Khufu's funerary monument. The trenches dug by AMBRIC revealed 4th-Dynasty ceramics and the remains of mud-brick buildings of a similar date on the Nazlet el-Sissi mound, to the north of the main entrance to Khufu's Lake. It is presumably here that archaeologists might expect to find traces of these port facilities and the associated early 4th-Dynasty major administrative centre.

The Wadi el-Jarf Papyri may not, then, in themselves contain the details that could solve the 'mystery' of the construction of the pyramid of Khufu at Giza – the precise construction methods or the type of ramps used to lift materials to the top of the structure as it rose, for example. But they do in an unexpected way shed light on part of the logistical effort that went into creating Khufu's funerary complex: namely, the river transport of some of the men and material that actually built it, and the systems that facilitated it. Although many questions remain unresolved, the papyri clearly indicate the conditions that were necessary for the construction of this monument: first an extremely elaborate logistical organization, and secondly maximum rewards for the very highly skilled workforce engaged in the achievement of this extraordinary project.

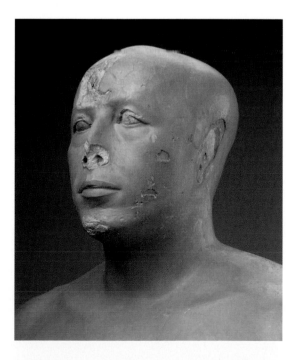

Bust of Ankh-haf, half-brother of Khufu and director of the king's port at Giza. Discovered in his giant mastaba tomb in the Eastern Cemetery, the statue portrays a mature and powerful man.

# CHAPTER 10

# FROM THE RED SEA
# TO THE NILE DELTA
## A Year in the Life of Merer
## and his Men

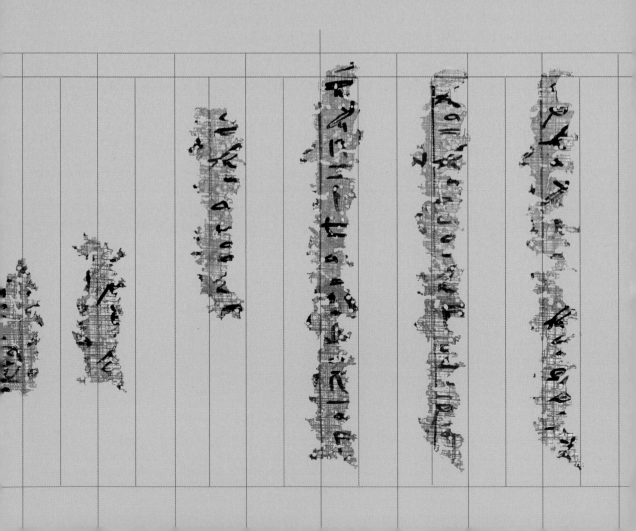

The 'Great' spends the day at the Portal of Ankhu Khufu ... giving textiles to Inspector Merer ...; while the 'Small' is on its way, the 'Great' is busy worshipping at this place.... The 'Great' spends the day at the Portal; giving fabrics ... as [reward?] ... The scribe Dedi goes to the Granary to bring back natron.

PAPYRUS D

The papyri from Wadi el-Jarf were probably all written in a period lasting just over a year, from the month of July in 'the year following the 13th census of Khufu', through to the next summer, which corresponds to the beginning of the 'year of the 14th census', during which the king likely died (*c*. 2605 BC). Throughout this period the work-gang undertook duties at a number of locations scattered all across the area controlled by the ruler of Egypt: from the zone surrounding the administrative capital across to the Red Sea coast, and up into the central Nile Delta, almost to the shores of the Mediterranean. The tasks the gang were engaged in are also highly varied, although most are linked in some way with shipping and specialist nautical work. They range from the transport of heavy loads along the Nile (Papyri A and B), sea-borne travel (Papyrus E), the construction of maritime coastal facilities (Papyrus C), and overseeing installations in the area surrounding the funerary complex of Khufu at Giza (Papyrus D).

From all the details recorded in the documents, we can build up a picture of the mobility and versatility of the work-gang whose archive we excavated. It is clear also that the royal court maximized the skills of this workforce, which seems to have enjoyed close relations with the central power. The strenuous work of supplying heavy materials to the pyramid construction site could probably only have been undertaken for part of the year, at the time of the flood when the Nile's level was high enough, and so they were put to work on other tasks they were experienced in. In addition, it seems that expeditions could alternate from one year to the next, so if Merer's team was on the Red Sea coast in the summer of the year of the 14th census – as seems to be the case from the documentation – a different work-gang must simultaneously have taken their place transporting Tura limestone blocks that year. A further possibility is that there was not the need for the transportation of Tura blocks in the last known year of Khufu's reign.

Part of Papyrus D, a logbook of the scribe Dedi, here tentatively reconstructed (see pp. 201–5).

Throughout the period covered by the papyri, the work-gang must have systematically carried their archives with them as they moved, explaining why the texts appear to have been abandoned at Wadi el-Jarf following the last mission to the coast of the Gulf of Suez. In fact, many of these documents must have been written on a daily basis by whoever was responsible for keeping the records, and we even detect the particular way in which the logbooks were written by reconstructing the writing technique of the scribe. In order to write his text, he needed regularly to dip his reed-pen in the ink, and the writing therefore gradually faded as the pen ran out of ink. It is noticeable that the beginning of each daily section of these reports systematically correlates with a time when the pen is loaded with the maximum amount of ink, which would certainly not be the case if the document had been written as a single text, compiled after the fact. It is this daily maintenance of the archives that explains why this batch of documents reached the shores of the Red Sea with the work-gang.

It is more difficult, however, to understand why they were left there, after the departure of the team, given that administrative documents such as these would certainly have usually been taken back to the capital at some point in order to be checked and then archived. One major event may explain this omission: the death of King Khufu at the very time that this last mission took place on the Red Sea coast. The administrative changes that may have been brought about by the death of one king and the accession of the next were perhaps of such magnitude that they might have rendered these routine documents completely useless, thereby justifying their abandonment at this remote site, when the work-gang headed home. An alternative explanation may be that the papyri discovered at Wadi el-Jarf were merely the original drafts of the official documents that were to be archived, and that only clean copies of the texts were then transferred to Giza. However, considering the care with which the documents were written, this second hypothesis seems less probable. In any case, regardless of how they happened to survive and why they were abandoned, the unique combination of data found in them allows us to follow closely the activities of the inspector Merer and his team over a long period of time. But beyond the details of the daily lives of these workmen, these documents also provide us with a fresh view of the activities of the royal court, as well as the functioning of its administration in several distinct spheres, at the very beginning of the 4th Dynasty.

## Merer and Dedi at Giza

Papyrus D survived only in a very fragmentary state, but piecing together some of the fragments makes it possible to propose at least a theoretical reconstruction of the original document. Another logbook, it is based not at the level of a simple phyle like Merer's, but deals with an entire *aper*-team led by a scribe named Dedi. It records two months of activity, probably partly contemporary with Papyrus A – indeed, one of the fragments mentions the feast of Thoth (the familiar Greek name for the Egyptian god Djehuty), which takes place at exactly the same time as the first month of the Akhet season, to which Papyrus A is dated. The contents of Papyrus D record the activities of a group of workers at the 'Portal' (*arerut*), a term used to refer to the entrance of an institution named Ankhu Khufu ('Khufu Lives!'). This institution seems to have been positioned in relation to the river, and was located near the Royal Residence (*khenu*), which is also mentioned in the text. Other administrative institutions are also referred to, such as the Royal Archives and the Granary (*shenut*), where a variety of products, including natron (a naturally occurring type of salt), were stored.

According to the surviving fragments of the text, which unfortunately represent only a very small percentage of the original document, it is obvious that the teams were working in alternate shifts to ensure that there was a permanent presence at this important royal establishment. They carried out various tasks, including guard duties, the supply of equipment and food, and the transport of personnel. There also seems to have been a religious aspect, since one of the fragments tells us that Merer's phyle was going to worship there (*iret khet*). Several passages written in red ink (here shown in **bold**) also indicate that numerous rewards were handed out to the work-gang by their superiors, including gifts of textiles, with Inspector Merer and his subordinates among the beneficiaries. The following passage, which is one of the best-preserved sections of the document, gives some idea of its contents:

> J11a [...] J11b [...] unload? [...] J11inf: [... Ankhu Khuf]u or J12a [...] J12b [...] J12inf [Khufu] J13a [...] the inspector Merer J13b [sailing to]? J13inf Ankhu Khufu J14a [...] J14b **Coming of the *iuat*-boat**; the scribe Dedi [goes] to the Granary J14inf. Ankh[u] Khuf[u] J15a The 'Great' spends the day at [Ankhu] Khufu Portal J15b [...] J16a The 'Large' spends the day at the Portal of Ankhu Khufu J16a [...] J16 margin [...] **x + 10; giving**

**textiles to Inspector Merer** [J17a] [...] [J17b]; while the 'Small' is on its way, the 'Great' is busy worshipping at this place. [J18a] The 'Great' [spends the day ...] [J18b] [...] [J19a] The 'Great' spends the day at the Portal; **giving fabrics** [J19b] **[...] as [reward? ...]** [J20a] [...] [J20b] The scribe Dedi goes to the Granary to bring back natron.

Ankhu-Khufu is clearly situated at the foot of the plateau – Merer's team of boatmen were able to gain access to it so that they could moor and spend the night there, according to some fragments of Papyrus B, a situation confirmed by the extract from Papyrus D above. The 'determinative' sign accompanying the place-name Ankhu Khufu varies according to context: it is sometimes accompanied by the house sign (⬛), indicating that a specific building or institution is meant, and sometimes by the city sign (⊗), which may designate a locality or even an extensive settlement. The toponym itself, which might be translated as 'Khufu Lives!', is particularly interesting because it refers to the living king, as opposed to Akhet Khufu ('Horizon of Khufu'), which refers to the deceased, deified king.

As already noted, Ankhu Khufu is clearly an area where numerous administrative buildings were located, most notably the royal palace, as well as archives and storage facilities. However, the religious function of the place is also apparent since the 'Great' phyle (Merer's phyle) is at one stage tasked with celebrating a cult, and natron, a material particularly used for ritual purification, including in the embalming process, is said to have been brought to Ankhu Khufu by the scribe Dedi. Throughout documentation dating to the Old Kingdom the term 'Portal' (*arerut*), which appears dozens of times in the surviving fragments of this papyrus, specifically designates the forecourt of a temple – even if in later times it may be used more generally for other official buildings. The conclusion is clear: we believe that Ankhu Khufu is primarily used to refer to the valley temple (sometimes also known as the 'reception temple') of Khufu's pyramid complex.

Khufu's valley temple is not known archaeologically because its remains are currently buried under the modern Cairo suburb of Giza, but it effectively served as the gateway to the entire royal funerary complex, including the pyramid itself, and was connected with the main waterway by a lake. It is also possible that the king's residence surrounded the valley temple, at the heart of the most

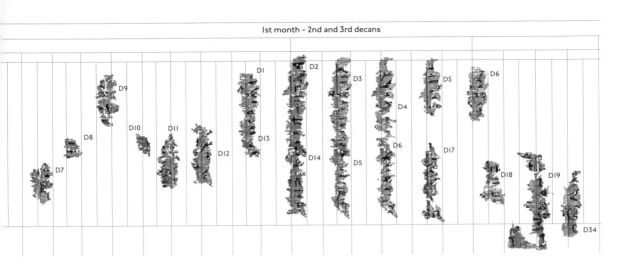

important construction site of his reign and alongside the majority of the main administrative structures. Most of the buildings housing state-employed workers may also have been located at this time in this well-defined sector, at the foot of the Great Pyramid. And since the teams led by Merer and Dedi were stationed in this same district of Giza, they therefore found themselves close to the most prominent hubs of state power. This is perhaps why the workers are also described as *setep za* ('the chosen phyle' or 'the elite') in the documents. The same term is regularly used to designate the royal court itself, and these teams of highly skilled workers were evidently an intrinsic part of the king's immediate surroundings, as a result of the important function they performed, their geographical location and their physical proximity to the king. Their close relationship with the monarch is unequivocally stressed by some of these groups – including one of the teams attested at Wadi el-Jarf, whose name 'Those who are Known to the Double Golden Horus' certainly tells us something. 'The Double Golden Horus' was one of Khufu's five royal names, so this collective name stresses that the team members were most likely admitted into the king's orbit, and perhaps even physically presented to him at some point.

The king's relationship with these teams of skilled workers was in fact even closer, bearing in mind that the fragments of Papyrus D suggest not only that these men worked on the construction of the royal funerary monument, but that they were engaged – during the king's lifetime – in the celebration of his personal cult. Nearly 150 years later, the Abusir archives, which concern the functioning of the 5th-Dynasty royal funerary complexes, show that the temple staff was made up of different phyles – by then there were five, but these still include the original four known from the 4th-Dynasty texts: 'Great', 'Asiatic', 'Prosperous' and 'Small'. The phyles take turns to be responsible for the operation of all different aspects

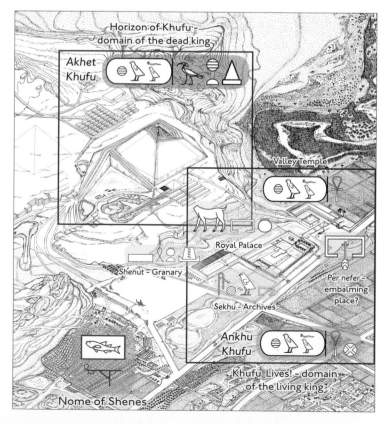

Map of named places appearing in Papyrus D, in their approximate relation to the Giza Plateau during the construction of the Great Pyramid. The red boxes outline the areas respectively of Ankhu Khufu, the domain of the living king, and Akhet Khufu, the domain of the dead king. Papyrus D also mentions the province or nome of Shenes, which incorporated the Great Pyramid valley temple, the 'Workers' Town' (Heit el-Ghurab) shown bottom left in the diagram, and the whole floodplain stretching east of the Giza Plateau. The underlying drawing was created in 1985, before Heit el-Ghurab was excavated and before waterways and harbour basins came to light. Archaeology and the Wadi el-Jarf Papyri now show many points of agreement with this original, drawn hypothesis, including the location of the royal river front, Khufu's palace south of his valley temple, and the vast 4th-Dynasty settlement south of the principal harbour basin.

of the sanctuary (provisioning, guarding and attending to the cult), operating on monthly shifts that are familiar from the roster schedules discovered in the funerary complexes of the kings Neferirkare-Kakai and Raneferef. It seems that the very origins of this system at Giza, from the beginning of the 4th Dynasty onwards, can be witnessed in the Wadi el-Jarf Papyri. In addition to their key role in the construction of the king's funerary monument, Merer's workers were most likely also entrusted with celebrating the royal cult while the king was still alive. The same kind of rostering is also perceptible in Papyrus D, with the Great, Asiatic and Small phyles each clearly taking their turn to guard the 'Portal' of the institution.

It was the key role that the work-gang played in the royal institutional domain that probably also explains the close attention paid to it by the monarchy. The king regularly rewarded the workforce, particularly with the frequent distribution of lengths of cloth – a luxury product that could even be used as a form of quasi-currency, as evidenced by the many red-ink 'rubrics' (relating to payment) that appear throughout Papyrus D. This is all a very long way from the stereotypical image of workers crushed under the weight of tasks required of them by a despot: the work-gangs that figure in the Wadi el-Jarf Papyri appear to be quite privileged members of contemporary society.

## Merer in the Nile Delta

The work-gang's prolonged period of work in the Giza region, well documented by Papyri A, B and D, probably came to an end when the level of the Nile waters dropped at the end of the inundation season, which would have made the transportation of heavy loads along the waterways of the Nile Valley less viable. The final surviving section of Papyrus B may already refer to these difficulties at the end of the flood cycle, since it reports on an individual named Hesi experiencing problems in sailing.

Merer's team was then sent on another mission, as reported by Papyrus C, which took them to the central Nile Delta. This papyrus was unfortunately not very well preserved, with only about fifty fragments of readable length surviving (some inscribed with five or six columns of text), most of which are missing their upper sections, preventing a reconstruction of the exact chronological sequence of the activities the document is concerned with. What remains of Papyrus C, however, does indicate that the work in the Delta lasted for at least a month. A fragmentary date preserved in one of the accounting papyri (Papyrus G), which seems to relate to the same operation, suggests the mission may have taken place at the end of the first month of Peret, that is at the end of November or early December in that year.

The team worked in two different locations, both of which seem to be associated with a Delta branch of the Nile: Ro-Wer Idehu (which may be translated as 'The Great River-Mouth in the Marshes') and Ro-Maa ('The True River-Mouth'). As noted earlier, by cross-referring with other sources, these places can be located in the 12th nome (province) of Lower Egypt, in the centre of the Delta, probably along the course of a waterway that preceded the current Damietta branch of the Nile. The same Ro-Wer toponym appears in precisely this geographical location in the biography of an early 4th-Dynasty high official called Pehernefer, while the Ro-Maa toponym was still associated with the 12th nome of Lower Egypt in Greco-Roman temple inscriptions. If the area around Ro-Wer Idehu and Ro-Maa is plotted on a map of present-day Egypt, it corresponds to the region of the modern city of Mansura, some distance from the Mediterranean coast. However, during the Old Kingdom period the Delta did not extend as far north as it does today, and reconstructions of the landscape place the 12th nome near the coast at the time of Khufu. The mention of marshes (*idehu*) in the first of the place-names may simply refer to the so-called 'hybrid zones' along the northern coast of the Delta.

The physical location of Merer's Delta operations may be relatively easy to determine, but the precise nature of the work the men were engaged in is less obvious. The team is said to be 'tamping or compacting' a stone structure that is described as a 'double *djadja*' (or 'second *djadja*'). The most likely interpretation of this word, which can have several meanings in ancient Egyptian, is provided by the context. Since the logbook is primarily reporting on the activities of a group of sailors, the *djadja* could be a dock or platform bordering an expanse of water. In support of this interpretation is the evidence from the ancient L-shaped jetty discovered at Wadi el-Jarf, which comprises two sections at right-angles to one another. As we examined this jetty, we noted that it had been very carefully built by packing down the material that forms the core, in order to make it more durable. Given that it dates to exactly the same period,

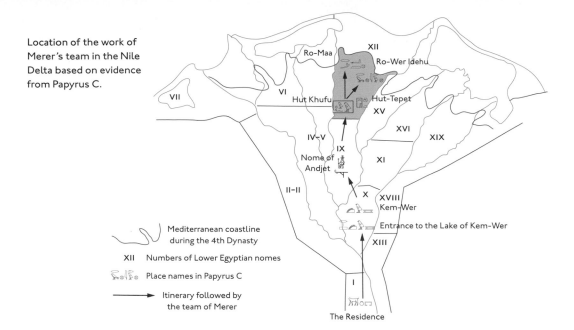

Location of the work of Merer's team in the Nile Delta based on evidence from Papyrus C.

Mediterranean coastline during the 4th Dynasty

XII   Numbers of Lower Egyptian nomes

Place names in Papyrus C

⟶   Itinerary followed by the team of Merer

this structure could be a good parallel for the one mentioned in the Papyrus C logbook. If this identification is correct, the document would be of great interest for the history of the early Old Kingdom, since it implies that already in the 4th Dynasty Egyptian rulers were pursuing a proactive policy of openness to the outside world, with the simultaneous development of port structures both on the Red Sea (demonstrated archaeologically at the port of Wadi el-Jarf) and on the Mediterranean coast (recorded textually in Papyrus C).

Contacts with the Levant and the Eastern Mediterranean seem to have increased at this time, with the earliest 4th-Dynasty rulers forging close links with the city of Byblos in order to obtain cedarwood and pine (both not found in Egypt), which were needed, among other things, for shipbuilding. The Palermo Stone (a stela inscribed with royal annals listing the activities of Old Kingdom rulers) makes several mentions of the importation of wood to construct large boats during the reign of Sneferu. In exchange for this timber, the rulers sent luxurious objects carved from Egyptian alabaster, often inscribed with the names of members of the royal family, including Queen Hetepheres, wife of Sneferu and mother of Khufu, as well as Khufu himself. Excavations in the early 20th century at Byblos recovered objects of this type, which may perhaps be regarded as diplomatic gifts.

Papyrus C provides us with yet further fundamental information on the functioning of the Egyptian state at the time. Throughout the period the gang was carrying out the work programme in the Delta, an official named Imery made regular trips to fetch bread and beer to feed the workers. As with the rewards of cloth, since this relates to provisions for the benefit of the gang, the information about these provisions was recorded in red in the document. A royal foundation, Hut Khufu, or 'the *hut*-mansion of Khufu', was responsible for the supplies, and this same institution was also the source of the building stone used to construct the 'double *djadja*', which was the workers' main project. These *hut*-foundations are well-known to Egyptologists: they were state-controlled structures, sometimes manned by prisoners of war, that were particularly established by 4th-Dynasty rulers in the more marginal areas of the Egyptian state with the aim of accelerating the development of these regions. The *hut*-foundations are therefore particularly numerous in the Delta, an area of Egypt that was still rather unevenly developed at this point in history, making it a kind of royal colonial project. Papyrus C gives us our first real inside view of the ways in which one of these institutions operated as it undertook a major strategic exercise in land stewardship.

## Merer on the Red Sea coast

At the end of the Delta mission, we have no knowledge of the missions on which Merer's workers were then engaged – our sources are silent for some considerable time. As suggested previously, it is possible that the men were permitted some respite during the winter season (January to March), allowing them to rejoin their families, from whom they would otherwise have been separated for most of the year while they were occupied with their duties. One thing we can be certain of, however, is that their last mission of the year took them to Wadi el-Jarf, on the Red Sea coast, since it was ultimately at this site that their archives were finally abandoned.

The Egyptians' maritime expeditions from the Red Sea coast are becoming increasingly familiar to us, thanks to the combined study of the three coastal ports that have been identified one after the other (see Chapter 2), and also thanks to the Sinai inscriptions which commemorate these missions at their destinations (Chapter 3). A series of precise dates provided by various Old and Middle Kingdom texts indicate that the so-called 'intermittent ports' created by the Egyptians were in use mainly between April and the end of the summer. This is undoubtedly the most favourable period for voyages across the Red Sea, an ocean that is still considered capricious and dangerous in winter, even today. It is difficult to calculate these dates precisely because of the 'floating' nature of the Egyptian calendar, given that their calendar year of 365 days shifts back by one day every four years compared to the real solar year (which is about six hours longer than the Egyptian one). Nevertheless, it is still possible to extract the chronological information with a fair degree of certainty. Thus, for the Old Kingdom:

- At Ayn Sukhna, on the Red Sea coast, an inscription includes the date 'year of the 7th census, 4th day of the 4th month of the season Shemu', in the reign of the late 5th-Dynasty ruler Djedkare-Isesi, which probably corresponds to an absolute date that is somewhere between June and July, *c.* 2454 BC.

- At Wadi Maghara, in the Sinai mining region, a stela set up by the 6th-Dynasty ruler Pepi I dates to 'the 5th day of the 4th month of the season Shemu in the year after the 18th census', which may correspond to an absolute date somewhere between July and August, *c.* 2357 BC.

Documentation from later in the Middle Kingdom is generally in line with this information from the Old Kingdom. An expedition to Ayn Sukhna in the reign of Amenemhat I can be dated to July 1964 BC, and another expedition from the time of Senwosret I corresponds to March–April 1935 BC. The Wadi el-Jarf documents also provide useful confirmation of this sort of timing for expeditions. Many documents – a note on a cloth bag in addition to several accounting documents discovered within the papyrus archive – relate to the provisioning of the work-gang during their stay at the port, indicating monthly dates between the second month of the Shemu season and the third month of Akhet, a period which, at the time of Khufu, would have corresponded to the interval between April and September. The team therefore probably stayed on the coast for a prolonged period of up to six months, between the end of 'the year after the 13th census' (year 27 of Khufu, *c.* 2606 BC) and the beginning of 'the year of the 14th census' (year 28).

The process of reactivating the 'intermittent port' would have certainly required a visit of this length. The sealed stores had to be opened up by moving or smashing the heavy stone blocking that securely closed the entrance, and the dismantled boats within had to be extracted and transported to the shore for reassembly. The workers would perhaps also have had to transport from the Nile Valley any boat parts that might be missing if the stored material had been damaged during the time the port had been left idle. The work-gangs then had to be ferried across the Gulf of Suez to the mines in Sinai. On the coast opposite Wadi el-Jarf, the Egyptians built a fortress at Tell Ras Budran (el-Markha) to secure access to the Sinai peninsula at this point, and this would have been manned by troops during the time the teams of royal workers were active in Sinai.

Once the expeditionary force was engaged in their work in the turquoise and copper mines – based at several sites simultaneously, including Wadi Maghara, where rock-cut official inscriptions include mentions of both Sneferu and Khufu – the duties of Merer's men were still not over. They had to make regular shuttle trips in their boats between the Egyptian and Sinai coasts in order to supply the teams of hundreds of miners with provisions that would have been impossible to find in Sinai. While on land at Wadi el-Jarf, Merer's team would also have had to manufacture the large pottery jars for storing the water fetched from the spring near the site to equip the boats with water-containers. In their stay at the site, Merer's team undoubtedly produced a total of more than 1,000 of these pottery vessels. A deposit of more than 500 of them (some bearing inscriptions giving a shortened version of the name of the escort-team of 'The Uraeus of Khufu is its Prow') was unearthed in the G22 and G23 galleries of the rock-cut storage system, and others have been found across all the activity areas of the site, including the sea edge and the harbour basin. Finally, long after the expeditionary force had finished their work and been repatriated, the gang would have had to ensure that the site was officially closed down once more by dismantling the boats, carefully stacking the parts in the storage galleries and probably renewing the stone blockage system.

Only a few small fragments of logbooks, now grouped together under the name Papyrus E, seem to correspond to this long stay on the coast with which Merer's year concluded. They include references to the toponym Bat (literally 'The Bushy Land'), which was probably the ancient name for Wadi el-Jarf and for other sites on the Red Sea coast, alluding perhaps to the bushes growing in the wadis that punctuate the landscape. These fragments also speak of sailing expeditions, mountainous areas and a place called Ineb Khufu ('Walls of Khufu'), which may refer to the Tell Ras Budran fortress at the port where ships, including Merer's, docked on the southwestern coast of Sinai.

It is with these last bits and pieces of texts that we finally lose track of Merer's work-gang. They probably headed back to the Nile Valley in the early autumn, leaving behind them our unexpected batch of archives, buried at the entrance to storage gallery G1 when the site was closed down. We know nothing of the subsequent fate of Merer himself, whose meticulous reports have taken us into the very heart of the functioning of the Egyptian state at this iconic period in pharaonic history. What happened at the end of such a pivotal year, which perhaps corresponded to the very end of Khufu's reign? Were the team required to work for Khufu's successor? Perhaps one day Merer's final resting place will be located in the pyramid-builders' cemetery at the southern end of Giza.

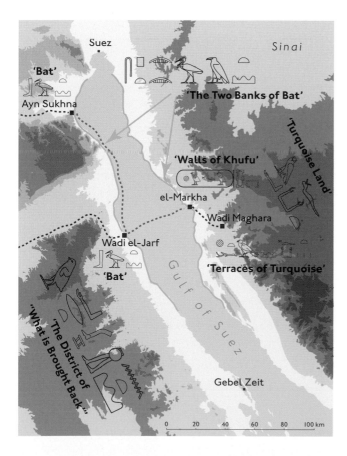

Place names and general organization of the expeditions to Sinai during the Old Kingdom.

# PART V

# HOW THEY
# BUILT THE
# GREAT PYRAMID

# CHAPTER 11

# FROM WORKERS' VILLAGE TO PORT CITY

Day 22: Spends the night at Ro-She Khufu. In the morning, sets sail from Ro-She Khufu; sails towards Akhet Khufu; spends the night at the granaries? of Ro-She Khufu. Day 23: The director of ten, Hesi, spends the day with his naval section in Ro-She Khufu, spends the night at Ro-She Khufu.

PAPYRUS B IV

What does archaeology tell us about the settlement where the people who built the pyramids lived and worked day to day at Giza? Are there any indications on or in the ground at Giza of where Merer offloaded his cargo of stone, or the state buildings where he was meant to file his logbooks? Where might the king's palace and valley temple – both now disappeared – have been situated? We need to use all pieces of an archaeological puzzle, along with indications in the Wadi el-Jarf Papyri, in order to visualize, in broad strokes, a land- and waterscape buried under 4–5 m of silt that the Nile deposited when it flooded between late June and early November every year. In addition, a blanket of modern buildings now covers the Giza floodplain. In spite of such limitations, some of the archaeological features fit remarkably well with what we can glean from the papyri.

## Giza: a tale of two settlements?

Since the first modern surveys of the valley floor along the base of the Giza Plateau, maps have shown two areas that rise higher than the surrounding floodplain – one to the north, the other to the south. As late as 1977, the village of Nazlet es-Semman stood isolated on the northern high ground that spread like butterfly wings north and south of where Khufu's causeway crossed the edge of the plateau leading to where his valley temple once stood. The combined villages of Nazlet el-Sissi, Nazlet el-Batran and Kafret Gebel occupied the southern high ground, southeast of the Sphinx. After the Aswan dams, built between 1900 and 1971, stopped the annual inundation, modern housing spread down from the village mounds and across the floodplain. Before that, the two conurbations had carried on a tradition of northern and southern Giza settlements that can already be seen in Old Kingdom titles of town administrators inscribed on their tomb walls at Giza.

In the late 1980s a British-American consortium (AMBRIC) carried out core drillings and excavated a network of trenches for

Two complete galleries excavated at the Heit el-Ghurab site at Giza form part of a major settlement complex (see pp. 223–31).

a wastewater project for the modern city at the base of the Giza Plateau. The core drillings logged the sediments that fill deep basins, and provided evidence of ancient settlements around these basins and along the levee of a buried western Nile branch, roughly on the course of the modern Mansouriyah Canal. A deep trench (for a main sewage pipe) along the Mansouriyah Canal cut through a basalt pavement that must have been part of the Khufu valley temple. To the south, the trench cut through settlement remains of the Pyramid Age, including thick mud-brick walls cased with limestone, about 100 m apart, that must have belonged to a buried royal building (a palace?). In their logbooks Merer and Dedi inform us of royal institutions – a state archive, granary and palace – attached to the Khufu valley temple as part of a larger settlement named Ankhu Khufu. Here, text and archaeology, as fragmentary as both may be, come together and provide pieces of the puzzle.

As for an ancient southern settlement at Giza, for 30 years I (Mark) have led a project with teams from Ancient Egypt Research Associates (AERA) which has mapped and excavated a 4th-Dynasty settlement 450 m south of the Great Sphinx. The site is named Heit el-Ghurab, Arabic for 'Wall of the Crow', the local name for a colossal stone wall on the northwest of the settlement, 200 m long, 10 m wide at the base, with a 7-m tall gateway. Our exposure of this settlement extends over 7 ha, between the escarpment on the west and the western edge of the combined modern villages of Nazlet el-Batran and Kafret Gebel. At Heit el-Ghurab we have gained detailed information on houses, workshops, bakeries and barracks; from intensive retrieval and analysis of ancient plant remains, animal bone, chipped stone, sealings and artifacts we know much about the diet and economy of the pyramid-builders.

## The 'Entrance to the Lake of Khufu' and the gateway settlements

Khufu's hydraulic works – his human disturbance on a geological scale – may be partly responsible for the separation of highland and settlement into the two identifiable zones in the Giza floodplain. He dredged a channel basin so wide and deep that it still left traces in the contours of the valley floor even after 4,500 years of annual Nile floods had filled and covered the basin with silt and built up the floodplain by up to 5 m. A channel basin is a wider waterway

Before the construction in the 1960s of the Aswan High Dam to control the flow of the Nile, the waters of the annual flood reached to the foot of the Giza Plateau – as in this historic photograph. In ancient times, the inundation season facilitated the delivery, by boat, of supplies and building materials to the pyramids.

A deep trench, dug for a sewage pipe in the 1980s by a British-American consortium (AMBRIC) along the Mansouriyah Canal, cut through a basalt pavement that must have formed part of the Great Pyramid valley temple.

Reconstruction of the 4th-Dynasty Giza floodplain and water transport infrastructure at low Nile, with a water level 7 m above sea level (asl). HeG = Heit el-Ghurab site. View to the north-northwest.

at the end of a canal that allows boats to moor and unload cargo without impeding the progress of other traffic, and gives room for turning – a landlocked harbour with quays and wharves.

Evidence suggests that Giza's central channel basin led from a westward bend in a western Nile branch, along the course of the old Libeini Canal, to the bottom of the pyramid plateau where it slopes from northwest to southeast. Here plateau bedrock met the floodplain east of where the pyramid-builders would later carve the Sphinx. To the south, the plateau slopes into a natural wadi that separated the Moqattam Formation, the pyramid plateau proper to the north, from the Maadi Formation outcrop to the south. The wadi provided a natural conduit up on to the plateau, while the area from east of the Sphinx to the Wall of the Crow proved optimal for delivering non-local stone and other building supplies, from where they could be hauled up to the pyramid then under construction. At the bend of the Libeini, the mound now occupied by the village of Nazlet el-Sissi stood as an island above the inundation water, while the companion mound to the south, now Nazlet el-Batran East (a satellite of the main village), was surrounded by water on three sides. The low ground between them extends westwards directly towards the Sphinx and Khafre's valley temple; its linearity and reach hint at a large, buried canal basin. Deep core drillings confirm this basin, and allow us to define its axis and estimate its size and depth – some 8 m deep, about 135 m wide and some 70 m long.

After people had stopped maintaining the central harbour basin at Giza, and centuries of Nile silt had filled it, they continuously built and rebuilt the mud-brick structures on the mounded settlements of Nazlet el-Sissi and Nazlet el-Batran East. These villages are reminiscent of the twin villages, El-Beirat and Ramla el-Alqata, erected on spoil heaps at the entrance to the great Birket Habu harbour basin that the 18th-Dynasty pharaoh Amenhotep III excavated on the west bank of Luxor, *c.* 1358 BC, some 1,250 years after Khufu. The mounded villages at Giza could have originated as outposts at the entrance to the central channel basin. If we can see the basin as the She Khufu, the 'Lake' or 'Basin of Khufu', that Merer so often notes, the twin peaks would mark its entrance, *ro* (literally 'mouth'). So here we can probably locate the Ro-She Khufu, the 'Entrance to the Lake of Khufu'. This institution, a port authority, plays such an important role in Merer's journal, and, as we learn from Papyrus B, Khufu's half-brother, Ankh-haf, served as director there.

Reconstruction of the 4th-Dynasty Giza floodplain and water transport infrastructure at peak flood, with a water level 13.5 m asl. View to the north-northwest.

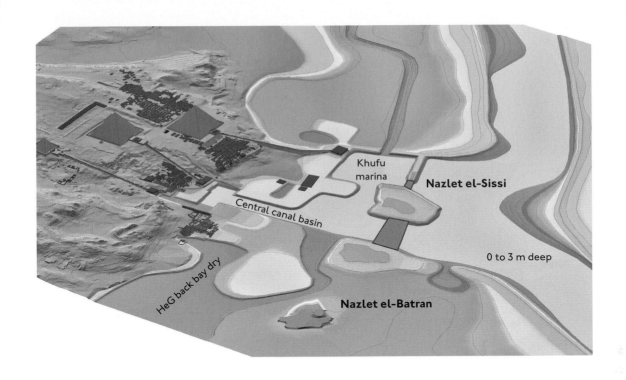

Khufu
marina

**Nazlet el-Sissi**

Central canal basin

0 to 3 m deep

HeG back bay dry

**Nazlet el-Batran**

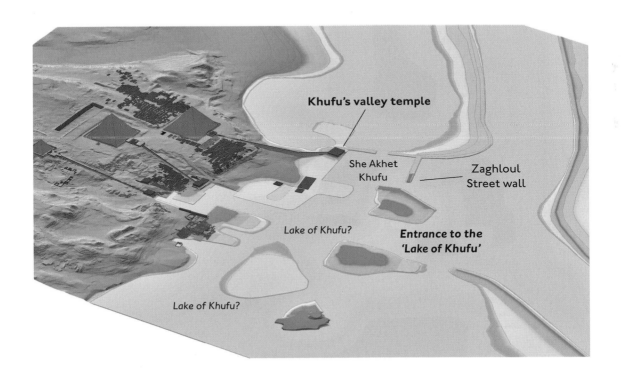

**Khufu's valley temple**

She Akhet
Khufu

Zaghloul
Street wall

*Lake of Khufu?*

***Entrance to the
'Lake of Khufu'***

*Lake of Khufu?*

## Giza North – 'Khufu Lives!', 'The Horizon of Khufu', Khufu's settlement

The Wadi el-Jarf Papyri tell us that the hub of Khufu's administration flanked his valley temple, in a place called Ankhu Khufu – 'Khufu Lives!' Here Merer and Dedi logged the various activities of their *aper* or work-gang. What can be gleaned of Ankhu Khufu from archaeology? Certainly not enough, but some of its broad features and the locations of two major structures have been discovered.

The AMBRIC trenches located Khufu's valley temple, which it seems was roughly as broad as Khufu's upper temple. Its builders paved part of the temple with black basalt on a massive limestone foundation, probably a central court, also matching the upper temple. The temple fronted on to its own separate dedicated marina, possibly named in Merer's journal She Akhet Khufu, the 'Lake (or 'Basin' or 'Harbour') of the Horizon of Khufu', after the name of Khufu's pyramid. When in 1993 construction workers excavated 500 m east of Khufu's valley temple for foundations of an apartment complex, they hit a colossal stone wall, at the same elevation (15 m above sea level) as the *in situ* basalt slabs of Khufu's valley temple. The Zaghloul Street wall, so-called because it was found a little east of a street of that name, is made of basalt on a limestone foundation – the same materials used in Khufu's upper temple and valley temple. The wall was part of a matching set with those temples. AMBRIC sewage trenches exposed other sections of similar walls running east–west, one to the north and the other on the south, also near elevation 15 m asl. A rectangle drawn to join those wall fragments on the northern and southern perimeters, the Zaghloul Street wall on the east and the Khufu valley temple location on the west, measures 400 m north–south by 450 m east–west. AMBRIC drill cores hit very deep clay and silt within this enclosure, suggesting a walled basin, dredged 8–10 m deep, that filled with Nile silt after people stopped maintaining it.

In Merer's time, when the annual flood raised the level of the waters of the 'Lake of the Horizon of Khufu', the temple town 'Khufu Lives!' must have twinkled with hearth fires at twilight. As Merer and Dedi sailed into the marina from the east, they could see Khufu's valley temple perched on a massive limestone foundation, which must have projected into the basin fronted by its own quay. State buildings, granaries and houses of retainers flanked the temple north and south, perched on the butterfly wings of high ground, which were probably spoil heaps from dredging Khufu's marina. Khufu provided his marina, surely, with an outlet into the main central harbour, She Khufu, and channel basin. At the peak of the annual flood, Khufu's 'lake' expanded to the south. Both core drilling and excavation show that the Nazlet el-Sissi mound lies at a juncture between this outlet, the bend in the Nile branch and the opening of the central canal basin, the reconstructed Ro-She Khufu.

The buildings of Ankhu Khufu continued south along this waterfront. In 1990, the AMBRIC trench along the Mansouriyah Canal encountered structures that Merer must have known. From a point approximately 50 m south of the Khufu valley temple, the contractors cut down through two major levels of Old Kingdom mud-brick buildings and settlement material for a stretch of 1.8 km. The lower layer was founded on a natural undulating surface of low mounds and desert-edge dunes on the levee of the western Nile branch. A trench across the Mansouriyah Canal encountered a high dune of sand, which sloped down to the west, apparently beneath both of the two phases of Old Kingdom buildings. A picture thus emerges of a settlement facing the Giza pyramids, but secluded between the high western levee of a Nile channel and the plateau. A layer of dense black ash between the natural surface and the bottom of the earliest walls indicated a large-scale fire that the builders may have set to burn off grass and scrub to prepare the ground for the buildings. The lowest settlement layer contained large quantities of animal bone from domestic cattle, pigs and sheep, as well as dung, charcoal and carbonized remains of other organic material between the foundations of mud-brick walls. The early occupation ended when its buildings were demolished and partly levelled with rubbish. It is possible that the lower layer dates to the 4th Dynasty, like the Heit el-Ghurab site, which could be its extension south of the central canal basin; and like that site, people abandoned it at the end of the dynasty. The higher phase suggests people settled in proximity to the valley temples of Khufu and Khafre in the 5th Dynasty.

Just north of where the Abu Taleb Bridge crosses the Mansouriyah Canal, the trench along the western side of the canal cut through two massive mud-brick walls, much larger than the rest, faced with squared limestone blocks. Unfortunately, no report on these features was published, but those involved recall the trench continued south for 50 to 100 m and then cut through another thick mud-brick wall with limestone casing. These walls belong to a building of monumental proportions. It is significant that the building aligns with the south side of Khufu's pyramid and the Nazlet el-Sissi village mound. This is a propitious place to build a palace.

Other AMBRIC trenches to the west along modern Sphinx Street revealed a mud-brick and limestone-paved floor extending east of a large wall and laid immediately over natural sand. This floor proved relatively clean; fallen brickwork, rather than accumulated rubbish, lay on it. Plotted on our reconstructed map of the 4th-Dynasty land- and waterscape, these features exist on

Reconstruction of 4th-Dynasty water transport infrastructure at Giza, with contour values in metres asl. White indicates low water at 7 m asl. Labels correspond to terms in Merer's journal.

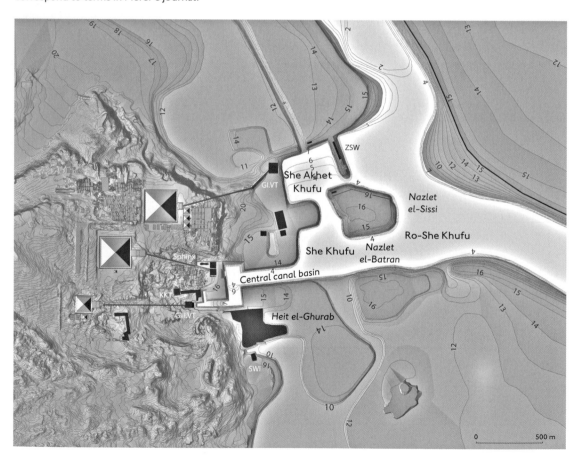

a broad terrace that extended north of the central canal basin (the She Khufu?), south of Khufu's valley temple, southwest of the valley temple's marina and west of the Nazlet el-Sissi mound (gatepost of Ro-She Khufu). From here to the valley temple was the royal zone at Giza, where Merer and Dedi and their gang joined in the activity at the hub of Khufu's administration.

Apart from the valley temple, all these elements, like the Zaghloul Street wall, appear to have been arrayed about 17 to 19° west of north, along the course of the old western Nile channel that ran parallel to the western desert edge. This is because just at this point, at Giza, the line between desert and cultivation begins to run southeast to northwest as the western side of the opening of the Delta.

All this is much more than we might otherwise have known, without the limited exposures and the information that small trenches have salvaged. But now, thanks to an entirely separate source of information – the Wadi el-Jarf Papyri – we also know that right here, along this stretch, lay the very hub and centre of Khufu's administration, including granaries and other storage, perhaps a treasury, an archive and one of Khufu's royal residences.

## The Heit el-Ghurab site

Heit el-Ghurab lay south of the central canal basin. According to our reconstructions, based upon indications in the papyri, during flood season Nile waters filled the low floodplain to the south and east to merge with water in the central canal basin as the She Khufu. The Heit el-Ghurab site must be understood as part of the major Nile port of its time. But which time? Was this vast infrastructure, with barracks and housing, already there in some form during the reign of Khufu? Or was it the case that what is found in Heit el-Ghurab existed in similar form near Khufu's valley temple further to the north? Most of what we have so far excavated and mapped dates to the later reigns of Khafre and Menkaure. We have reason to suspect, however, that it could have begun in Khufu's time.

By 2004, our teams from AERA had mapped what we called the Gallery Complex – four blocks of galleries transected by three broad east–west streets. Bakeries and other structures dedicated to production flank the Gallery Complex east, west and south. An enclosure wall runs from the Wall of the Crow south along the western side of the site, then turns to the east to enclose the Gallery Complex on the south and connects to the Royal Administrative Building (RAB). Most of this building remains buried under a modern, derelict soccer field, soon to be removed, but we know this large compound at the southeast limit of our excavations contained a sunken court of large storage silos.

On the far eastern limit of our investigations, we have recovered part of what we call the Eastern Town, a series of small chambers and courts that reflect an 'organic', village-like order. A relatively high frequency of grinding stones found in the Eastern Town suggests that, along with other craft and industry, its

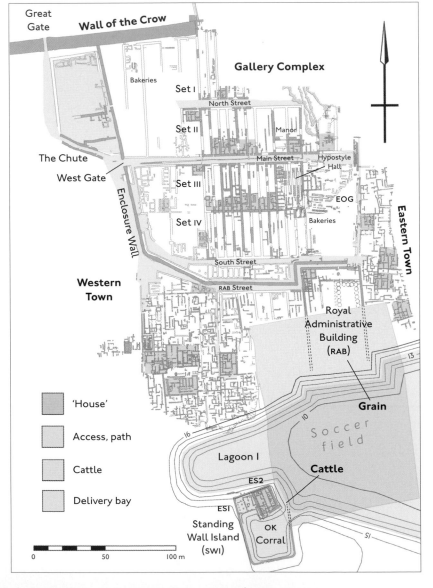

Plan of the Heit el-Ghurab site, the Giza 'Workers' Town', dating mostly to the reigns of Khafre and Menkaure. Excavations have also revealed an underlying, older phase, perhaps of Khufu's time.

inhabitants produced flour for the many bakeries that surround the Gallery Complex using grain from the storage silos in the Royal Administrative Building. In spite of the proximity of these state storage facilities and bakeries, Eastern Town people created their own hearths and baking facilities, and stored grain, most probably provisioned to them by central authority, in their own small silo granaries.

This part of the settlement continues east, beyond the limits of our salvage work, under the modern road and urban sprawl, possibly as far as the Mansouriyah Canal. As mentioned, that canal probably tracks an ancient waterway, a far western Nile branch, that was, perhaps, navigable only during flood season. Merer may have approached Giza on this waterway, or certainly on one close by, when he sailed to Giza from Tura South (he would have taken a different route from Tura North). This southern area of Giza, where the Heit el-Ghurab settlement was founded, projected in peninsular form out east into the floodplain. In order to reach his off-loading place at the end of the central basin canal (She Khufu), or to get into Khufu's own marina, the 'Lake of the Horizon of Khufu' (She Akhet Khufu) in front of the valley temple, Merer had to pass this eastern projection. From here, he could sail straight north into the marina in front of the valley temple, but to dock at the end of the central basin he had to turn west. The information from Merer's journal piques our interest in the housing, most probably for minor officials of about Merer's rank, that would have lined the site's eastern rim.

Southwest of the Gallery Complex, in a maze of walls that we call the Western Town, we can recognize thicker walls defining large, 'elite' houses. In our excavations of four of these houses, the high status of the proprietors is shown by the size of the houses (up to 400 sq. m), the thickness of the outer walls, the large amounts of prime meat cattle bone, and some of the highest-ranking titles of the time on 'sealings', dabs of clay used to seal string locks on bags, boxes, jars and doors. Before the clay dried hard, seal-bearers would roll across it a little cylinder etched with hieroglyphs that left an impression. The titles include 'Scribe of the Royal Documents', 'Overseer of Scribes of the Tutors of the Royal Children' and 'Overseer of Scribes of All the Kings Works'. In each of four large houses, we could distinguish a large central audience hall, all about the same size and always oriented north–south, with pilasters of a projecting frame, plastered and painted red, that define a niche at the southern end. Here the master of these official residences, or residential offices, would conduct business. Scribes, attendants and petitioners could have lined the long walls, perhaps holding their document boxes, in front of the master who sat framed by the niche of authority. Audience halls with just these features have been found in an Early Dynastic palace at Buto in the Delta, in other Old Kingdom sites (including all the large houses of the Khentkawes Town at Giza), and, in the last few years, in the large elite houses north of Sneferu's valley temple at the end of his own central canal basin, which serviced his two Dahshur pyramids.

Immediately south of the Western Town, we lost traces of the site at a sand-filled depression, which we named Lagoon 1. Then, about 65 m further south again, walls of fieldstone reappeared, remarkably standing up to a metre high, prompting us to name the area Standing Wall Island (SWI). Two enclosures (ES1 and ES2) opened south into a much larger enclosure with curved corners and a ground plan characteristic of ancient Egyptian corrals as pictured in carved scenes from the Early Dynastic Period to the New Kingdom, and similar to corral structures excavated at other sites. Here, in what we dubbed the 'OK (Old Kingdom) Corral', the inhabitants kept cattle, sheep and goats, and processed the large quantities of meat that the inhabitants of Heit el-Ghurab consumed across the site, according to faunal analyst Richard Redding's study of the animal bone from our excavations. A thick-walled, elite house occupies the northeast enclosure (ES2), which we see as the residence of the official who administered this establishment. The adjacent sub-enclosure (ES1) likely served as an abattoir.

We believe Lagoon 1 served in the dry season as a delivery route that became a southern service harbour during flood season. People brought protein (live cattle) up into the enclosure of Standing Wall Island, to the south, and carbohydrates (grain) into the silos of the Royal Administrative Building to the north. Cattle could have also been brought through the gate in the Wall of the Crow and kept in the northwest enclosures. But headmen of the community fitted their large houses into the head of this bay, between the Royal Administrative Building and the escarpment, so that, like the officers of customs houses, they could supervise the delivery and allocation of the commodities passing through – goods that satisfied the needs of the royal works and city infrastructure.

## Barracks and phyles

Before we undertook the broad clearing and mapping that gave us the whole footprint of the Gallery Complex, our smaller excavation trenches revealed structures similar to workers' houses from other ancient Egyptian sites and periods, with off-axis entries, hearths and rear living areas with cooking and baking chambers. When the larger layout was exposed, it was clear that authorities had placed these small domiciles in the backs of long, corridor-like galleries, with a width to length ratio of 1:7 and defined by very thick walls. We mapped four blocks of these long galleries, stretching 150 m south from the end of the Wall of the Crow and traversed by the three broad paved streets, North Street, Main Street and South Street, each 5.2 m wide.

When we excavated two complete galleries in Gallery Set III (GIII.4 in 2002 and GIII.3 in 2012), we discovered that they consisted of long, open, front (northern) ends divided approximately down the centre by a low wall with round limestone column bases embedded on top every 2.6 m (5 cubits). Thin wooden columns once rose on the bases so that the fronts of the galleries formed a colonnade, where we found several sleeping platforms raised slightly above floor level – six in GIII.4 and five in GIII.3. A person reclining on platforms at the ends of the long sides could monitor any coming and going. There were also larger sleeping platforms across the doorways leading from the house-like structures to the rear cooking chambers. These belonged to team leaders, who could in this way keep guard while sleeping, not unlike the doormen (*bowabs*) who sleep at night across building entrances in modern Cairo.

The interpretation of these structures as barracks addresses the apparent disparity between the amount of empty space seen in the Gallery Complex, with its fewer than 20 house-like structures, and the immense deposits of material culture and dozens of bakeries against the eastern, western and southern sides of the complex. Here production on an industrial scale and its consumption would far exceed the needs of that number of small households. In the area we call East of the Galleries (EOG), we excavated bakeries embedded in an expansive 'gravel' of concentrated bread-pot fragments, nearly a metre thick. On the basis of the cattle, sheep and goat bone found within the galleries zone, together with some assumptions from our limited excavations, Richard Redding estimated that around

Galleries III.3–4 at the Heit el-Ghurab site, after excavation. They formed part of the whole Gallery Complex, which was an early institutional building for accommodating and organizing temporary residents, comparable to our hospitals, prisons, schools, hotels, or barracks.

The Gallery Complex rose some 7 m high, with an interior loft, vaulted ceilings, and a common, flat roof terrace.

30 sheep and goats and 11 cattle per day could have provided meat for thousands of people. Where, and who, were all these consumers?

From experiments with volunteers, we determined that about 40 people could stretch out in the 4.6-m width and 16.5-m length of the colonnade of Gallery III.4. This result, along with ancient Egyptian texts known before the discovery of the Wadi el-Jarf Papyri, led us to estimate that each phyle enlisted in a work-gang (*aper*) numbered 40 men. And if each gallery served as a barracks for workers or royal troops who answered to an overseer, ensconced in the rear domestic area, we reasoned that each gallery housed a phyle, a *za*. Since documentary sources, principally the Abusir Papyri, record that phyles rotated through temple service, we assume that groups of conscripts likewise rotated through the Gallery Complex, living there while they worked on the royal project and then returning home. In gallery blocks II and III, we found eight galleries to the west of two larger structures, the Manor compound and Hypostyle Hall. Each block could therefore have housed two work-gangs, with four phyles per gang, a total of 320 men.

The discovery of galleries, albeit of a different sort, at Wadi el-Jarf began to provide support for our inferences about the Gallery

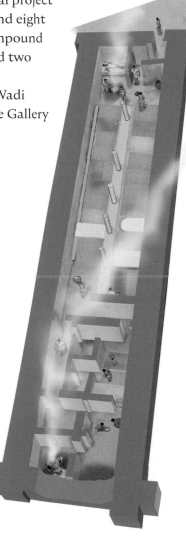

Gallery III.4. Features shown are a sleeping niche and hearth for guards near the front (north) entrance, a long columned colonnade with sleeping mats and platforms, a back domicile and rear chambers.

How many people could sleep in the galleries at any one time? The experiment shown here, conducted by excavation team members in Gallery III.4, demonstrated that 40–50 people could be accommodated.

Complex and labour organization within it. The distribution of work-gang names inscribed in red ink on water jar fragments found in the rock-cut galleries there shows a correspondence between gangs and galleries – a relationship that must have extended also between the gangs, or crews, and the disassembled boats that were stored in the galleries. In the middle of the coastal plain, halfway to the seashore from the rock-cut galleries, Pierre and his team also found a structure made from dry-stone walls consisting of 13 elongated galleries that both resembles and is of comparable size to the gallery blocks at Heit el-Ghurab, though less formally built. These galleries could have served as 'workmen's barracks' for expeditionary troops in transit through the Wadi el-Jarf on their way to and from the Sinai mining areas. There is an even greater resemblance between this coastal building and a double set of galleries found near Sneferu's pyramids at Dahshur. What all these structures share is an evident penchant for organizing people, activities and commodities in parallel rows – galleries – resulting in comb-like buildings.

The journal of Merer presents yet another match with Heit el-Ghurab and the barracks hypothesis. On the basis of monthly rations listed for Merer's team, Pierre estimated that Merer's phyle numbered 40, and related this to the estimate that each Heit el-Ghurab gallery could accommodate the same number of men. The two sources, archaeology and papyri, mutually enhance our understanding of this extraordinary time when the giant Egyptian pyramids were being constructed at Giza.

### The port and interregional links

The fact that the Heit el-Ghurab site and the Gallery Complex lie south of the major delivery zone and central canal basin suggests they functioned as a major part of the pyramid-builders' port. Gallery-like structures where shipments can be immediately and temporarily stored before distribution are a standard feature of ports. The Gallery Complex may thus have served in part for warehousing imported goods. The northern galleries could have opened on to the central Giza waterways, but unfortunately, as erosion has removed most of the northern part of the northern Gallery Set I, we cannot know what access there was here. It is significant that the tall Wall of the Crow ends at the northwest corner of Gallery Set I, as though to allow openings through a shared northern wall of the galleries of that block.

The correspondences between the Gallery Complex and details in the Wadi el-Jarf Papyri additionally require that the Heit el-Ghurab site should not be seen as just a 'workmen's town', any more than Merer's team were mere grunt workers. Drafted into royal works, the phyles could be required at various times to move large blocks for a king's monument, march to distant quarries to obtain fine stone and minerals, and crew a ship that might cross the Red Sea to Sinai for copper or sail along the Mediterranean coast to Lebanon to fetch olives, olive oil, wine, resin and cedarwood. Confirmation of such interregional networking comes from analysis of material culture recovered at Heit el-Ghurab. Charcoal derives from Levantine wood such as cedar, oak and olive, with significant concentrations in the galleries. We have found Early Bronze III Levantine combed ware pottery, most likely from jars for importing olive oil, but possibly also wine and resin. Members of expeditions to such places were ensured food and provisions, including prime meat, and sometimes rewards of gold and fine products including textiles, again as recorded in the Wadi el-Jarf Papyri.

Merer sometimes refers to his team as *setep za*, literally 'choosing a phyle', i.e., a 'chosen phyle' – a select, elite group. At one point, the team joins 'those who are on the register of the *setep zau*'. While the work was hard, the Wadi el-Jarf Papyri confirm that these 'chosen ones' (*setep zau*) were relatively privileged because of their closeness to the king. The term *setep za* raises a final possible link between the Heit el-Ghurab site, the Wadi el-Jarf Papyri and Khufu's palace at Giza.

## Khufu's palace

Merer delivered stone for Khufu; most of what we have mapped and excavated of the Heit el-Ghurab site dates to the later reigns of Khafre and Menkaure. But we have glimpses of a lower, earlier phase at Heit el-Ghurab that includes older galleries under Gallery Set I at the end of the Wall of the Crow. Most of the earlier architecture was razed when the site was remodelled, probably under Khafre. This lower phase may date to Khufu. When Khafre's workers removed most of the older architecture, for reasons not entirely clear they carried the mass of debris up and over the western escarpment and

This small seal impression or sealing, numbered 5848 by AERA archaeologists who found it in material dumped from the Heit el-Ghurab site, shows the hieroglyphs for *setep za*, with the house determinative sign, which could designate the royal palace.

dumped it behind the Gebel el-Qibli ('Southern Mount', the Maadi Formation knoll), leaving a huge deposit 6.5 m thick spread over 5 ha. Between 1971 and 1975 the Austrian prehistorian Karl Kromer excavated this area and found sealings relating to Khufu and Khafre. At the Heit el-Ghurab site we have, so far, found only sealings of Khafre and Menkaure. Some of Kromer's Khafre sealings, however, match those we have found in the large, 'elite' houses of the Western Town. In 2018 we returned to the site of Kromer's excavations, with more meticulous methods, and with the hypothesis that the dumped material derives from the older phase of Heit el-Ghurab.

Both the Kromer and AERA excavations identified a deeper, older phase of dumping that came from the east, the direction of Heit el-Ghurab. This represented a massive demolition of buildings in a single event. It included fragments of mud bricks and painted plastered walls, roofs, floors, corners and hearths. At least some of the buildings must have housed people of high status, as plaster fragments showed bands painted in various colours – deep red, orange, black, light and darker grey, beige, and lighter shades of red or orange. The dump also yielded objects of everyday life – copper needles, spatulas, fish hooks and faience beads, as well as small figurines and even organic material including wood, palm fibre and cloth.

So far we have found no sealings of Khufu; of those published by Kromer only five bore Khufu's name and 38 that of Khafre. The Khafre sealings found by both excavations include titles of very high-ranking officials, some of which were made with exactly the same cylinder seal as sealings we found in the large houses in the Western Town. But sealing number 5848 from the dumped material, a small fragment, is the most important. It shows the bottom of a Horus name and, underneath, the hieroglyphs ⌇⌇, for *setep za*, the same term Merer uses to designate his phyle.

However, *setep za* written, as here, with the house idea-sign (⌂, the determinative) makes it securely a place noun, and a reference to the palace. Before this little clay fragment, no example of *setep za* written with the house sign, therefore signifying the palace, was documented before the Middle Kingdom. One of five major terms for the palace (or aspects of the palace), *setep za* was where the king sat to make decisions, in consultation with his advisers, about craftwork, building or construction. As a verbal noun *setep za* could mean 'escort', or 'bodyguard'. Watching and attending to the needs of the king are among the activities Merer's men were tasked with, as indicated in the Wadi el-Jarf Papyri. People closest to the king were sometimes treated as a collective body (his larger 'body', as in his corporation).

Could this little sealing 5848, along with the other high-status indicators, be telling us that the Gallery Complex and Heit el-Ghurab hosted that part of the *setep za* – the barracks – that accommodated royal crews and troops organized into work-gangs? As Austrian Egyptologist Manfred Bietak has noted, Egyptian palaces, in addition to their large features of public display, 'also included offices, especially of the chief administrators of the state' (Western Town houses?), 'barracks and arsenals for troops' (the Gallery Complex?) 'and ... considerable storage areas for collecting and distributing commodities' (the Royal Administrative Building).

The Wadi el-Jarf Papyri refer to Khufu's palace under the general term *khenu* (*hnw*), which enjoyed a special status among the terms for palace as indicating the Royal Residence, that is, where the king actually stayed. From contexts within the texts themselves, Khufu's *khenu*/Royal Residence must have been in the northern settlement, near his valley temple, the place called Ankhu Khufu. Could Khufu's *khenu* be that large building encountered in the AMBRIC trench along the Mansouriyah Canal, aligned with the southern side of the Great Pyramid and the Nazlet el-Sissi mound?

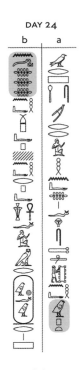

DAY 24

Merer used the term *setep za* to designate his phyle or team, and in this extract from Papyrus B, he logs that they joined with 'those who are on the registry of the *setep zau*'.

We know that even more royal structures lie under the modern buildings in this zone. We also know that in Heit el-Ghurab, the southern settlement, we have uncovered only part of a 4th-Dynasty proto-city. We are seeing different parts and elements from both the fragmentary archaeology and the fragmentary papyri. All the major structures in Heit el-Ghurab, including the barracks and bakeries, could have belonged to the *setep za*. Along with the administrative structures attested in the Wadi el-Jarf Papyri, they could have been sections of one gigantic palace layout, a kind of Old Kingdom Egyptian equivalent of Versailles, or, better, New Kingdom Amarna or Malqata in Thebes, and like those royal layouts, this palace-city included various royal apartments, halls and institutions. What the two zones of 4th-Dynasty settlement north and south of the central waterway, and separated by it, could represent is not the relocation of the palace, with its buildings and infrastructures, over time. Rather, this was one gigantic royal port-city that served three generations of pyramid builders, starting with Khufu.

# CHAPTER 12

# ANKH-HAF, DIRECTOR OF THE PORT OF KHUFU

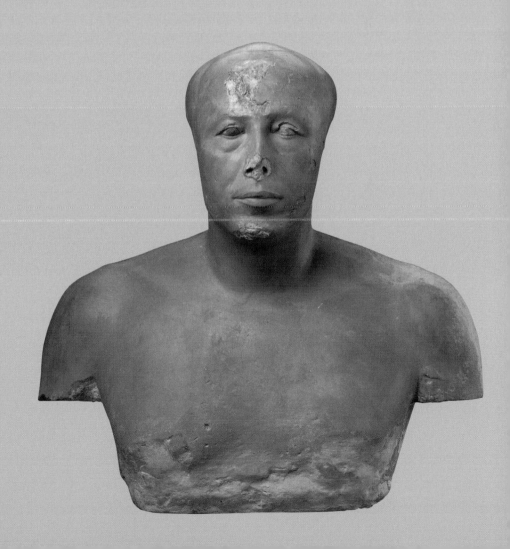

Day 24: Inspector Merer spends the day with his phyle hauling (crafts?) with those who are on the register of the elite, the *aper*-teams and the noble Ankh-haf, director of the Ro-She Khufu.

PAPYRUS B IV

With its immensity and the hints that it was once finished to near perfection, the Great Pyramid has stood for centuries enigmatic, non-human, seemingly people-less – as its creators intended. Yet marks of human hands are everywhere, and now in Merer's journal we can read the names and daily activities of individuals and groups who actually built the Great Pyramid for Khufu. Of course, Egyptologists have long known names, titles and even found physical remains of the people who belonged to the society that built the Great Pyramid. But titles on tomb walls are just that – bare statements of role or condition. Only at the end of the 4th Dynasty did résumés of titles begin to evolve into the first biographies. Now, in the Wadi el-Jarf Papyri, we can follow the movements and activity of one typical team – Merer and his phyle – morning, afternoon and night. The papyri give us 'individuals in history', and not only Merer. We see a 'director of six', named Ideru, sailing from Tura to Heliopolis for food and returning three days later with bread and 40 sacks of grain. A man named Hesi, 'the director of ten', spends the day at Ro-She Khufu, 'Entrance to the Lake of Khufu', with his naval section. We learn of Dedi, who seems to be the head of the four phyles including Merer's team, and who keeps his own logbook, rewarding Merer with cloth.

Merer's journal mentions another individual who directed this cast of dramatis personae, and who also had a decisive historical impact in the 4th-Dynasty royal administration – a prince named Ankh-haf. On a particular Day 24 of one of his ten-day cycles (as recorded in Papyrus B IV), Merer noted down that he and his phyle spent time hauling something, possibly boats, probably in the Ro-She Khufu. His phyle joined other chosen phyles (literally 'those who are on the register of the elite'), *aper*-teams and, significantly, the noble Ankh-haf, 'Director of the Ro-She Khufu', a title that is documented only here. As we saw in Chapter 11, the Ro-She Khufu must have been a kind of port authority for receiving all kinds of deliveries – from places as far apart as Lebanon and Aswan, provisions from all over Egypt, and fine limestone from Tura – into what was, essentially, Khufu's central harbour at Giza, where scribes

PREVIOUS PAGE
Prince Ankh-haf, in a finely carved limestone bust, painted in orange-red ochre, which is surely a portrait of the real man. In Papyrus B IV, Inspector Merer refers to him specifically as Director of the Ro-She Khufu, that is, director of the king's port at Giza.

PART V    How They Built the Great Pyramid

must surely have accounted for all goods incoming as meticulously as Merer accounted for the daily labours of his team. Now, thanks to the Wadi el-Jarf Papyri, we can identify prince Ankh-haf as in charge of this place – the Director of Khufu's port.

## An individual in history

In the obscure history of the Great Pyramid Ankh-haf stands out because of the extraordinary realism of his famous portrait bust, which American archaeologist George Reisner found in the 1920s in the mud-brick building attached to the stone chapel of his tomb, G 7510, in the Eastern Cemetery at Giza. In a layer of plaster applied over the beautifully carved limestone sculpture, the artist had moulded finer details, including a short beard and ears, that had broken off and are now missing. The whole piece, which ends just below the chest and with the arms cut off below the shoulders, was then painted in orangish-red ochre. It is a sensitive portrait of a mature man who looks rather weary, with pouches under his eyes and a bald head, the lines of his receding hair marked on the sides – all suggesting keen observation by the sculptor of the characteristics of a real person. Ankh-haf's bust is in surprising contrast to the formal, stylized canon of Egyptian sculpture in the round and relief, including the life-size standing figure of Ankh-haf himself on the west wall of his inner stone chapel. Here, his figure shown in full, he wears a long kilt and leans on his staff. Ankh-haf's portrait bust is so exceptional, even with the broken nose and missing ears, that when curators at the Museum of Fine Arts, Boston, where the bust is held, painted eyes, eyebrows and hair on a faithful replica and dressed it in a hat, suit and tie, they were struck by the modernity of the face. It seemed a physical likeness of an actual person who had once lived, breathed and thought. The German Egyptologist Jan Assmann has observed that, if slightly restored and cast in bronze, and put on display in an official building, it could easily pass as a portrait of a modern politician or businessman.

As well as his role as Director of Khufu's port and harbour, Ankh-haf also held other important positions and titles, judging by fragmentary inscriptions from his tomb, though under which king and exactly when is still debated by Egyptologists. We need, therefore, to study the clues provided by his tomb.

## The tomb of Ankh-haf

Ankh-haf's impressive tomb (G 7510) in the Eastern Cemetery took the traditional form of a mastaba, like many others arranged in rows beneath the Great Pyramid. Named after the low benches found outside Egyptian houses, mastaba tombs had walls that sloped inwards and a flat roof. Measuring 105 × 52 m, Ankh-haf's is one of the two largest at Giza, second only by a trifle to the gigantic anonymous mastaba G 2000 in the Western Cemetery. George Reisner and William Stevenson Smith believed Ankh-haf served as the first Vizier under Khafre, after the reign of Khufu's immediate successor Djedefre, who moved north to Abu Roash to build his pyramid. Reisner, who excavated the cemeteries beneath the pyramids at Giza, believed the Eastern Cemetery (which he designated G 7000) expanded from west to east: Khufu's builders first raised his three queen's pyramids and then built eight large mastabas (from an original twelve cores) for the king's closest family members. In Reisner's view, Ankh-haf's gigantic mastaba was the first addition to the east of these original tombs, built early in Khafre's reign.

Since Reisner's interpretation, several scholars have argued strongly that Ankh-haf built his mastaba and served as Vizier during the reign of Khufu, rather than Khafre. They base their re-evaluation on the architecture and decoration of the tomb – the corridor-like type of stone chapel built into its southeast corner, the two false doors in the western wall and the style and technique of scenes and inscriptions carved in delicate low relief, of which only pieces remain. In his masterful study of 4th-Dynasty Giza, Austrian Egyptologist Peter Jánosi deduced that G 7510 was, in fact, the very first mastaba in Khufu's Eastern Cemetery, based on the way in which it aligns between lines extended from the southern side and centre axis of the Great Pyramid, and the first two of Khufu's queens' pyramids (GI-a and GI-b).

Ankh-haf's inner stone chapel consisted of a narrow north–south chamber accessed by a corridor on the north, which gave it an L-shaped ground plan. With two false doors sunk into the western wall, the chapel is similar to ones attached to the eastern sides of queen's pyramid GI-b and to the chapels of the mastaba of Hemiunu (G 4000), discussed below, and G 2000 in the Western Cemetery. Craftsmen inscribed the larger, southern false door for Ankh-haf, and the northern false door for his wife, who was named Hetepheres, although no second burial shaft has been found for her in the tomb. A statue of Ankh-haf must have stood in a *serdab* (an enclosed statue chamber) behind the southern false door, but no trace of it was found.

Mud-brick walls, rendered with white plaster, extended the chapel to the east. Within, beyond what was possibly an open court, lay the oblong north–south chamber where Reisner's excavators found Ankh-haf's bust lying on its back in front of a white-plastered mud-brick pedestal projecting from the west wall. When they lifted the bust, they saw broken ceramic bowl stands and 94 plaster models of food offerings, apparently Ankh-haf's last ritual meal. A low bench north of the pedestal served as a shelf for these offerings. How did the attendants who made these offerings experience Ankh-haf's bust?

A marked peculiarity of the bust is the way, as mentioned, it is cut horizontally just below the chest and both arms are cut horizontally just below the shoulders. Such truncations are seen in ancient Egyptian sculptors' models and trial pieces. Andrey Bolshakov, who studied the bust in detail, suggested that it would have attached to another piece sculpted with the lower chest and outstretched arms. If so, this would form an image like the well-known bust of a 6th-Dynasty priest named Idu, found in his tomb at the northern edge of Giza's Eastern Cemetery. Idu appears from the chest up at the bottom of his false door, as though rising from the Underworld, his relief-carved arms stretching out, palms up, to receive offerings. Bolshakov suggested Ankh-haf's bust could have been Idu's model and prototype. The pedestal in Ankh-haf's chapel is just wide enough to accommodate the bust, with its back against the wall and the presumed missing outstretched forearms and hands in proportion. Set up on the pedestal, Ankh-haf would have been at eye-level with those who attended to him in death. Ankh-haf's image, positioned at the north end of this rear room, stood aligned with his false door at the southern end of his inner stone chapel, and with his statue in the serdab. As Bolshakov says, in the dark, lamp-lit room Ankh-haf's bust would have provided an 'illusion of the deceased suddenly appearing from deep within the tomb to gaze at the visitor who has brought offerings'.

## Overlooking the Ro-She Khufu

If Ankh-haf's mastaba and Khufu's queen's pyramid GI-a were the two first monuments raised in the Eastern Cemetery, it is all the more

curious that Ankh-haf built so far to the east, 117 m east of
pyramid GI-a. With Ankh-haf's mastaba and the first two queens'
pyramids, the builders established a frame into which they then
inserted the other mastabas for Khufu's family members. The
size and priority of Ankh-haf's tomb in the building sequence
certainly suggest the highest princely status, and the position
is also meaningful in view of Ankh-haf's title in the Wadi el-Jarf
Papyri, Director of the Ro-She Khufu.

At that time a steep escarpment plunged 36–40 m down
from the Giza Plateau to the floodplain; Ankh-haf perched his huge
mastaba only 30 m from its edge, and his mud-brick chapel extended
another 13 m east, bringing its eastern façade to within just 17 m of
where the cliff falls away. From his chapel, Ankh-haf's bust looked
out over the very water transport infrastructure that he had overseen
as Director of the Ro-She Khufu.

Other alignments are also significant. Ankh-haf's mastaba lines
up with the mound of Nazlet el-Sissi, which, as already discussed,
is a very ancient, strategic place that forms the northern gatepost
of the entrance to Khufu's port. The mastaba also aligns with the
approximate centre of the large building framed by massive stone
walls, possibly a buried palace, and with the royal terrace that
thrusts east along the north side of the central canal basin, indicated
by other AMBRIC excavations and drilling. The southern sides of
the building, terrace, mound and Ankh-haf's mastaba align with
the south side of the Great Pyramid. Mastaba G 7510 was located
appropriately for a prince in charge of Khufu's port authority.

## The puzzle of Ankh-haf's role and relationships

Scraps of relief-carving from Ankh-haf's mastaba bear witness
to his title of 'King's Eldest Son'. The king in question is generally
identified as Sneferu, making Ankh-haf the half-brother of Khufu.
Of course, if an eldest son dies before the father, the title moves
on to the next eldest son. Inconvenient though it is for writing neat
historical narrative, however, such titles cannot always be taken too
literally. Nefermaat, who was buried in Mastaba 16 at Meidum, held
the same title and with respect to Sneferu. Two men, Hemiunu and
Kawab, also display the title 'King's Eldest Son' in their tombs at
Giza. (We have six 'eldest sons' in the reign of Khafre.) Although this
is a minority opinion, it is not entirely impossible that Khufu, rather

The bust of Ankh-haf
may once have been
attached to another
piece portraying the
chest and outstretched
arms, like the sculpture
of the 6th-Dynasty priest
Idu shown here, found in
his tomb at the northern
edge of Giza's Eastern
Cemetery.

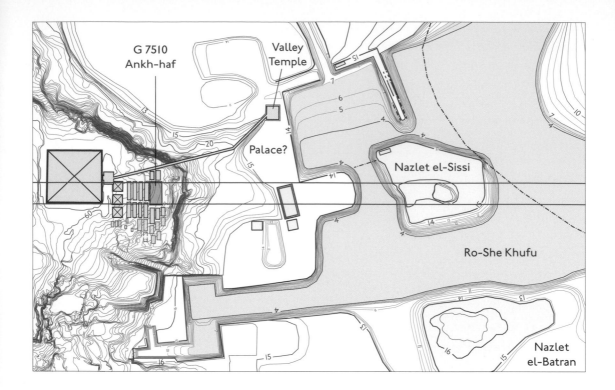

G 7510
Ankh-haf

Valley
Temple

Palace?

Nazlet el-Sissi

Ro-She Khufu

Nazlet
el-Batran

Ankh-haf's huge tomb
G 7510 in the Eastern
Cemetery is one of
the two largest at Giza,
measuring 105 × 52
m. The mastaba tomb
overlooks and aligns
with the mound of
Nazlet el-Sissi, at the
northern flank of the
Ro-She Khufu, of which
Ankh-haf was in charge.

than Sneferu, was Ankh-haf's father, though here we will continue with the majority view.

Ankh-haf's wife was named Hetepheres, spelled out clearly in beautiful hieroglyphs above the northern false door of Ankh-haf's inner stone chapel. She bore the titles 'Eldest King's Daughter' and 'Priestess of Sneferu', and is generally regarded as the daughter of King Sneferu and Queen Hetepheres I. Ankh-haf's wife is one of three prominent women named Hetepheres of this time. The first, Hetepheres I, Sneferu's wife, is generally seen as the mother of Khufu and is known from a secret shaft tomb (G 7000x), where Reisner's team excavated her magnificent burial assembly only to find her body missing when they opened her alabaster sarcophagus. From the next generation, Ankh-haf's wife must have been among the most important members of the court, but, as she was not a queen, Egyptologists do not assign her a Roman numeral. The third Hetepheres (II) was a daughter of Khufu who married his son Kawab, gave birth to Meresankh III and later married one of Khufu's successors, though it is not certain which. It is interesting in this line of names that Hetepheres II built the very first mastaba south of Ankh-haf's (G 7520) for her tomb (to be in proximity to a close family member?), but donated it and a black granite sarcophagus to her daughter, Meresankh III, who perhaps died before her.

The titles of Ankh-haf's wife Hetepheres – Priestess of Sneferu and King's Eldest Daughter – combined with Ankh-haf's title, King's Eldest Son (honorific or not), probably signify that Ankh-haf and his wife were born into the royal house in the generation before Khufu's children, and this raises a question. If Ankh-haf was a true son of Sneferu, by another, unknown wife, why would he locate his tomb in the cemetery where Khufu's children were buried and not at Meidum or Dahshur like others of his generation – Nefermaat, for example? And Ankh-haf's appearance now in the Wadi el-Jarf Papyri as the Director of Khufu's port raises another question, this time concerning the titles and order of succession of the post of Vizier and Overseer of All the King's Works.

## The mystery of two viziers

The Wadi el-Jarf Papyri fragment mentioning Ankh-haf informs us that he served as Director of the Ro-She Khufu, and the date found in another papyrus from the same collection would place this at the end of Khufu's reign. This title, however, has not turned up in the fragments of relief carving that once decorated Ankh-haf's chapel (or anywhere else, so far), though those same bits and pieces do convey that Ankh-haf served as Overseer of All the King's Works and Vizier. These were both highly important and influential positions – but when did he hold them? Here, we have something of a puzzle, a tale of (at least) two Viziers who also served as Overseers of All the King's Works for Khufu.

If Ankh-haf was Overseer of All the King's Works and Vizier under Khufu (and so far nothing says explicitly it was for this king), we then have to contend with Hemiunu, who has long been cited as the overseer of Khufu's pyramid project following Hermann Junker's excavation of his large mastaba (G 4000) in the Western Cemetery. This revealed Hemiunu's titles of Vizier and Overseer of All the King's Works, as well as his powerful limestone seated statue in his serdab, showing him as a rather heavily built figure. Hemiunu probably inherited the offices from his father, Sneferu's son Nefermaat, who had served as Sneferu's Overseer of All the King's Works, as well as Vizier, early in that king's reign, and whose mummy was buried (and plundered during his own generation) in his giant Mastaba 16, at Meidum. Scenes in the chapel of that mastaba show a man named Hemiunu three times, with titles and prominence that suggest he was Nefermaat's oldest son, and so a grandson of Sneferu. This Hemiunu shares titles found also on the base of the statue of Hemiunu from G 4000, written with incised hieroglyphs filled with coloured paste like Nefermaat's reliefs in his chapel. The name and titles, the hieroglyphic style, the father–son relationship, the fact that Hemiunu's mastaba G 4000 is one of the largest (*c.* 53 × 28 m) and oldest in the Western Cemetery of Khufu's officials, all suggest that Hemiunu took charge of Khufu's works early on (following one other Overseer of All the King's Works; no other Viziers of Sneferu are known after Nefermaat). Did Ankh-haf in turn then take over from Hemiunu during Khufu's reign?

On the other hand, as noted above, recent studies date the tomb of Ankh-haf to Khufu's reign, rather than Khafre's, and it is likely that Ankh-haf's was the first mastaba built in the Eastern Cemetery at the foot of the Great Pyramid. In his study, *The Administration of Egypt in the Old Kingdom*, Nigel Strudwick placed Ankh-haf *before* Hemiunu, rather than being his successor.

If Ankh-haf did take over as Overseer of Works and Vizier from Hemiunu, then we have to accept that an older man, a member of the generation of Khufu and Nefermaat, Hemiunu's father, took over from a younger person, a nephew, thus violating the notion that, as Strudwick says, 'promotion to high offices and ultimately the vizierate was made on the basis of seniority, providing the individual was still in favour'. But if Hemiunu took over as Overseer of All the King's Works and Vizier from Ankh-haf, how does that fit in with the fact that in his logbook Merer documents working with Ankh-haf at the end of Khufu's reign as Director of the Ro-She Khufu? Was Ankh-haf also Vizier and Overseer of All the King's Works at this time? The papyrus texts are silent on this.

Could it be that Ankh-haf had stepped down from the high offices of Vizier and Overseer of All the King's Works by the time Merer composed his logbook? We have to wonder. Would Merer have documented working in the presence of the Director of the Ro-She Khufu but not mentioned that the same person was also Overseer of All the King's Works or Vizier? If I were a stevedore or the captain of a cargo boat and wanted to record a day working in the presence of the Executive Director of the Port Authority of New York and New Jersey,

and if that person was also Secretary of Commerce, or, closer to the title of Vizier, the President, or, in another country, the Prime Minister, would I record only the lesser title? Perhaps it was more meaningful for Merer that he worked under Prince Ankh-haf in his capacity of director of Khufu's port. Merer's task in delivering stone for the Great Pyramid was, after all, specific to that office.

The idea that Ankh-haf deliberately located his mastaba (G 7510) directly above the entrance to Khufu's port, reflecting his title, Director of the Ro-She Khufu, together with the argument that this tomb was the first in the Eastern Cemetery, would suggest he held that title when Khufu's builders began the Eastern Cemetery. The very first pieces in the Eastern Cemetery were the shaft tomb intended for the queen mother Hetepheres I (G 7000) and the cutting for the passage of an unbuilt pyramid, GI-x, which builders shifted 28 m west where they completed queen's pyramid GI-a. These structures defined the northern boundary of the Eastern Cemetery. Because the queen mother's secret tomb, where her funerary equipment was buried (G 7000x), and this boundary align with the axis of the King's Chamber in the Great Pyramid, the builders may have started the Eastern Cemetery about the time that they had raised the Great Pyramid to that height and while the King's Chamber still lay open to the sky. This could have been around Khufu's regnal year 18–20. The latest date from the mastaba of Hemiunu relates to the 10th census, and he may have died between the age of 55 and 65. If the builders' dates from Hemiunu's tomb are from the reign of Khufu, it could be that Hemiunu died and Ankh-haf, an older man, subsequently became Overseer of All the King's Works and Vizier. It is then possible that Ankh-haf himself directed the layout of the Eastern Cemetery, giving him liberty to mark his authority over the royal port he directed by building one of the largest mastabas (twice the size of Hemiunu's) at the edge of the plateau, directly overlooking the Ro-She Khufu.

Still, we wonder again why Merer did not mention Ankh-haf's high-ranking titles, especially Overseer of Royal Work and Workforces (the longer variant), since Merer's assignments between Tura and Giza and between Wadi el-Jarf and Sinai were precisely about building the Great Pyramid. Also, Overseers of Works had charge of expeditions. Is it possible that either Hemiunu or Ankh-haf served as Overseer of All the King's Works while the other served as Vizier, or vice versa? Could individuals move in and out of office, so that Ankh-haf took on the office of Vizier but passed it on by the time he was supervising Merer as Director of the Ro-She Khufu?

Truth be told, Egyptologists do not really know the rules of succession for officials, or even for kings for that matter. Strings of titles etched in stone in tomb chapels were summaries of an official's whole career, or most of it. Certainly, no official held all the titles listed at any one time. Four of Khufu's sons buried in large mastabas in the Eastern Cemetery attained the title Vizier, at some point, as did three of Khafre's sons who were buried in the royal rock-cut cemetery in front and to the right side of his pyramid. And this is before the promotion of private individuals to this highest office. Just as we find too high a number of 'King's Sons' and 'King's Eldest Sons' for our expectation that the eldest son became king, we find 'an embarrassingly large number of Viziers' in the Old Kingdom, as Strudwick puts it – 16 from the capital zone of Memphis during the 4th to the early 5th Dynasty. In his study of Old Kingdom officials, Wolfgang Helck concluded that the title of Vizier was, like 'King's Son', honorific and conveying the highest 'command authority'. Could Viziers, that is, the ones who really carried out the duties that went with the title, have overlapped, or could there have been more than one at a given time? This is possible at the end of the 4th Dynasty and probable for much of the rest of the Old Kingdom, when a 'multiplicity of Overseers of All the King's Works' could be understood as different individuals holding the title for each separate building project. For the entire 4th Dynasty we know of more than half a dozen people holding these high titles. So far, there is no evidence of overlap for the time of Khufu. But now we must factor in Ankh-haf's appearance in the Wadi el-Jarf Papyri under the title Director of the Ro-She Khufu, with no sign of the title Vizier or Overseer of All the King's Works.

Perhaps late in life, Ankh-haf took on the office of Vizier and Overseer of All the King's Works under Khafre, as Reisner surmised, following the reign of Djedefre, Khufu's successor. Egyptologists have thought that Djedefre only ruled for some eight years. Michel Valloggia's work at Djedefre's Abu Roash pyramid shows that he may instead have ruled for nearly a quarter of a century (23 years), but not all scholars are certain that this is correct. If Ankh-haf was born in the last few years of Sneferu, by the time Khafre took the throne, he would have been 36 to 40 years old, working from the 28 years assigned to Khufu and 8 years of Djedefre. But if Djedefre reigned for 23 years, Ankh-haf would have been older than 51 (Khufu 28 years + Djedefre 23 years). In either case, it is possible he came out of retirement and served as Overseer of All the King's Works and Vizier for part of Khafre's quarter of a century on the throne. This would have taken him into his sixties and maybe seventies.

The immense size of mastaba G 7510 indicates Ankh-haf's elevated high status. If Ankh-haf was not yet Vizier and Overseer of All the King's Works when Khufu's tomb-makers built mastaba G 7510, his status as Director of the Ro-She Khufu, royal son, Khufu's half-brother and member of the princely class (*iry paut*) clearly must have brought a privileged first place among the tombs of the royal family in the Great Pyramid's Eastern Cemetery. What we do know, what the Wadi el-Jarf Papyri now tell us, is that at the end of Khufu's reign, Ankh-haf was certainly in charge of Khufu's port, through which passed much of the materials and manpower that fed into the construction of the king's colossal building project.

# CHAPTER 13

# FEEDING AND SUPPLYING THE WORKERS

[First day <of the month>] the director of 6 Idjer[u] casts off for Heliopolis in a *iuat* transport-boat to bring us food from Heliopolis while the elite (*setep za*) is in Tura. ... [Day 4 ...] the director of 6 [Idjer]u [comes back] from Heliopolis with 40 *khar*-sacks and a large *hekat*-measure of *beset*-bread while the elite haul stones in Tura North.

PAPYRUS B II

The logbooks from Wadi el-Jarf provide vivid daily reports of the activities of the work-gangs who were involved in the construction project centred on the Great Pyramid at Giza. Numerous accounts included in the same batch of archives fill out the picture, adding information about the supplies of food and other materials that were allocated to the teams by the royal administration throughout the year. These minutely detailed accounts confirm the evidence obtained by archaeology through the excavation of the facilities at Giza where these same workers were housed. It is clear the teams involved in the construction of the royal funeral complexes were not badly treated. Like their counterparts in the New Kingdom community of Deir el-Medina, a millennium later, who were also tasked with building royal tombs (although very different in type and scale), these workers were very well looked after by the state, and they probably depended entirely on the government for their livelihood as well as that of their families. Occasionally they also gained access to products that were rare – even luxurious – and which might have been thought to be reserved for a limited social elite restricted to the immediate entourage of the king.

## A rich and varied diet

**PREVIOUS PAGE**
Part of Papyrus H from Wadi el-Jarf, a document accounting for the delivery primarily of grain to the work-gang (see pp. 253–56).

Among the foods that are recorded by the papyri, some of which were handed out by the 'Granary' (*shenut*) that formed part of the royal administration, were different types of birds and poultry (such as ducks, geese and cranes), fish, fruit (including figs), a very wide variety of breads and/or cakes (*shaut*-bread, *gaua*, *hetch*, *pesen*) and several kinds of drinks, ranging from *henket*-beer, the most common, to varieties of alcoholic beverage that were clearly highly desirable, such as the *seremet* and *sekhepet* forms of beer. The workers were also provided with dates (the fruit of the date palm was probably less common at that time in the Nile Valley) and honey, a product that is only very rarely attested in the early pharaonic period, and which it is safe to assume was mostly consumed within the royal entourage. Archaeobotanical analyses of remains found at Wadi el-Jarf by Claire Newton have confirmed this diverse range of plants in the diet. She has been able to identify cereals (emmer wheat and hulled barley), legumes (vetch and pea), garlic and various types of fruit, such as watermelon, figs, sycamore figs and fruits of the *Balanites aegyptiaca* tree (the so-called 'desert date'). More unexpectedly, she was also able to identify dates and olives, albeit in small quantities. The study of faunal remains, conducted by Joséphine Lesur, showed that the main meat being consumed at the site was beef, but the diet also included ovicaprids (sheep and goats) and a number of wild species such as ibex and dorcas gazelle. The day-to-day reality of livestock consumption at Wadi el-Jarf is also demonstrated by a series of seal impressions naming animal-herders and butchers that were found in various parts of the site.

The basic diet, however, was dominated by cereals – the vast majority of surviving documents concern deliveries of grains in various forms (*zut*-grain, *djedju*-flour, *besha*-barley) or different kinds of loaves. Some of the dispatch notes consist of summaries of an entire set of supplies provided by the administration to the work-gang as a whole, while others are obviously for local internal use, recording rations that were allocated on a daily basis to individual workers. These 'local' texts systematically involve a combination of three products. First was the type of bread baked in the large bell-shaped *bedja*-moulds that are found both at Giza and at Wadi el-Jarf (*beset-* and *hedj*-loaves). Secondly, there was a variety of flat cake-style bread, probably baked in open pottery vessels resembling shallow platters (*pesen*-loaves). And finally *henket*-beer, a beverage that seems to have been low in alcohol and high in carbohydrate, and was clearly considered to be one of the staples of this daily diet.

These rations were allocated to the workers according to their role within the expedition, as well as where they were at the time. When Inspector Merer was constantly making round trips between Tura and Giza to transport limestone blocks (as reported in Papyrus B), the monthly food supply for his workforce took the form of 40 *khar*-sacks of *beset*-bread, a very dense loaf baked in *bedja*-moulds and probably designed to remain edible for up to a month (see also p. 182). Since in this instance the royal administration was quite near to the places where the gang was working, it was

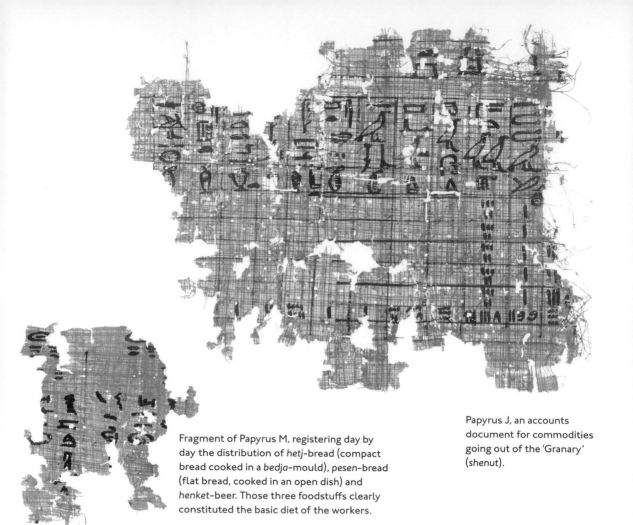

Fragment of Papyrus M, registering day by day the distribution of *hetj*-bread (compact bread cooked in a *bedja*-mould), *pesen*-bread (flat bread, cooked in an open dish) and *henket*-beer. Those three foodstuffs clearly constituted the basic diet of the workers.

Papyrus J, an accounts document for commodities going out of the 'Granary' (*shenut*).

convenient to supply them with a finished product that was fetched from the reserves in the city of Heliopolis. It seems likely that in this instance the loaves had been made in state-organized facilities similar to the numerous large bakeries identified by Mark's work-gang at Giza in the Heit el-Ghurab settlement. Things were very different, however, when the same team was located much further away from the central administrative base, as would be the case at Wadi el-Jarf, a remote desert site more than 120 km from the Nile Valley. Given the distance and isolation, the supplies regularly delivered to the workers would have taken the form of a raw or semi-refined product (such as grains of wheat and barley, or coarse flour), leaving it to them to bake it into bread or brew beer, according to their daily requirements.

## A glimpse of the economy at the beginning of the 4th Dynasty: Papyrus H

Papyrus H provides us with insights into the early pharaonic economic system and also allows us to analyse in greater depth some of the administrative practices of Khufu's time. Discovered within the batch of archive material buried at the entrance to the GI storage gallery site at Wadi el-Jarf, Papyrus H has survived almost intact, primarily comprising two large fragments that could be fitted back together. Its original length is estimated at 81 cm, but almost all the text has been preserved on the surviving 67.5 cm, which reveals that it is an accounts document, summarizing grain deliveries made to the work-gang over a period of about five months. The stretch of time covered by the text is between 'the year after the 13th cattle-count' of Khufu (i.e. years 26–27 of his reign) and the beginning of the following year, that of the 14th census (years 27–28). It is interesting to see that the document devotes a special section to the so-called *heriu renpet*, the five additional ('epagomenal') days in the Egyptian calendar which were added to the twelve months, each of thirty days, in order to create a complete 365-day year. The records therefore correspond to a period between May and September, which is exactly when we would expect conditions to be right for this work-gang to undertake an expedition on the Red Sea coast.

Once the document had been unrolled, its subject was immediately clear from a vertical column of writing on the verso identifying it as 'bread accounts'. The details written on the recto provide a window into the accounting methods in use at the beginning of the 4th Dynasty and how the system of feeding the workers was organized. On the upper part of the roll, the scribe recorded the numbers of each of the months covered by the accounts, with the months forming the subject of individual columns of writing clearly delimited by vertical lines. Four of these columns are well preserved, and two others could be reconstructed almost in their entirety with the help of some small fragments of the document excavated at the same time as the main pieces. The details in the columns consist of the origins of the recorded foodstuffs, with the name of the province ('nome') which supplied them, followed by a more precise locality. Deliveries of cereals listed in the document came from different provinces in the Delta, including the Harpoon Nome (in the northwest Delta, close to the spot where Alexandria would later be located) and the Dolphin Nome (in the northeastern

Papyrus H (recto),
an accounts document
for bread, flour, grain
and dates.

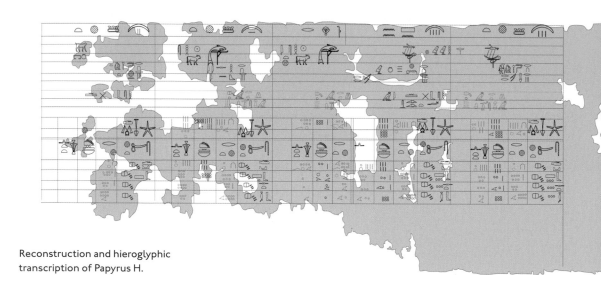

Reconstruction and hieroglyphic
transcription of Papyrus H.

Translation of Papyrus H.

### Section IV

| [2nd month of] Akhet | | | |
|---|---|---|---|
| The Residence | | | |
| 1/10e Ny-hedjet[.our] | | | |
| 1/6e Khen[...] | | | |
| | | | |
| | | | Overall total |
| Arrears | Delivered | Full amount | Detailed account |
| | | 101.25 | ftour |
| | | 17 | barley |
| | | 15 | [grain] |
| | | 8.5 | [dates] |

### Section III

| 1st month of Akhet | | | |
|---|---|---|---|
| Town of Ibet-Hesire | Dolphin Nome | | |
| 1/10e Hesi | | | |
| 1/6e Qeni | | | |
| Deliveries in hekat of cooked bread: 6 | | | |
| [63.25] | 78.5 | 141.75 | Overall total |
| Arrears | Delivered | Full amount | Detailed account |
| 41.25 | 60 | 101.25 | flour |
| 9 | [8] | 17 | barley |
| 8 | [7] | 15 | grain |
| 5 | [3.5] | 8.5 | dates |

### Section II

| Epagomenal Days | | | 4th month of Shemu | | | |
|---|---|---|---|---|---|---|
| Town of Ibet-Hesire | Dolphin Nome | | Harpoon Nome | | | |
| | | | 1/10e Khementnu | | | |
| | | | 1/6e (Sen) Merer(?) | | | |
| Deliveries in hekat of cooked bread: 6 | | | Account of this(?) by Irtysen | | | |
| 7.37 | 16.31 | 23.69 | [51.75] | 90 | 141.75 | Overall total |
| Arrears | Delivered | Full amount | Arrears | Delivered | Full amount | Detailed account |
| 4.87 | 12 | 16.87 | 41.25 | 60 | 101.25 | flour |
| 1 | 1.87 | 2.56 | 5 | 12 | 17 | barley |
| 1 | 1.5 | 2.5 | 3.5 | 12 | 15 | grain |
| 0.5 | 1 | 1.5 | 2.5 | 6 | 8.5 | dates |

### Section I

| 3rd month of Akhet | | | |
|---|---|---|---|
| Town of Ro-Huu(d) | Harpoon Nome | | |
| 1/10e Ny-hedjet-ur | | | |
| 1/6e Sen-Merer | | | |
| Deliveries in hekat of cooked bread: 6 | | | |
| 52.25 | 89.5 | 141.75 | Overall total |
| Arrears | Delivered | Full amount | Detailed account |
| 41.25 | 60 | 101.25 | flour |
| 5 | 12 | 17 | barley |
| 3.5 | 11.5 | 15 | grain |
| 2.5 | 6 | 8.5 | dates |

Delta). Other notations specify the individual who had calculated the account, and probably also the person who was responsible for the dispatch of the commodities.

The lower part of Papyrus H consists of the actual accounts, which are presented in the form of a table. On the right the scribe lists the different cereals that were part of this particular allocation, preceded by the total volume, given in the form of quantities of *khar*-sacks (10 *hekat*-measures). The following three columns of text are then used to record: 1. the quantity of the allocation that theoretically should be delivered to the workers (in red ink); 2. the quantity that has in fact been allocated to them (in black); 3. the remainder that is still anticipated (again in red). This use of different colours of ink thus distinguishes between the situation in reality and what it should theoretically have been. Exactly the same method of accounting is found in the later papyri from Abusir, organized in the same way into 'spreadsheets' that allowed the accounts to be checked at a single glance.

Detail of the verso of Papyrus H, giving the title of the document when rolled, 'Account of bread' (*heseb en te*).

In the case of Papyrus H, it is interesting to note that the work-teams are never actually paid the full amount that is due to them – the different allocations systematically correspond to just 63 per cent of the initial expected total. This shortfall is confirmed both in the individual monthly columns (all identical) and in the section devoted to epagomenal days, where exactly the same percentage of actual delivered supplies is shown, proportionately, over the period of the five days. This may not necessarily reflect the failure by the administration to deliver the full wages due. It is possible that some of what was described as being provided in the form of grain deliveries was actually provided in another form, such as equipment or other types of foodstuff, and that they were registered simultaneously on other accounts that would have served as supporting documents. In short, these cereal rations may have functioned at least partly in the role of 'currency', providing a general estimate of a salary. The actual amount of that salary could instead have been provided in a diverse range of materials that added up to this original value.

Also of great interest in the accounts is the record of the geographical origins of the products being delivered, which clearly change according to the month in question. In the first two monthly columns (reading right to left), the Harpoon Nome is logged as the region in charge of the deliveries, but in the third and fourth

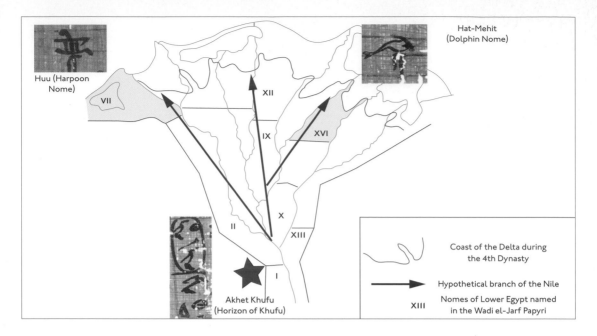

Papyrus H – an account of grain and dates – gives us a glimpse of the 'nomes' or 'provinces' system at the beginning of the Old Kingdom. It shows that the commodities paid to the work-gangs were delivered every two months from different parts of the Delta, in quantities calculated by the state to distribute the weight of this responsibility.

months the Dolphin Nome – at the opposite end of the Delta – is recorded as taking over the responsibility. This rotation of provincial levies must surely be regarded as a shrewd procedure by the administration, spreading the effort involved in the maintenance of the work-gangs equitably across the whole territory controlled by the king. Throughout Khufu's reign, the various provinces were clearly contributing on an ongoing basis to the construction of the royal funeral complex – the great national project – but each was participating according to their individual means and resources. Some provided raw materials or labour, while others (and this is probably the case for the whole Delta region) were probably mainly called on for their agricultural wealth. The varied nature of these different levies thus undoubtedly gave the overall supply model a certain flexibility, which in turn meant that it could operate more effectively.

# CHAPTER 14

# HOW THEY MIGHT HAVE RAISED THE STONES

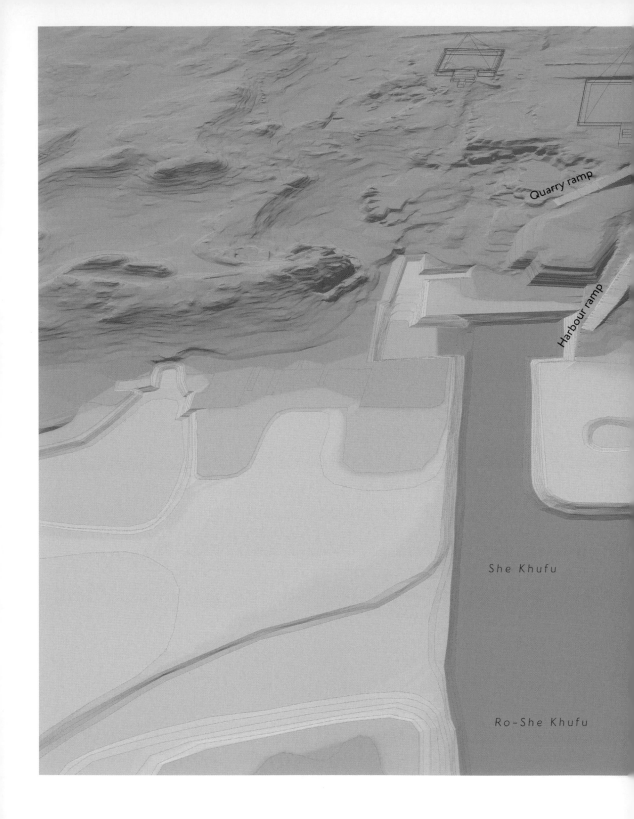

Quarry ramp

Harbour ramp

She Khufu

Ro-She Khufu

PREVIOUS PAGE View along the south side of the Great
Pyramid, looking east, with modern-day Cairo in the
background (see pp. 273–76).

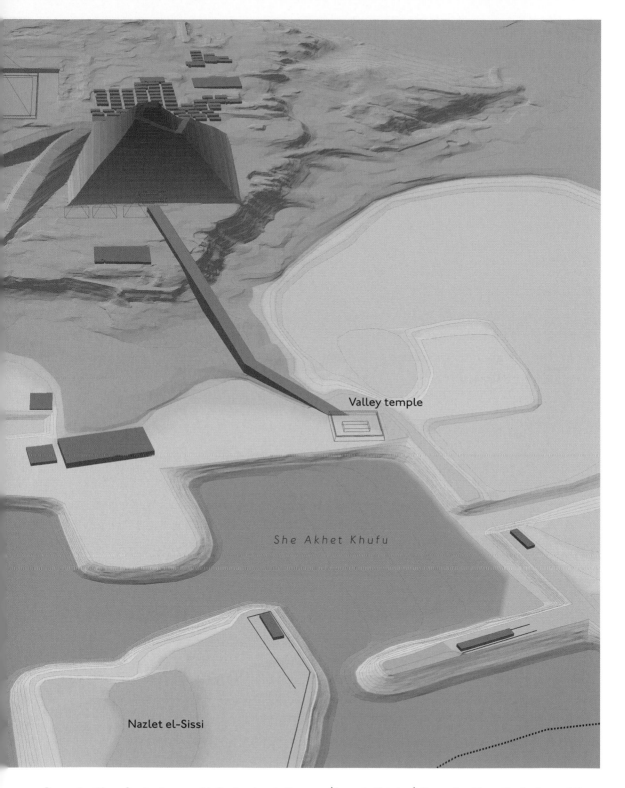

Valley temple

She Akhet Khufu

Nazlet el-Sissi

Reconstruction of water transport infrastructure in the Nile floodplain east of the Giza Plateau, during Khufu's reign. Dark blue: low water (7 m asl) during planting and harvest seasons (November–May). Light blue: water at flood peak (13.5 m asl) during inundation season (August–October). Ramps lead from the harbour at the end of the central canal basin, and from the southern quarry, to 40 m above the pyramid base at the southwest corner of the Great Pyramid.

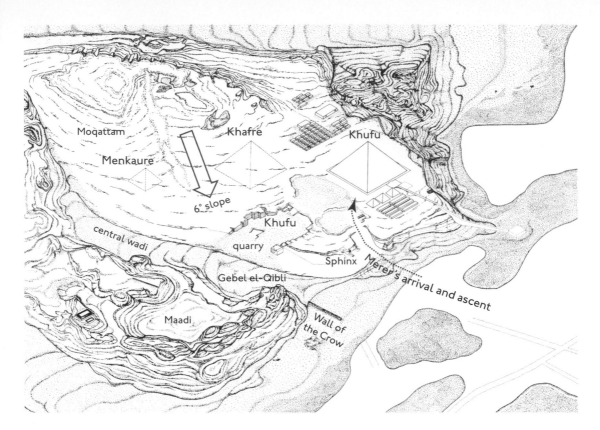

Isometric drawing of the Giza Plateau with features identified for the Khufu Pyramid project, showing the 6° southeasterly dip of the Moqattam Formation outcrop and the Maadi Formation. The original width of the central wadi is extrapolated from this dip. The spot immediately northeast of the Sphinx was the most efficient access up to the Khufu Pyramid, arriving at its southeastern corner (dotted line). Access to Khufu's main quarry, which furnished local (as opposed to Tura) limestone for the Khufu Pyramid, lay farther south, through the central wadi.

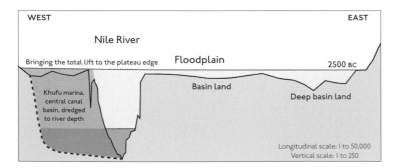

Why would Khufu have dredged a large central canal basin to river depth? In order to use the 7-m rise of flood water in the main Nile branch to lift cargo boats like Merer's, bearing Tura limestone, as high as possible, and as close as possible to the Giza Plateau to reduce the distance that stone had to be transported overland up to the pyramid building site.

Day 25: Inspector Merer spends the day with his phyle hauling stones in Tura South; spends the night at Tura South. Day 26: Inspector Merer casts off with his phyle from Tura [South], loaded with stone, for Akhet Khufu (the Great Pyramid); spends the night at She Khufu (Lake of Khufu). Day 27: Sets sail from She Khufu, sails towards Akhet Khufu, loaded with stone, spends the night at Akhet Khufu.

PAPYRUS B I

When Merer and his men arrived at the Great Pyramid on that Day 27 they must have unloaded the special, fine white limestone they brought from the eastern quarries of Tura South across the Nile Valley. What happened next? How did the stones get up to the Great Pyramid, which Merer identifies as Akhet Khufu ('Horizon of Khufu')?

## The natural hydraulic lift of the Nile flood

Merer's cargo boat had to cross Giza's central harbour, She Khufu, a broad canal basin that stretched from a western Nile branch to the foot of the Giza Plateau, 46 m below the base of the Great Pyramid when the flood waters were at their peak. If Merer's stone was intended for the pyramid itself, rather than its temples and causeway, he must have docked at the low, southeastern base of the plateau, somewhere between the Wall of the Crow to the south and the area east of where Khafre would later carve the Sphinx out of the bedrock escarpment. Only here does the Moqattam Formation, the pyramid plateau proper, dip invitingly 6° to meet the Nile floodplain.

The channel basin was itself the first mechanism for raising stones up to the pyramid site. By dredging the channel 10 m deep, as deep as the western Nile branch that flowed close to the plateau, the builders could take advantage of the 7-m rise in water level during flood season, from low water in early summer to its peak in mid-August, followed by a gradual drop in September to October. Using this natural hydraulic lift, Khufu's work-teams could float cargo boats loaded with stones to the very base of the plateau, and raise them 4 m over the general level of the floodplain.

In Papyrus A Section 11 Merer logged how his team were engaged in an operation to augment this hydraulic lift at the 'dyke' or 'dam' (*djenet*) of the Ro-She Khufu. Merer's phyle joined some

15 other phyles, subdivisions of *aper* work-gangs, amounting to some 600 men, to remove wooden piles or posts, under the supervision of a member of the *iry paut* ('princely class'), whose name is missing but who is most probably Ankh-haf, identified as the Director of the Ro-She Khufu in Papyrus B IV (where his name is preceded by the title *iry paut*). The reason they are removing the piles is that the dyke of Khufu held back water at the entrance to Khufu's basin. After the Nile had risen sufficiently, Merer and cohorts pulled out the posts to open the canal basin, allowing cargo boats to sail in and bring stone during the high-water season. This operation was critical enough that Prince Ankh-haf himself directed it.

### Landing platform – Terrace I

Merer mentions loading stone in Tura a number of times, but unloading only once. At Tura, quarry workers must have assembled stacks of blocks at loading bays, where Merer's men could collect and load them. At Giza, there must have been a corresponding off-loading bay where stones could be stored and recorded before hauling teams took them up to the pyramid.

A broad, flat terrace carved from bedrock at the western end of the She Khufu basin served this purpose, Terrace I as it is now called. Khafre later built his valley temple and the Sphinx Temple on this terrace, but it is likely that Khufu had already created it as part of his water transport infrastructure. Excavations have exposed the terrace, which slopes gently down east of Khafre's valley temple to an elevation of 12.9 m above sea level, almost the level of the 4th-Dynasty floodplain. After building his valley temple, Khafre then added long, thin Tura-limestone ramps aligning with the temple's doorways and reaching out over the terrace, following the slope down to the east. The builders laid these ramps over an older bedrock surface whose gentle slope formed a perfect slipway for docking cargo boats with broad bottoms, low hulls and abruptly truncated ends, such as we see in Old Kingdom tomb scenes, reliefs and models, including the relief of boats carrying granite columns from the causeway of Unas. At some location on this terrace, Merer would have docked the *hau-* and *imu-*boats mentioned in Papyrus B on which his crew carried stones to Giza.

This terrace extends south to the mouth of Giza's central wadi, which cuts between the Moqattam and Maadi Formations

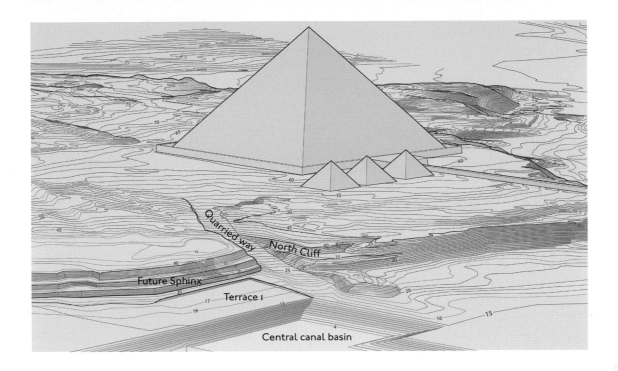

Labels on image: Quarried way · North Cliff · Future Sphinx · Terrace I · Central canal basin

of the plateau and leads directly to the mouth of Khufu's main quarry for his pyramid core stone – the 'hole' corresponding to the 'pile' of his pyramid. But, arriving this far south would make less sense for Merer's deliveries of Tura limestone (and no sense at all if his Tura stone was actually used to finish the work on Khufu's lower causeway and valley temple). However, to the north, in front of where Khafre later built the Sphinx Temple, core drilling and excavation revealed that Terrace I drops more than 12 m almost in line with the escarpment to the east of Khufu's pyramid. This drop, subsequent core drillings confirmed, must be the quay at the end of the central canal basin, long buried and now under the stage and seating for the Sound and Light show and the modern buildings of Nazlet es-Semman.

When Merer arrived at the pyramid site of Akhet Khufu, he would have docked at this quay and his men would have levered and tumbled the stones off their boat onto Terrace I. They then turned their craft around, sailed back east and moored or anchored for the night in the soft twilight reflecting off She Khufu, which expanded south and east at flood season, beyond the confines of the deeply dredged canal basin. No doubt their boat was one among many that dotted the lake, alongside barges that had brought granite beams

Reconstruction of the Giza Plateau eastern escarpment before the creation of the Sphinx, with a way cut through the escarpment to deliver material from the end of the central canal basin up to the Great Pyramid of Khufu. Terrace I extends east of the location of the Sphinx, yet to be quarried out of bedrock. View to the northwest.

from Aswan, gypsum and basalt from the Faiyum, timber from Lebanon, cattle from the Delta and people from all over Egypt.

In this way, Merer's phyle and others like it brought stones to about 44 m below the base of the Great Pyramid, which had been rising course by course over the previous 20 years; its closest (southeastern) corner lay 500 m to the northwest. The next task, probably taken on by other teams, was to move the stones up to where they were needed on the pyramid.

## Direct ascent to Khufu's pyramid

When Khufu's quarrymen cut into the natural escarpment at Giza to create Terrace I, they left a stepped rock face, 20 m high. Later, Khafre's masons cut a U-shaped ditch into this face, reserving a core block from which they carved the Sphinx. Blocks cut from the ditch, weighing many tens of tonnes, were moved to the east to build Khafre's valley temple on Terrace I. As they quarried deeper, the workers then took blocks to make the Sphinx Temple. This sequence of quarrying and construction has removed most traces of Khufu's quarry cuts and ramps.

The most direct way from the end of the central canal basin up to Khufu's pyramid is now marked by the track of a modern asphalt road, ascending from the modern piazza in front of the Sphinx (which lies above the ancient, buried central canal basin), and passing 50 m north of the Sphinx. The road ascends along the 'North Cliff' that quarry workers cut east to west through the natural escarpment and could possibly follow the course of an ancient supply ramp for delivering stone to the high plateau. Did Khufu's forces begin this cut through the eastern escarpment to create a hauling track up to his pyramid? We cannot know: when quarrymen cut a series of officials' tombs in the North Cliff, they probably removed any traces of builders' ramps that might have existed here.

In fact it is more likely that haulers bringing stone for Khufu's pyramid used a ramp that bridged the natural escarpment a bit further north. The 1-m contours mapped in 1977 show a buried protrusion extending here from the escarpment down to the northwest corner of the reconstructed canal basin, very similar to the contours of the buried Khufu causeway foundation crossing the escarpment further north, which could be the remains of an old ramp.

## Rise, run and the harbour ramp

For lifting blocks, the builders used two basic tools: the inclined plane and the lever. Some assembly of ropes, wood and stone might also be possible. To get the stones first to the site of Khufu's pyramid, a ramp from the area east of where the Sphinx was later created would have brought the stone haulers to the level of the pyramid base only 100 m from its southeast corner. If the track ran close to the surface visible now, it would have sloped at a comfortable 5°. But then to lift the stones that Merer delivered

Terrace I (left), the Northern Ledge, the road up to the southeast corner of the Great Pyramid (right), and the North Cliff (= 'Amphitheatre cut'), which is the northern border of the greater Sphinx quarry. View to the west-northwest.

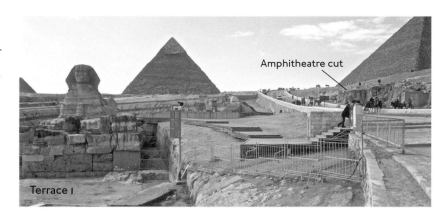

Amphitheatre cut

Terrace I

Contours at 1-m intervals showing protrusions (highlighted yellow) extending from the north and south ends of the escarpment east of the Khufu Pyramid. The northern protrusion marks the buried foundations of the Khufu causeway. Could the southern protrusion mark the remains of an ancient access ramp? Green highlight: Terrace I and the modern road. Blue highlight: west end of buried canal basin.

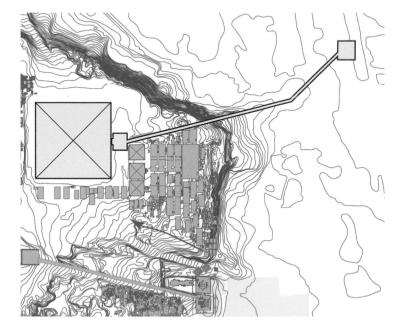

up to the level on the pyramid where masons needed to set them as they worked on it, Khufu's builders had to raise their ramp as they raised the pyramid.

Any straight-on ramp needs a long enough run to accommodate a rise at a practical slope of between 6 and 10°. Over the 500 m from Terrace I to the southeast corner of the pyramid, the natural slope of the plateau formed a ready inclined plane of about 6°. A ramp from Terrace I to a height of 30 m above the pyramid base, would have risen 44 m in total and sloped gradually more steeply, to about 8° 25′ 7″. If the ramp then rose 40 m above the pyramid base, it would have sloped 9° 32′ 12″.

This ramp would have been massive. A rough estimate of its volume, assuming a width of 30 m, is 225,000 cu. m. for a ramp rising 30 m above the pyramid base, and 300,000 cu. m for one 40 m above the base. But pyramid-building supply ramps need not have been as wide as that at the top, and they certainly splayed out at the bottom as a series of accretions. Compare the ramp that Khufu's builders made of stone (and probably debris-fill) at the northern end of this same escarpment as a foundation for his causeway. It ran 500 m from the valley temple (at 15 m asl) to the top of the escarpment (at 50 m asl), with a slope of only 4°. Given a generous estimate of 30 m width, its volume would amount to 262,500 cu. m.

## Quarry ramp

Builders used the fine, white stones from Tura, such as Merer delivered, for the outer pyramid casing and for lining the pyramids' inner passages, and the Queen's Chamber and the Grand Gallery as well. Most of the stone for the bulk of the pyramid – the 'core stone' – was taken by Khufu's workmen from a large quarry to the south. Creating in the process a large bedrock basin that lines up with the pyramid, they removed up to 2,760,000 cu. m of stone, which is 170,000 cu. m more than the estimated 2,590,000 cu. m of stone in the Great Pyramid. However, it is not possible now to measure the full extent of the quarry, as its southern end remains buried by the sand that fills Giza's central wadi.

A ramp could run from the northern rim of this quarry to 30 m above the southwest base of the pyramid, a distance of 320 m, at a functional slope of just over 7° and with a volume of 210,000 cu. m – a rough and generous estimate assuming it was 30 m wide. At that

(OPPOSITE) Contour map of the Great Pyramid, with reconstructed contours (at 1-m intervals asl) of putative ramps from the harbour and the quarry, and a ramp spiralling up and around to the top of the pyramid near its apex. The contours have also been reconstructed west of the harbour, where the bedrock was extensively quarried under Khufu's successor, Khafre, and where he had the Great Sphinx carved out of the bedrock.

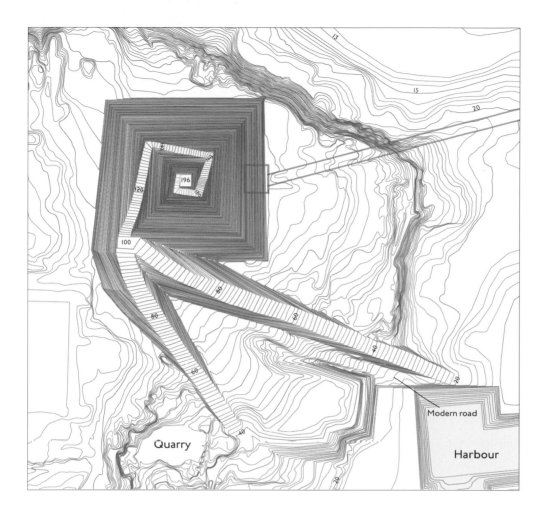

height above the base, the pyramid already contained close to 50 per cent of its mass. If the ramp started further back in the quarry, giving a 100 m longer run, it would have sloped at approximately 5½°, with a volume of 270,000 cu. m, assuming again a generous width of 30 m. If the builders raised this ramp to 40 m above the pyramid base, it would then have sloped at 7° with a volume of 327,600 cu. m.

Ancient Egyptian engineers clearly did conceive of ramps on such scales. Specifications for a ramp or embankment in Papyrus Anastasi I include a width of 55 cubits (just under 29 m), a length of 730 cubits (382.5 m), a height of 60 cubits (31.44 m) and a side batter of 15 cubits (7.86 m). Khufu's builders may have used both a harbour ramp swinging up on to the pyramid from the southeast and a quarry ramp from the south.

The surface now, from the area east of the Sphinx, where Merer
might have docked, to the base of the Great Pyramid, is covered
by a modern road and the Khafre Pyramid causeway, which ascend
at a comfortable slope of around 5°. View to the north–northwest.

## Fabric and framework of a pyramid supply ramp

What were Khufu's pyramid supply ramps made of? Examples of large construction ramps and embankments left by the pyramid-builders at Giza – that survived the large-scale excavations of the early 20th century – consist of walls of broken limestone pieces set in desert clay mortar (tafla). The walls define compartments filled with a debris of limestone chips, gypsum and tafla, a mixture that occurs in millions of cubic metres at the site and fills vast quarried areas along the southeast of the plateau. Rows of these compartments form accretions with sloping (inclined) outer

Walls of a ramp embankment that ran from quarries west of the Sphinx to the queens' pyramids and mastabas of the cemetery east of the Great Pyramid. Builders formed ramp walls of broken limestone pieces, from quarrying and stone trimming, set in desert clay mortar (tafla). View to the northwest.

Cross wall

Accretion

Remains of a ramp embankment against an unfinished wall of large limestone blocks west of the Great Pyramid. The colossal wall defines the southern border of the Western Cemetery of mastaba tombs. Partial excavation has revealed how builders formed the ramp, and enlarged it incrementally, with cross walls and accretions that lean in like the skins of an onion. View to the northwest.

faces plastered in Nile silt and desert clay. These layers, like onion skins, lean in against an inner core formed against the side of the wall (or pyramid) under construction. As the wall or pyramid rose, the builders raised the core and inner accretions and added outer accretions as stepped buttresses, not unlike the internal structure of the earlier step pyramids.

These embankments and ramps were massive, solid structures, yet with pick hammers they were easily de-constructed into their constituent parts. The builders then reused the debris in other ramps and embankments, or left it filling the quarries. In their large-scale excavations to uncover ancient stone structures, early modern excavators sometimes did not recognize intact ramps and so removed them along with the similar debris that buried them.

Supply ramps of this kind were raised incrementally by the builders up to about one-fifth of the height of the entire Great Pyramid. How did they then lift the stones to build the rest of the pyramid?

## Challenge of the monoliths

As the builders raised the pyramid toward its apex they naturally had ever fewer stones to set, and, as visible today on Khufu's pyramid, the core and backing stones become smaller towards the top. The blocks of fine white Tura for the original outer casing, now missing, would likewise have decreased in size, as can still be seen in the intact casing at the top of Khafre's pyramid.

However, Khufu gave his builders a special challenge – that of moving the largest and heaviest stones in the pyramid up to between one-third and nearly half its height. The King's Chamber, where Khufu was buried in his granite sarcophagus, and the five, stacked relieving chambers above it, are situated 43 m to 66 m above the pyramid base. The 44 colossal granite beams that roof the King's Chamber and also separate the five upper chambers, one from another, weigh a total of 2,000 tonnes. If the blocks lining the walls and floor of the King's Chamber are added to this, Khufu's workforce raised up to this level and then set 1,100 cu. m of granite – about 3,307 tonnes. The largest of the granite beams has been estimated to weigh 70 tonnes. We do not know the thickness of the 22 (or possibly 24) limestone beams that were set in eleven gabled pairs to form the roof of the highest relieving chamber, Campbell's Chamber.

Campbell's Chamber, the highest of the five stress-relieving chambers above the King's Chamber, west end, with the gabled limestone ceiling and one of the 44 colossal granite beams that roof the King's Chamber and separate each of the five chambers above. Red hieroglyphs – on the gabled wall – and a red horizontal line on the granite beam remain where Khufu's builders painted them as they constructed this stack of chambers.

Nor do we know whether there is yet another, upper set of gabled beams, like those over the entrance to the Descending Passage, now exposed where blocks were removed in the past, and those over the chambers of 5th- and 6th-Dynasty pyramids. Petrie measured the gabled entrance beams as 0.84 m thick, which would mean they each weigh around 25 tonnes.

Moving 44 granite and 22 (possibly 24) limestone monoliths to between level 49 and level 60 on the pyramid required a straight path, because the 480 to 800 pullers that were needed to move such loads on sledges up ramps and along embankments would have been strung out for 48–80 m, even if four to eight abreast, and it would have been hard for them to pull their load around a corner. The haulers must have off-loaded these blocks from boats at the southern end of Terrace I, dragged them along over the edge of the southern quarry, and then straight up the quarry ramp to the southwest corner of the base of the pyramid.

## Wrap-around accretion ramp

Having reached the base, in order to raise the monolithic granite and limestone beams between 30 and 40 m up to the required level on the pyramid, Khufu's builders needed another straight length of ramp. Once they had reached this height, they could move the monoliths across the top of the truncated pyramid to their final planned locations in the structure of the chambers.

From the pyramid's southwest corner, the builders might have raised the roadway by increments from the ground up, as the pyramid rose, on an accretion (composed of the usual compartments and debris fill) against the west side of the pyramid. This could be buttressed with additional, stepped accretions that would have expanded it at the bottom. At 40 m above the pyramid's base at the southwest corner, the roadway could then continue its run on this accretion ramp north for 250 m, sloping up 7° 44′ 1″ to 74 m above base level at the northwest corner. This would more than allow the train of pullers to pull the sleds loaded with the roof beams of Campbell's Chamber – the topmost of the monoliths – to the level at which they needed to be set and then drag them across to the centre of the structure.

An accretion ramp such as this could have wrapped around the pyramid as it rose, at increasing slopes and with a narrowing roadway. However, accretions built from the ground up to support the road on all sides of the pyramid, combined with the initial straight-on ramp up to 30 m or 40 m high, would amount to 50 per cent more volume than the pyramid itself. If we add up the volumes of the harbour ramp, quarry ramp and the western accretion ramp with its lower buttressing accretions, we arrive at a total of 2,271,557 cu. m, or 86 per cent of the volume of the Great Pyramid and more than 82 per cent of the volume of material removed from the southern quarry (2,760,000 cu. m). So where could Khufu's builders have obtained so much debris? It appears they would have needed some other kind of ramp to lift the stones and raise the pyramid.

## Of sledges and sheer legs – a spiral ramp

Could the builders have founded the entire ramp on the sloping face of the pyramid itself as it rose, rather than on the ground? This would have been a huge saving in material. To answer this, we need to look at how masons dressed the outer face of the pyramid's casing after they had completed the structure almost to its apex and as workers removed the ramps from top down. Unfinished casing at the bottoms of Khufu's queens' pyramids shows the builders set Tura casing stones that stuck out far beyond the final plane of the pyramid face. As they set each course of casing stones, they lightly chiselled the lines where the sloping plane of the pyramid face would

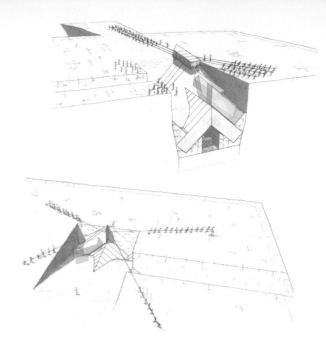

Casing stones at the base of Khufu's queen's pyramid GI-c. Builders left extra stock of stone on courses where they stopped trimming the casing from the top down. Extra stock protrudes here from untrimmed casing half a metre or more.

Workers pulling chevron stones across the pyramid course where they would have lowered them into place to form gabled vaults over a pyramid chamber of the 5th or 6th Dynasty. The chambers of these later pyramids lay close to ground level. Khufu's design presented the challenge of constructing gabled vaults for the Queen's Chamber and Campbell's Chamber, at 21.19 m and 64 m above the pyramid base respectively.

The sheer side of the Great Pyramid. Would extra stock of stone on the untrimmed casing (missing here) have supported a spiral ramp founded on such steeply sloping sides of the pyramid? View to the east along the south side.

intersect each stone, and the top of each course. Then they bevelled the extra stock of stone on the outer face of each block back to the intersection with the intended plane of the pyramid.

Would this extra stock left on the outer face of the casing stones before they were smoothed project out enough to support a ramp on the sloping pyramid face? If the masons left the same amount of extra stock as on the bases of the queens' pyramids – 50–80 cm – on all the casing stones of the Great Pyramid, or on select courses at certain intervals that extended out like a step or ledge, it might have been enough to support the stout retaining wall of a wrap-around ramp while being anchored in the pyramid. Perhaps projecting casing stones staggered diagonally across the pyramid face could have accommodated the rise of the ramp. Alternatively ones could have been left projecting further out in horizontal courses at intervals, so that the base of the retaining wall of the ramp was level but was stepped up at these courses, while the roadbed rose at a functional gradient on top of the ramp as it spiralled up.

If builders anchored the stretch of ramp along the west side of the pyramid on projecting casing stones, the roadbed on top could have sloped at 1:6 (a *seked* of 6 – a *seked* is the ancient Egyptian unit of ratio of run to rise, forming the slope), or almost $9\frac{1}{2}°$, for 154 m to arrive at 75 m above the pyramid base. From this point the pullers could move across the roofing beams for Campbell's Chamber. Reducing the width of the top of the ramp and roadbed would have contributed to a huge saving in material compared with the accretion ramp. Rising higher than this level above the base, the spiral ramp sections could narrow at the same time as the slope had to increase, until the pyramid narrowed so much near its apex that a ramp was no longer viable. Within the last 10 m of the top, the builders could have used A-frames as sheer legs, similar to those that served as bi-pod masts of Old Kingdom boats shown in models and relief-carved and painted scenes. Workers standing on the steps of the untrimmed courses could haul up blocks tied by ropes that ran up and over the tops of the frame's legs to gain mechanical advantage, lifting them step by step to the course under construction. Here, they would also raise blocks in short increments using levers, and push them into place. Including a supply ramp from the southern quarry to the pyramid, the volume of a spiral ramp founded on the slope of the pyramid could have been as little as 110,000 cu. m, less than 5 per cent of the pyramid volume.

The concern is whether *any* kind of ramp supported on the 52° sloping face of the pyramid, even with protruding casing blocks, would have supported those monoliths weighing tens of tonnes, in addition to the sleds and hundreds of pullers. For this reason, Khufu's builders might have invested in the time, effort and materials to build an accretion ramp along the west side of the pyramid, founded on the ground, for the critical operation of lifting the heaviest stones up to 75 m above the base, together with a spiral ramp for the levels above, up to 136 m. They could have obtained the required debris from creating Terrace I, from the extension of the southern quarry and from the Gebel el-Qibli, the knoll of the Maadi Formation south of the central wadi, which they exploited mainly for the broken stone and tafla clay to make ramps and embankments, not for blocks of stone.

## Of gangs and graffiti

The Wadi el-Jarf Papyri inform us about various operations, direct and indirect, critical to building the Great Pyramid – hauling and transporting stones, record keeping and using water transport infrastructures. However, there is nothing in these papyri to inform us about how the pyramid-builders raised the stones to the higher levels on the pyramid. But the work-gangs who moved the monoliths did leave their names in the form of graffiti on the walls of the Relieving Chambers above the King's Chamber, like the control marks naming the gangs on the stones closing the rock-cut galleries at Wadi el-Jarf.

Builders' graffito from the southern ceiling beam of Campbell's Chamber that reads 'Friends of Khufu'.

PART V   How They Built the Great Pyramid

One Giza gang compounded their name with the cartouche-name of the king, Khnum-Khuf ('The God Khnum Protects'), leaving their traces on ten blocks on the northern side of the stack of the Relieving Chambers. Another gang compounded their name with the king's Horus name, Horus-Medjedu (something like, 'Horus Who Crushes'), which they wrote on seven blocks on the southern walls. The physical distribution suggests that the two gangs competed. The full name of the southern gang was 'The (Two Lands) Purifiers of Horus-Medjedu', and that of the northern, 'The Followers of the Powerful White Crown of Khufu' (or, in parallel with a Wadi el-Jarf gang, 'The Escort Team, the Powerful White Crown of Khufu'). A third gang name occurs twice, appearing clearly on one of the southern ceiling beams: 'The Friends [or Companions] of Khufu' (*semeru* Khufu).

Because the graffiti occur on both the granite and the limestone blocks in the long north and south walls of the Relieving Chambers, these must be the names of the gangs who actually transported the granite monoliths and the limestone blocks of these chambers, rather than those who quarried them, as they derived from different sources. These particular gangs must have been at work several years earlier than the boat transport crews attested at Wadi el-Jarf. The papyri recording the boat crews' activity contain a date near the end of Khufu's reign, by which time these blocks and the chambers they form would have been fully embedded in the completed pyramid. While their names do not suggest nautical insignia, 'The Followers of the Powerful White Crown of Khufu' and 'The Purifiers of Horus-Medjedu' did transport the stone – both the granite and limestone blocks – from stockpiles on the ground up to the required place, high above the plateau surface. They were the ones who dragged the huge monoliths up the sloping ramps and across the pyramid's unfinished structure in order to build the Relieving Chambers.

## The year of Merer, and the stones he brought

Merer and his men delivered fine Tura limestone to the Great Pyramid in the penultimate year (26–27) of Khufu's reign. It is therefore unlikely that any of this stone was raised onto the pyramid itself for the casing. Although the builders set in place the casing stone from the bottom up, as the pyramid rose, they trimmed it from the top down, as they removed ramps and embankments that may have cloaked the face of the pyramid. Judging from the elements Khafre and Menkaure left incomplete in their pyramid complexes, the valley temple and lower causeway were among the last major parts of a pyramid complex to be built. Entrance to the pyramid itself was only accessed through the valley temple and up the long causeway. Finishing work could very well have been in progress on these lower features of Khufu's pyramid complex at the time Merer was an eyewitness to its construction.

If the stone Merer and his men delivered was for Khufu's lower causeway and valley temple, they would not have off-loaded on Terrace I. Coming from Tura North, sailing through the Ro-She Khufu, the entrance to Khufu's Lake, they would have turned right (north) to enter the She Akhet Khufu, the 'Basin [of the Pyramid] "Horizon of Khufu"', in front of the king's valley temple. If they were arriving from Tura South, they could have sailed across the lake directly north into the She Akhet Khufu.

By the time of his death, we sense that Khufu had largely finished all the major parts of his pyramid complex, including the valley temple. The Subterranean Chamber, carved painstakingly out of the bedrock deep below the pyramid superstructure, was left unfinished, a task the builders might have given up on, or suspended, during the life of the project. The Eastern and Western cemeteries of mastaba tombs flanking the pyramid also stood incomplete. Could some of the Tura limestone Merer delivered have been used for the mastabas? Or did Khufu provide only the mastaba cores, leaving it to his courtiers to finance their casings as well as their chapels?

What else still might require the fine, hard, white limestone that Merer and his men brought from Tura North and Tura South in the final years of Khufu's works? The builders also needed the massive beams for roofing and sealing the rectangular pits on the south side of his pyramid for the cedar barques that would be used for Khufu's funeral. When in 1954 Egyptian archaeologists removed the huge limestone slabs that covered the eastern pit, still containing Khufu's disassembled cedarwood solar boat, which was later reconstructed, they exposed 'builders' graffiti' that included 18 cartouches of Khufu's successor, Djedefre. These graffiti testified that this king had tended to his predecessor's burial in the magnificent pyramid he had built. Djedefre's cartouche is part of yet another work-gang name, with both a short version, 'Djedefre is Ruler', appropriate if he was new to the throne, and a longer version which can be translated as 'The Coptite-nome Gang "Radjedef is Ruler"'.

When a Japanese mission from the Institute of the Solar Boat lifted the cover slabs from the second of Khufu's southern boat pits in 2015, which also contains boat parts, they documented graffiti from two stages of work. They noted newer graffiti written over older graffiti, and marks on rough, older surfaces in contrast to ones on smoothed, newer surfaces. The older surfaces are visible mostly on the ends of the blocks, whereas the sides, tops and bottoms reveal more of the newer, smoothed surfaces, which masons must have created when placing the stones side by side as they covered the pit.

Signs on the older surfaces mark the destination – 'pyramid', 'pyramid on the horizon', 'temple' – to which the stones were taken

The eastern of the two southern boat pits, view underneath the slabs that remain in place. These may well have been the last Tura limestone deliveries to the Great Pyramid.

from the quarry. Some also might indicate groups that brought the stones from the quarry. Of course, this was one of the main jobs Merer documented for his group in his logbook. But the marks taken as group-signs are very simple – single hieroglyphs, including 'life' (*ankh*), 'offering' (*hetep*), 'beauty' (*nefer*) and 'great' (*wer*). *Wer*, possibly also meaning 'old' or 'senior', might have been the name of Merer's phyle. The other signs would correspond more to divisions or sub-units of a phyle (*za*).

On the newer, smoother top, bottom and west side surfaces of the covering slabs, the signs could be read as 'enclosure wall', 'boat' and 'sail'. These are thought to mark the movement of the stones from the storage area at Giza to the boat pits. Gangs with names compounded with the cartouche of Djedefre were responsible for this movement, along with other possible gangs named 'Waswy' (the two *was*-sceptres), 'Followers of Netjeru Gang' and a gang name that the Japanese scholars read as 'Followers of Khufu', written with Khufu's cartouche. If this reading is correct, it is the same gang name as found on a gable roof beam of Campbell's Chamber. It would be convenient if the Khufu-named gang occurred on the older surfaces, and the Djedefre-named gang was on the newer surfaces, but both cartouches were found on second-stage surfaces. This means that workers had already begun to cut the stones to the right size and put them in place to span the pit during Khufu's reign, and that Khufu's teams, including Merer's, could have delivered these stones.

The Japanese team also found on the older surfaces four examples of an unequivocal date: 'The 14th Occasion (census), Month 1 of Shemu'. A regular, biennial 'cattle count' would make this date a regnal year 28–29, which must be Khufu's last regnal year. Since the newer surfaces include names of gangs of both Khufu *and* Djedefre, we have to conclude that Khufu's gangs began to drag the stone from an off-loading station, probably Terrace 1, to the

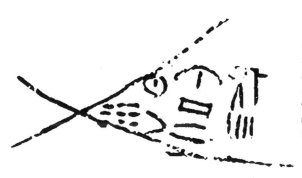

Date from the older surfaces on cover blocks over the western boat pit on the south side of the Khufu Pyramid, the 14th Occasion (census), Month 1 of Shemu.

southern boat pits, where masons began to trim and fit them side by side on the pit. This transfer and trimming continued in the reign of Djedefre, most probably at the beginning of his first year.

Of course, we do not know the circumstances of Khufu's death. Perhaps members of his royal house and entourage were aware for some time during his last year that the end was near and they had begun to ready his funeral equipment, including the two wooden ships and the pits that would receive them once they had fulfilled their function and been dismantled. It is interesting to consider how this fits with the date documented in the Wadi el-Jarf Papyri. As Pierre has written here, these papyri were probably all written during a period of just over a year, from July in 'the year after the 13th census of Khufu' through to the next summer, corresponding to the beginning of what would be the 'year of the 14th census', when the king must have died. Merer and his team carried out their Tura–Giza, Delta and Wadi el-Jarf–Sinai missions during the last year of Khufu's reign, but the king must have lasted for some time into his census year 14.

By this time the Great Pyramid stood complete, so too its long causeway and valley temple, which, as the hub of Khufu's administration, already bustled with activity, including Merer's services for the king's sustenance in life in his palace and for his spiritual well-being in his temple. The gigantic stone-raising ramps had been removed, the debris dumped into the southern quarry. In the following year, as Merer and his trusted team worked at Wadi el-Jarf, the king died. The last stones that Merer and his phyle had delivered from Tura before departing to the Delta and thence to Wadi el-Jarf may have been raised not much farther than from Terrace I, up the track corresponding to the modern road, to Khufu's southern boat pits, a short distance from the top of this slope.

Because he had served the king while he was still alive in his palace and valley temple at Ankhu Khufu ('Khufu Lives!'), perhaps at some point Merer returned to Giza to give prayers and offerings to his departed king, laid to rest in the pyramid, Akhet Khufu ('Horizon of Khufu', whence he could rise and set with the sun). We are most grateful that Merer left his logbooks behind at Wadi el-Jarf, in a place that favoured their preservation.

# PART VI

# LEGACY

# CHAPTER 15

# HOW THE PYRAMIDS CREATED A UNIFIED STATE

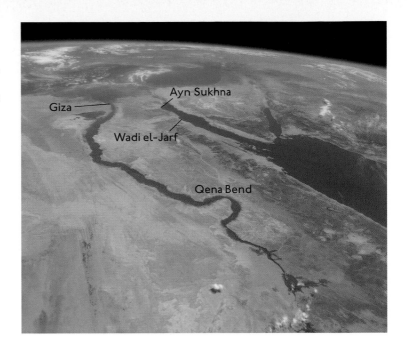

Google Earth image of Egypt, looking from the Qena Bend, homeland of the first pharaohs, north to Giza at the apex of the Nile Delta, showing the locations of the Old Kingdom Red Sea ports of Wadi el-Jarf and Ayn Sukhna.

The Wadi el-Jarf Papyri give us rare insight into an intriguing question – how did the pyramids build Egypt? In other words, how did the pyramids create a unified Egyptian state? Early Old Kingdom rulers who constructed pyramids in the process colonized their own country, primarily Middle Egypt and the Delta, to feed the royal project. They mobilized people to travel and come together at the work site, socialized conscripts from the provinces, set up institutions, educated young scribes and established a bureaucracy to keep track of tasks in the way Merer did. The consequences, intended or not, unified Egypt as a territorial national state. Egypt's unique geography and early population history help us understand how.

## Internal colonization

The population of Old Kingdom Egypt is estimated to have been around 1.1 million, as compared to today's 100 million. Settlement was concentrated in two main locations. One was in the south in the Qena Bend, where the Nile Valley makes its great eastward bend between Hierakonpolis and Abydos, concentrated between modern Luxor (ancient Thebes) to the south and Qena to the north. And the second was in the northern 'capital zone' between the entrance to

OPPOSITE Evidence for central administration: seal impressions left on clay fragments from the 'Workers' Town' at Giza, made by cylinder seals belonging to royal officials (see pp. 298–300).

the Faiyum and the apex of the Delta, where the valley narrows to as little as 3 km and pyramids line the western high desert. Three times over three millennia (in the Late Predynastic, early Middle Kingdom, early New Kingdom) rulers emerged from the Qena Bend region and marched north to take the Delta. They tied together the 'Two Lands', Upper (southern) and Lower (northern) Egypt, by establishing a capital just above the Delta apex.

As Djoser in the 3rd Dynasty and Sneferu at the beginning of the 4th built the first of the gigantic pyramids, they regularized great flood basins to expand agriculture and also formalized provincial administrative districts in Upper and Lower Egypt that Egyptologists call nomes, each of which had its own emblem or symbol. On the broad green valley floor of Middle Egypt (regarded as part of Upper Egypt) and the Delta the royal house created new estates and villages. Land was plentiful and freely available, but more people were needed to work it and to tend the herds. So Egypt's rulers raided peripheral lands, captured people and settled them in new farms and ranches that would support their pyramid projects.

At Khor el-Aquiba in Nubia, north of Abu Simbel, a governor of Upper Egyptian Nome 17 named Khabaubat inscribed a text in stone in which he records leading 20,000 men 'to hack up Wawat', a Nubian province. In another inscription in the same place, Zauib, governor of 'the northern part of the Eastern [Delta] Nome' tells how he had taken 17,000 Nubians. These governors may have been capturing people to expand Sneferu's labour force. An entry in the Palermo Stone annals for one of Sneferu's census years reads: 'smiting Nubia, bringing in 7,000 males and female live captives, 200,000 sheep and goats; building the wall of the south and north-land, "Mansions of Sneferu"'. For the following census year the annals mention 'creating 35 estates with people (?) [and] 122 cattle-farms'. Next is the entry for Sneferu's 8th census year: '… erecting (the building) "Sneferu, High of the White Crown" (at) the base (?) of the southern gateway, (and the building) "Sneferu, High of the Red Crown" (at) the base (?) of the northern gateway; making doors for the royal palace of pine; eighth occasion of the census'. These are the back-to-back census years, which were normally biennial, when Sneferu moved from Meidum to Dahshur to start a new royal necropolis and continue his pyramid-building project.

Capturing people and internal colonization thus came in tandem with pyramid building. But the captured did not remain

A comparison of the distribution of estates of Sneferu and locations of 3rd-Dynasty monuments. The latter cluster in the Qena Bend and the narrow part of the Nile Valley below the apex of the Delta, while the estates are distributed in the broad valley of Middle Egypt and the Delta.

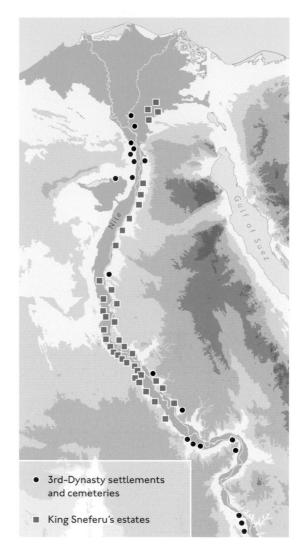

● 3rd-Dynasty settlements and cemeteries

■ King Sneferu's estates

Recto of the Palermo Stone, with a detail of the bottom register (VI) that includes records of three years of Sneferu capturing Nubian people and cattle, establishing new estates, and building a new palace.

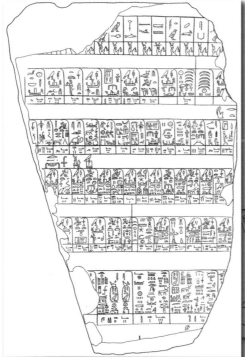

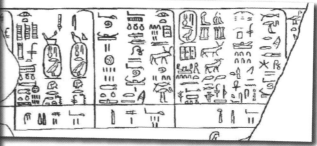

enslaved. The royal house integrated them into the Egyptian economy and society. Even those persons designated by Egyptian words we might translate as 'slave' enjoyed many of the juridical rights of other dependent people. Certainly in the New Kingdom, and perhaps also in the Old Kingdom, 'slaves' could become staff members of temples they helped to build, and might be promoted upwards in social rank to attain greater freedom from labour than other Egyptians.

In the valley temple attached to his Bent Pyramid at Dahshur, Sneferu personified his estates as female offering-bearers with names like 'Joy of Sneferu', 'Dancers of Sneferu', 'Road of Sneferu', 'Sneferu is Luscious of Pastures' and 'Nurse of Sneferu'. He grouped the estates by nome, with five of them in Nome 16 of Middle Egypt. Menat Sneferu ('Nurse of Sneferu') and Menat Khufu ('Nurse of Khufu'), possibly referring to the same estate, were probably located in this nome at a wadi mouth south of Beni Hassan. Local rulers, empowered by the 4th-Dynasty kings to look after their estates, later began to build their own mastaba tombs, modelled after the large mastabas at Giza.

The purpose of the colonization of Middle Egypt and the Delta by early kings was to set up a centripetal inflow of produce to feed their pyramid projects at Egypt's centre. Intentionally or not, they also set up a simultaneous counter motion – a centrifugal development of the provinces that became miniature states in their own right, with local rulers and capital towns. Both processes helped to consolidate the Two Lands into a unified, territorial state. Wadi el-Jarf Papyrus H reveals how Khufu's administration alternated deliveries from the Harpoon Nome, in the western Delta, with deliveries from the Dolphin Nome, in the eastern Delta, to supply Merer's team with food and other rewards. Such coordination between Egypt's nome districts certainly helped unite the kingdom.

## Mobilization

How did the royal house mobilize people throughout the land for building Khufu's Great Pyramid? Did the state override an existing social order of families, households and villages, or work with it? As the Wadi el-Jarf Papyri make clear, a key term is *za*, which as we have seen Egyptologists translate as 'phyle', Greek for 'tribe'. The *za* hieroglyph depicts a rope tied in a series of loops to make a cattle

Phyle
(za)

Green,
Fresh
(wadjet)

Gang
(aper)

Known of
(rekhu)

Menkaure

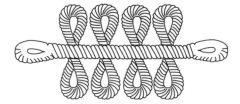

Builders' graffito from the Menkaure pyramid
temple giving the name of the gang, 'Known
of Menkaure', the phyle (za), 'Green' (or 'Fresh'),
and the district sign for Upper Egyptian Nome 17.

The hieroglyphic sign
for za, 'phyle', a rope tied
in eight or ten loops to
form a cattle hobble.

hobble that would bind together the legs of a number of animals
so that they had to move as one and could therefore be controlled.
*Za* can mean 'protection', but even before the Wadi el-Jarf Papyri the
term was known also to designate people rotating through periods
of labour on building projects and in temple service as seen in the
Abusir Papyri. Merer begins many of his entries, 'Inspector Merer
together with his *za*' (his phyle). As the Wadi el-Jarf Papyri and
graffiti found on blocks that closed the rock-cut galleries make
clear, phyles (*zau*, plural) made up an *aper* (or *aperu*, plural) –
a work-gang, crew or team.

Two or more calves with
feet tied to a cattle hobble
(za) from a carved scene
in the tomb of the priest
Ka-em-nefret at Giza.

When George Reisner excavated the upper temple of the
Menkaure Pyramid, the third built at Giza, between 1906 and 1907,
he found graffiti left by builders' gangs on the multi-tonne limestone
blocks of the unfinished temple walls. Of all builders' graffiti from
the Old Kingdom, these are the most complete formulations of a
labour organization, and they happen to be contemporary with the
final occupation of the Heit el-Ghurab site at the base of the Giza
Plateau below Menkaure's valley temple. In each graffito, the name
of a *za* (phyle) follows one of two gang names. On the southern side
of the temple, two graffiti named an *aper*-gang as 'Friends [*semeru*]
of Menkaure'. On the northern side of the temple, 13 graffiti named
another *aper*-gang, 'Known Ones [*rekhu*] of Menkaure'.

Hieroglyphs at the end of these workers' graffiti could designate
'divisions' into smaller sub-groups and home districts, or simply the
home base of the phyle itself. Most of the division hieroglyphs carry
positive meanings, like 'strong', 'first', 'noble' and 'rising', which can
be taken as praise of the workers and their work. Some of the division
signs match emblems for Upper Egyptian nomes: 10, possibly 16 and
17. These nomes are geographically in Middle Egypt, where texts,

tradition and archaeology attest that 4th-Dynasty pyramid builders established estates. Among the graffiti are also signs for Lower Egyptian nomes 3 and 15. Merer's own phyle may have hailed from Lower Egyptian Nome 2, close to the apex of the Nile Delta where the river begins to divide, as the scribe added the emblem for this nome in a horizontal margin below the daily entries in Papyrus A.

Later Old Kingdom (6th-Dynasty) royal decrees that show the mechanics of recruitment for the town of Coptos are directed to the 'Overseer of the Pyramid Town', 'all the Chiefs of the Coptite Nome', 'Overseers of the Phyles of Upper Egypt' and also 'families of the nome of Coptos'. The royal house called upon labour from a

The Gebelein Papyri consist of five rolls found in a wooden box accounting for people of a village named 'Two Rocks' or 'Two Mountains'. The accounts, parts of which were inked onto the box lid, reveal government penetration of the countryside, to track all kinds of people of various trades, as well as *neferu*, young recruits, possibly for work on royal projects like the pyramids. The documents are thought to date to the 4th Dynasty, possibly the reign of Menkaure.

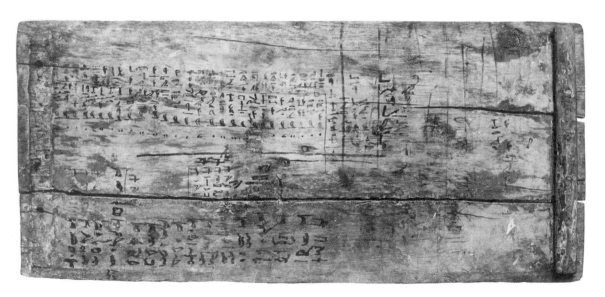

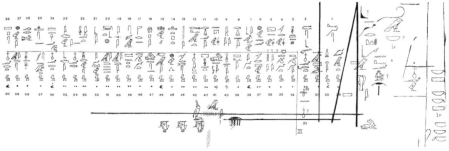

　　　　PART VI　　Legacy

national network that reached down through the hierarchy of nome, village, estate, household and family. We see the penetration of state bureaucracy in the Gebelein Papyri from near the site of that name ('Two Mountains') at the northern border of Upper Egyptian Nome 3.

The Gebelein Papyri possibly date to the reign of Menkaure, exactly contemporary with the main phase excavated at the Heit el-Ghurab site and the *aper*-gang and phyle graffiti in that king's unfinished upper temple. From two villages that comprised an estate, the papyri list 300 people in categories – bakers, brewers, craftsmen, boat-makers, sailors and rowers, masons, metalworkers, stockmen, hunters, nomads, grain measurers, a sealer of the granary and 'young recruits' (*neferu*). Why make an inventory of these villagers? Perhaps for expeditions and labour mobilizations away from home, possibly even for the king's pyramid project. The spreadsheet organization of the Gebelein Papyri, similar to the 5th- and early 6th-Dynasty Abusir Papyri accounts of the pyramid temple of Neferirkare-Kakai, reveal a pan-regional, long-term, bureaucratic mindset for keeping track of products and people. And now in the Wadi el-Jarf Papyri we can see the earliest known expression of this same bureaucratic mindset, and the system of recruitment and organization for nothing less than building the Great Pyramid.

## Institutionalization

The Gallery Complex at Heit el-Ghurab was an incipient, precocious institutional building for accommodating regularly changing cohorts of people, like modern schools, hotels, hospitals, prisons and barracks. Built to accommodate steady recruitments of workers for some 35 to 50 years, the Gallery Complex is more massive and formal than the galleries-cum-barracks that have been found recently in the vicinity of Sneferu's Dahshur pyramids and at ports on the Red Sea coast, including the large comb-like dry-stone building of Zone 5 at Wadi el-Jarf.

Institutional buildings like those listed above reverse the relative positions of inhabitants and visitors that exist in normal buildings like houses, temples and churches. In the latter, inhabitants, in the sense of those who own and control the purpose of the building, occupy the deeper, more restricted spaces, and receive visitors in the more frontal, less restricted, open, circulatory spaces. For example, owners of a house occupy the private areas of bedrooms, bathrooms and kitchens, and receive visitors in living rooms and parlours. In institutional buildings, 'visitors' (guests, students, patients, prisoners, conscripts) occupy the deep, restricted cells (prison cells and classrooms), while 'inhabitants' (guards, teachers, hotel staff and so on) control access and circulation.

While the Gallery Complex as a whole functioned like an institutional 'reversed building' along the lines of prisons, hospitals and schools, each individual gallery expanded the architectural components (though not the social composition) of a normal household unit (albeit with a width to length ratio of 1:7).

Giza galleries as compressed team houses. Pyramid builders took the 'normal' house model – which included open areas for 'visitors' (rotating troops) to the front and the more private domicile to the rear – stretched it out, width to length 1:7, and replicated it many times over to achieve an economy of scale for accommodating and organizing people. The Gallery Complex as a whole formed a kind of public institutional building, where 'inhabitants' controlled access and the larger open circulatory spaces, while living in the sub-complexes of the Eastern and Western Towns.

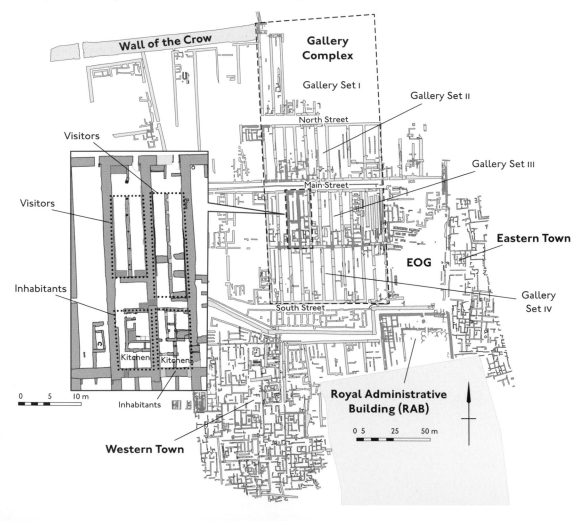

An off-axis entrance gave access to more open public and communal space towards the front, with more interior private and domestic space behind, and finally food-preparation spaces at the back. Typically for large institutions of 'reversed' character, the service personnel and administrators – the 'inhabitants' in the technical sense – lived in sub-complexes, with normal and traditional relations between inhabitant and visitor. At Heit el-Ghurab residential sub-complexes are located in the so-called Eastern and Western Towns. We can imagine that the experience of staying in the structured space of the Gallery Complex differed dramatically from everyday life in home villages and neighbourhoods.

## Socialization

On the basis of how members of phyles rotated through temple service, as documented in the Abusir Papyri, we assume that groups of conscripts rotated through the Gallery Complex, staying there while they worked on the royal project and then returning home. Merer and his men might have enjoyed time back at home between December and March, since none of the documents contains any reference to this period.

Home for most Egyptians at this period was in a small village. Even the populations of larger settlements and towns would compare to villages of more recent centuries. For the early Old Kingdom, we can imagine Egyptians living in village houses joined by 'organic' pathways that emerged 'bottom up' through local rules related to kin, path distance and proximity to wells and other resources.

Young men and their families may have slept close together in their villages, in small rooms in small houses. The Gallery Complex, however, must have been unlike anything back home. Conscripts must have spent nights in the Gallery Complex pressed tightly together. The compression and regimentation must have suppressed individual thinking, except for group leaders, who occupied the house-like rooms, domiciles, at the back of each gallery. But compression also leads to *esprit de corps*, a unified team-body politic, as with military troops and sports teams. As archaeologist Mary Shepperson put it in her study of architecture in early Mesopotamia, *Sunlight and Shade in the First Cities*: 'Buildings and cities ... structure not just what people perceive, but also *how* they perceive.'

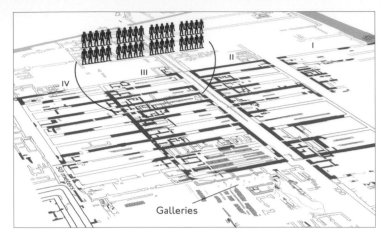

The fit between phyles, gangs and galleries. Each gallery, between 4.5 and 4.8 m wide, and 55 m (Set I) or 34.5 m (Sets II–IV) long, could have housed a phyle, and each of the four blocks (Gallery Sets I–IV) could have accommodated two gangs of four phyles, or one crew.

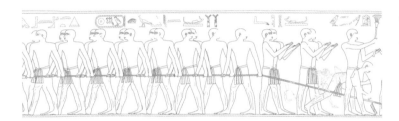

A team of men with ropes dragging a stone – in fact, the capstone – for the 5th-Dynasty pyramid of Sahure. Line drawing of a scene carved in relief on Sahure's pyramid causeway.

Life on the roof of the Gallery Complex at Giza. By infilling the springing of the vaulted ceilings, the builders could have created one broad, flat terrace over each block of galleries, where people could sleep in the open air, keep animals, or store wood, reed and charcoal for cooking. Food was prepared in the caboose-like back chambers, a cook and kitchen for each phyle. Water jars and other utensils marked with phyle names were found at Wadi el-Jarf, which may indicate that teams brought their own items with them. Inhabitants were additionally fed from a series of bakeries and food-processing facilities outside the Gallery Complex.

When on the job, members of a phyle slept, ate, moved and worked in unison, as the cattle-hobble hieroglyph suggests. When we look at the partially worked, but unfinished, granite casing on the Menkaure Pyramid, we can imagine teams chanting as one voice as they rhythmically hammered with heavy pounding stones, or when pulling the multi-tonne monoliths on which they painted their graffiti. Traces left by workers in the New Kingdom granite obelisk quarry at Aswan also help us imagine Old Kingdom phyle members working and chanting in unison. Here, quarrymen pounded to pulverize and sink a granite surface ever deeper in a trench that outlined and formed each obelisk. As they pounded in synchrony to chants, the whole labour ensemble became an orchestrated, human, stone-cutting machine. Reginald Engelbach, who studied the Aswan obelisks, cited a work song of his day (the 1920s), in which the lead singer called out: 'Bash you boys, what's up with you?' (*duqq ya awalâd, khabar eh ummâl?*). Sound and movement amplified collective energy. Engelbach suggested that some 200 workers who formed the giant Unfinished Obelisk (130 bashers plus support personnel) rotated positions in synchrony for maximum efficiency and order. It is easy to imagine a similar dance and chorus for many of the orchestrated acts in the opera of pyramid-building.

Conscripts in the Gallery Complex at Giza may have experienced more freedom of movement after their labours on the broad rooftop terrace of each set of galleries, created by infilling the spring of the vaults that roofed each individual gallery. It is noteworthy that internal lateral doorways giving access from one gallery to another are found only at the rear of the galleries, behind the overseers' domicile. But up on the roof, members of different teams from different villages and provinces could mix and mingle, sleep in the open air, enjoy sunset and twilight, look at the stars and watch the movement of the moon. The lunar calendar set the timing of feasts that brought special allocations of meat (which arrived at Giza on the hoof). Up on the roof, they escaped the restricted and restrictive space of the Gallery Complex footprint.

This was one of the earliest instances of absolute rulers forming a unified social, corporate body by packing individuals into a crowd that breathes, shouts and feels in unison. Anyone who took part in this Cecil B. DeMille epic – the largest and most formal collective action of the time – returned to a home village and neighbourhood changed, imbued with a sense of national identity.

## Intensification – economy of scale

If many people are compressed into one large structure for days on end, in a hotel for example, a large kitchen or food factory is needed to feed them. How did the pyramid-builders achieve this? Ancient Egyptians had been intensifying production beyond household capacities since the Predynastic period – as seen for instance in brewing far in excess of domestic needs at the nascent capital at Hierakonpolis – but nowhere near on the scale required for feeding all the people involved in building the Great Pyramid. We get an idea of the operations required when we look at the facilities for bread-baking in Heit el-Ghurab.

People here baked bread in *bedja*-pots on an industrial scale in large, open-air enclosures. The numerous bakeries we have found in

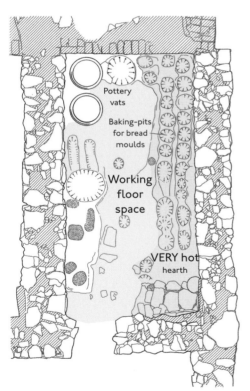

Schematic plan of one of the Heit el-Ghurab bakeries, with green for working floor space, and pink for baking-pits fashioned like egg-cartons to receive the bottoms of the bell-shaped *bedja*-pots in which the pyramid-builders baked conical loaves of bread.

Pottery vats

Baking-pits for bread moulds

Working floor space

VERY hot hearth

A *bedja*-pot in its receptacle, with another pot placed upside down as a lid.

a variety of settings produced bread in quantities beyond the amount that could be consumed by any one household. The pyramid-builders intensified production by expanding and replicating many times over basic household modes of production, but also further extended aspects beyond that domestic system. Even in the size of individual bread moulds, the Heit el-Ghurab bakers reached for an economy of scale greater than household baking.

## Bureaucratization

After the discovery and translation of the Wadi el-Jarf Papyri, we now see how one 40-person team such as Merer's kept a daily written record of their every move and task. The Tura limestone required for the Great Pyramid casing could have been delivered by only three or four phyles of 40 men like Merer's (120 to 160 men), while many other phyles brought granite from Aswan, timber from the Levant, gypsum from the Faiyum and people from the provinces. Other teams hauled stone up to the course under construction and set stones in place. If each and every team kept their own daily record, we have to wonder, as Pierre has written here, 'how many other logbooks equivalent to that of Merer must have been kept by the numerous teams that gravitated to the pyramid of Khufu during the 25 or so years that the construction site probably existed? Certain projections are mind-boggling: if each group of roughly 40 men was responsible for keeping a day-by-day account of its activities, how many tens of thousands of rolls of papyrus would have been needed to record it all?' It is, as he says, certain we have lost untold masses of information.

All this scribal work required a bureaucracy to check and archive incoming records and allocate payments, a requirement of every complex state. Stimulating the growth of a bureaucracy was one major way that the giant pyramids helped to build Egypt. A bureaucracy that is recognizable in modern terms developed as kings organized labour and produce from the countryside to support their pyramid projects. At first, Sneferu relied on brothers, sons and uncles to keep track of it all, led by the Vizier in the person of one of his sons, Nefermaat, buried in Mastaba 16 at Meidum, as seen in Chapter 12. The Vizier, a kind of prime minister, also acted as the Overseer of All the King's Works, who marshalled labour and directed foreign expeditions. Nefermaat's son, Hemiunu, served as

Khufu's Overseer of Works and Vizier. Ankh-haf, named as Director of the Ro-She Khufu in the Wadi el-Jarf Papyri, was probably another son of Sneferu, and Khufu's (and Nefermaat's) half-brother; he too may have served as Vizier to Khufu, as we saw in Chapter 12. A hierarchy of overseers and other officials, such as Controller of the Palace, Master of Largesse (rewards and gifts), down to the level of an 'Inspector' like Merer answered to these two offices. From the early 4th Dynasty we also find the title Overseer of the Treasury.

As Sneferu kept on building one pyramid complex after another at three different sites (Seila, Meidum and Dahshur), the organizing of the necessary supply and labour became increasingly complicated and required more high-level oversight. This must be why there are so many 'King's Sons' and 'King's Eldest Sons' and, as noted, 'an embarrassingly large number of Viziers' in the Old Kingdom, titles that the king had begun to bestow on men who were not his real, bodily sons, in order to convey the highest authority of command. Over the course of the 4th Dynasty, people who were not members of the king's immediate family, or a king's son – honorific or otherwise – begin to take on a greater variety of high-ranking titles that reflect an increasing and diversifying administration, culminating in the 5th Dynasty. A threshold from royal to non-royal family professional bureaucrats was crossed in the reign of Menkaure.

This, and almost everything we once knew about the administration that built the pyramids, comes from the hieroglyphic titles that the officials carved in the chapels of their tombs at the end of their lives. We are, therefore, seeing a time-lag in administration that evolved over the course of careers and lifetimes. Confounding our understanding is the fact that Egyptologists cannot agree about when, in which reign, or even in which dynasty, many of the tombs were inscribed with titles that are important to the study of government.

We do, however, get a glimpse of administration at the time of its operation from sealings found at Heit el-Ghurab. Sealings are the impressions left when seal-bearers rolled a cylinder etched with hieroglyphs across small lumps of damp clay to secure string locks on bags, boxes, jars, doors and documents. Only under the seal-bearer's authority could anyone break the seal to open the box, door or document. Seals of state offices bear the title and the Horus name of the king reigning at the time, his *serekh* (but not the name of the title holder). The titles form an index to the organization of government when the seal was in use.

Pottery Mound, a heap of trash that residents dumped in dead space between two of the houses in the Western Town, provided one such index. The mound of rubbish was next to House 1, the largest house excavated at Heit el-Ghurab, with spacious central rooms, bins and benches. Excavation of around 20 sq. m yielded 1,039 seal impressions, 424 of which were made by just 12 'core' seals, all belonging to officials claiming the title 'Scribe of Royal Documents'. Through their meticulous analysis, John Nolan and Ali Witsell were able to reconstruct most of the original design of the 12 seals, which showed that they were used by officials active in the reigns of Khafre and Menkaure. The individual cylinder seals were probably each assigned to a different official.

Excavation of Pottery Mound, the dump from a scribal workshop in House 1 on the Heit el-Ghurab site, produced 1,039 sealings with seal impressions, 424 of which had been impressed by only 12 cylinder seals – all of them Seals of Office, and most bearing high-ranking scribal titles. From bits and pieces of sealings (indicated by the thin lines in the rolled-out pattern),

John Nolan reconstructed much of the texts engraved on the seals, presenting a rare opportunity to study a coherent group of Old Kingdom officials in a defined time and place.

The cylinder seal, possibly of gold, shown reconstructed here bears the Horus name of Menkaure and the title 'Scribe of Royal Documents'.

Three cylinder seals, fragments of which were found in the lower strata of Pottery Mound, impressed clay sealings during the reign of Khafre. They bear the simple, unspecialized title 'Scribe of the Royal Documents', a title apparently created in the 4th Dynasty but most popular in title sequences etched in tombs of the 5th Dynasty. But one of the Khafre seals also bore the title 'Keeper of Royal Instructions'. Nine other officials used their seals to impress sealings whose fragments were found in higher strata. Their seals accordingly bore Menkaure's *serekh* along with the same general title, 'Scribe of the Royal Documents'. However, some of these royal document scribes now specialized, having new titles: 'Scribe of Royal Documents for All [Royal] Work' and 'Scribe of Royal Documents for Royal Instructions', an office apparently expanded from the title 'Keeper of Royal Instructions' under Khafre.

This small keyhole look at administration in practice shows both that the number of scribes increased in the reign of Menkaure and that they had begun to specialize. Recognizing the need for more scribes to read, act on and file documents like Merer's accounts and logbooks, the royal house at this time made a concerted effort to train more scribes. The titles recovered from Pottery Mound suggest that House 1 served as a scribal workshop where high-ranking officials trained young scribes. The 'instructions' in these titles would have been part of the education of men like Ptahshepses,

Granite-carved head of Sheshem-nefer II, from his mastaba tomb (G 5080) in the Western Cemetery at Giza. He bore the title 'Scribe of Royal Documents for Royal Instructions', also found on sealings from House 1 in the Heit el-Ghurab site.

who left an account of his long career under several kings, spanning the 4th to the 5th Dynasties, on the false door of his tomb chapel in Saqqara, now in the British Museum. In the missing first part of four vertical columns of hieroglyphs on the right, Ptahshepses probably began, 'a child who was born', and then, in what is preserved, he states:

> ... during the time of Menkaure ... [he] was educated among the royal children in the palace of the king and in the privacy of the royal harem ... [A youth who tied on the girdle ... during] the time of Shepseskaf, who was educated among the royal children in the palace of the king and in the privacy of the royal harem ...

Ptahshepses, and others like him, staffed the more elaborate bureaucracy of the 5th Dynasty. We might even know the name of one of the five seal owners from Pottery Mound who held the title 'Scribe of Royal Documents for Royal Instructions' and so would have taught in House 1. So far, only one person is known who inscribed this title in his tomb chapel, a man named Seshem-nefer (II). He added this to his other high-ranking titles in his chapel in Khufu's Western Cemetery, most likely late in his career, during the mid-5th Dynasty. Seshem-nefer II was also one of the first to claim the title 'Overseer of Scribes of Royal Documents', a title which was to become the exclusive prerogative of Viziers later in the 5th Dynasty. Like the clues in the Wadi el-Jarf Papyri, the trail leading from this new evidence from Pottery Mound helps to bring individuals back into history.

Ironically, Khafre and Menkaure educated scribes and expanded the bureaucracy just before subsequent administrations scaled down the size of their pyramids, instead putting far more effort into the finely carved relief work in their pyramid temples and building separate sun temples. The necessary infrastructure created for 4th-Dynasty pyramid gigantism had itself become more important than the initial reason for creating and expanding that infrastructure. Now it was essential to keep open the international, long-distance trade routes for procuring cedar, wine, olive oil, copper, gold, incense, pigment minerals and people, and to maintain provincial farms, ranches, villages and nome capitals for a steady supply of meat animals, cereal grains and linen. And a more complex bureaucracy was needed to keep track of it all.

## Neighbourhood to nation

When conscripted from their communities for missions that supported pyramid-building, Egyptians interacted with teams and their leaders from other Egyptian towns and villages, and potentially with people from abroad – the Levant, the far Western Desert, Aswan, the Red Sea and Sinai – people who specialized in procurement and transport of material from their homelands.

The Heit el-Ghurab settlement, together with the broader area of Ankhu Khufu, with its waterways and transformations under Khafre and Menkaure, formed a proto-city at the end of the half-millennium that saw some of the world's first cities appear in north Syria, Mesopotamia, the Indus Valley and China. For three generations, 'downtown Egypt' moved 14 km north from Memphis to Giza. In this proto-city, which first developed for the project of building the Great Pyramid, or in missions to the Delta, the Red Sea coast and Sinai, individuals like Merer and his team members experienced many more and more varied social interactions than back home. Everyone involved must have returned to their villages and neighbourhoods changed by their experiences within national and interregional social networks. In this sense, even with restrictions on intra-site movement and social interaction, the Heit el-Ghurab site and the larger settlement functioned like modern cities. The Great Pyramid builders proactively reached for economy of scale in people and products.

Immediately after Menkaure died and left his pyramid unfinished, downtown Egypt moved back south to Memphis and Saqqara. The national and interregional network catalysed for building the Great Pyramid became itself the end rather than the means. As pyramids shrank, almost immediately after Giza's 4th Dynasty, and took increasingly standard forms, the state, now with a bureaucracy stretching beyond royal family members, was more invested in the network itself, and how it could sustain the Egyptian nation.

# FUTURE DISCOVERIES
# ON THE RED SEA COAST?

PREVIOUS PAGE
View of Sinai from the
Wadi el-Jarf site, with
our archaeological
expedition tents.

The rediscovery of Egyptian activities on the Red Sea in the pharaonic era has undoubtedly been one of the most important achievements in Egyptology over the last 20 years – it has also been an exciting adventure. The identification and exploration of the three 'intermittent ports' that were developed along this coast by the pharaonic state in the Old and Middle Kingdoms – Mersa Gawasis, Ayn Sukhna and Wadi el-Jarf, the last two involving Pierre and his team – has made it possible to shed light on hitherto unknown aspects of pharaonic civilization. The highly important documents uncovered must now be taken into account in any history of Egypt written in the future. This includes not only the Wadi el-Jarf Papyri, but also the abundant epigraphic material discovered at the other two ports.

At a time when press releases on archaeological discoveries seem to be ever increasing and making ever more dramatic claims, some thought should be given to the question of the real significance of 'finds'. The originality and rarity of any newly discovered find contributes a great deal to its ultimate importance to historical research. The clearance of a new private tomb in the cemeteries at Saqqara or Giza, or elsewhere in Egypt, beautiful as it may be, will not necessarily provide us with as much genuinely new data on ancient Egypt as a humble rock inscription found somewhere in the desert, or even an analysis of palaeobotanical or archaeozoological remains from some early, poorly known settlement site. It is often in the more remote areas that we might expect to encounter the most significant and unprecedented new evidence, far away from the famous sites, some of which have been explored, excavated and studied for more than a century already. All archaeological research is fundamentally based on the assessment of value for money, and a guarantee of return on our investment with regard to scientific information gained.

Are there still important sites waiting to be discovered on the Red Sea coast? The three ports that have been found in recent years probably operated alternately, with only one of the three being in use at any specific point in time. The port of Wadi el-Jarf, the oldest known at present, operated for quite a short period, at the beginning of the 4th Dynasty, and was soon replaced by Ayn Sukhna, which seems to have been periodically occupied for more than a millennium, from the mid-4th Dynasty to the end of the 18th Dynasty (*c.* 2597–1349 BC). The port of Mersa Gawasis was more specifically geared towards long-distance trade with the land of Punt to the south and was probably used for this purpose for only part of the 12th Dynasty (*c.* 1920–1785 BC), at a time when the port at Ayn Sukhna was clearly temporarily abandoned. Together, these sites have undoubtedly given us a greater understanding of most of the ways in which the Red Sea coastline was exploited during the pharaonic period.

Some grey areas persist, however: certainly this maritime activity by the ancient Egyptians did not begin with the 4th Dynasty, although it is likely that they did not fully develop the system of 'intermittent ports' until the Wadi el-Jarf experiment. From the Naqada period to the 3rd Dynasty, there is evidence for a great deal of trade that may have involved maritime expeditions. From the Predynastic period onwards, the Red Sea was the conduit by which such exotic materials as obsidian and probably also lapis lazuli (neither of which occur naturally in Egypt) were obtained for use in the manufacture of artifacts in the early days of pharaonic culture. Recent surveys of South Sinai have similarly highlighted the presence of expeditions that reached this region from the Nile Valley between the Naqada III phase of the Predynastic period and the 1st–3rd Dynasties.

Other embarkation points may have existed on the Red Sea coast, particularly in the south, in the region of Hurghada, Safaga, Quseir and Mersa Allam, since this whole coastal area was accessed by several desert routes leading to the Red Sea; these routes originated in Upper Egypt, including from the main centres of development of the Naqada culture.

Information about Egyptian activities in the Red Sea in later periods is also scarce, including for the whole of the New Kingdom (*c.* 1539–1069 BC). At Ayn Sukhna there are rock inscriptions dating to the reigns of Amenhotep I and III (the second and ninth 18th-Dynasty rulers), but no occupation levels corresponding to this period have yet been discovered there. The embarkation point for Queen Hatshepsut's great expedition to the land of Punt in the first half of the 15th century BC – so well described and documented in her mortuary temple at Deir el-Bahri, in Luxor – is still not known. The site of Mersa Gawasis, which has often been suggested as the port where this mission set out from, has not yet yielded any material clearly dating to the New Kingdom. The Punt expedition from the time of Ramesses III in the late 12th century BC (mentioned in a summary of his reign forming part of the Great Papyrus Harris) seems to have sailed from the head of the Gulf of Suez. A large storage jar bearing cartouches of Ramesses III was discovered at the ancient site of Clysma (el-Qulzum) at the northernmost point of the Red Sea by an Egyptian archaeological mission in the 1960s, indicating activities in the Suez region at the beginning of the 20th Dynasty (c. 1180 BC). More evidence would be required, however, to confirm that there were port facilities at the head of the Gulf of Suez in the late New Kingdom.

Our knowledge of the Red Sea during the pharaonic period would be considerably enriched by the discovery of one or more new coastal archaeological sites in the future, whether these might be highly organized ports like those that we already know of, involving systems of storage galleries, or less complex installations that simply served as staging posts for long-distance routes. Archaeologists working at the site of the major Greco-Roman port of Berenice, at the southernmost end of the Egyptian stretch of Red Sea coast, recently discovered a stela there inscribed with the name of Amenemhat IV (the penultimate 12th-Dynasty ruler, c. 1794–1785 BC), suggesting that this port was already being used in much earlier times. Systematic exploration of the Red Sea and the Gulf of Aden (along the coasts of Sudan, Saudi Arabia, Yemen, Eritrea, Ethiopia and Somalia) may also provide evidence of ancient Egyptian activity, although such surveys – considering what they would involve – are perhaps unlikely to be conducted by Egyptologists.

A different line of enquiry in future might be research projects along the main lines of communication linking the Nile Valley with the Red Sea. These could potentially locate the remains of the temporary camps of expeditions heading towards the coast, as well as traces of their exploitation of water sources and the creation of artificial landmarks, supply depots and checkpoints. A good example of this is a survey recently conducted by a team from the French Institute of Archaeology in Cairo (IFAO) directed by Yann Tristant along the Wadi Araba, the main route between the Nile Valley and Wadi el-Jarf. Whatever the aims and routes explored by any investigations, it is now becoming a matter of urgency to undertake surveys of this kind. The enormous increase in tourist resorts which are gradually springing up along the coast, as well as the appearance of new roads cutting through the desert margins, has already condemned some archaeological remains in these areas of the Red Sea and the Eastern Desert to oblivion.

When the Ayn Sukhna site was discovered in 1998, it had already been damaged by numerous modern developments, including several pipelines, a tarmac road and a high-voltage line, and a major area of its remains had been irreparably destroyed by the construction of a hotel on the coast. The maritime section of the Wadi el-Jarf site is, in turn, threatened with being erased from the map when the government decommissions the military zones in which it is currently located, which will inevitably lead to the construction of tourist facilities there. Further ancient ports – in addition to the ones already recorded – must have certainly existed all along the Red Sea coast, but for all we know they may have already been completely destroyed, before they could even be identified.

Because of this, any new discoveries that we can plausibly expect to find on the Red Sea coast are primarily likely to be the results of continuing work at the three major sites already being investigated. At Mersa Gawasis, Kathryn Bard and Rodolfo Fattovich have still not excavated a section of the gallery storage system, and they have not yet systematically cleared part of the terrace that gives access to the galleries. At Ayn Sukhna, the excavations, currently led by Claire Somaglino and Mahmoud Abd el-Raziq, are now focused on a huge area of encampments where there are not only settlements dating to different periods, but also large numbers of workshops for the processing of copper ore. At Wadi el-Jarf, areas not yet excavated include a dozen of the storage galleries, a craft workshop and several areas of settlement. Excavations and investigations also continue at Giza, of course. And even at this best-known of all sites, new evidence does turn up. It is not very likely, however, that we will discover another batch of archives as important as the papyri that have been the main subject of this book, but ... one of the most appealing things about archaeology is that we can never really be certain what we might find.

# CHRONOLOGY

Egyptologists divide the kings of ancient Egypt into 31 dynasties, following the system of the Egyptian priest Manetho, who wrote in the 3rd century BC. Dates before the Late Period are much debated, especially so for the earliest periods. The chronology given here is adapted from *L'Egypte pharaonique: Histoire, société, culture*, by Pierre Tallet et al. (Paris, 2019). Names and dates of individual kings are listed only to the end of the Middle Kingdom, the main time period covered by this book and the scrolls.

## PREDYNASTIC PERIOD

| | |
|---|---|
| Badarian (Upper Egypt) | 4500–3800 BC |
| Maadi–Buto | |
| (Lower Egypt) | 3900–3400 |
| Naqada I–Naqada IIA/B | |
| (Upper Egypt) | 3900–3600 |
| Naqada IIC/D | |
| (Unification of Egypt) | 3600–3200 |
| Naqada IIIA/B | |
| (Dynasty '0': Iry-Hor; | |
| Ka; Scorpion (?)) | 3200–3100 |

## EARLY DYNASTIC PERIOD

| | |
|---|---|
| 1st Dynasty (Naqada IIIC) | |
| including Narmer; Hor-Aha; | |
| Djer; Djet; Den; Adjib; | |
| Semerkhet; Qa'a | 3100–2900 |
| 2nd Dynasty (Naqada IIID) | |
| including Hetepsekhemwy; | |
| Raneb; Ninetjer; | |
| Sekhemib; Peribsen; | |
| Khasekhemwy | 2900–2750 |
| 3rd Dynasty | 2750–2675 |
| Djoser (Netjerykhet) | 2750–2720 |
| Sekhemkhet | 2720–2710 |
| Khaba | 2710–2700 |
| Nebka | 2700–2690 |
| Huni | 2690–2675 |

## OLD KINGDOM

| | |
|---|---|
| 4th Dynasty | 2675–2545 |
| Sneferu | 2675–2633 |
| Khufu (Cheops) | 2633–2605 |
| Djedefre | 2605–2597 |
| Khafre (Chephren) | 2597–2573 |
| Menkaure (Mycerinus) | 2572–2551 |
| Shepseskaf | 2551–2545 |
| 5th Dynasty | 2544–2413 |
| Userkaf | 2544–2534 |
| Sahure | 2534–2515 |
| Neferirkare-Kakai | 2515–2501 |
| Shepseskare | 2501–2495 |

| | |
|---|---|
| Raneferef | 2495–2490 |
| Niuserre | 2490–2478 |
| Menkauhor | 2478–2468 |
| Djedkare-Isesi | 2468–2432 |
| Unas | 2432–2413 |
| 6th Dynasty | 2413–2250 |
| Teti | 2413–2394 |
| Userkare | 2394–2393 |
| Pepi I | 2393–2343 |
| Merenre I | |
| Nemtyemsaf | 2343–2334 |
| Pepi II | 2334–2260 |
| Merenre II | |
| Nemtyemsaf | 2260–2250 |

## FIRST INTERMEDIATE PERIOD

| | |
|---|---|
| 7th–8th Dynasties | 2250–2200 |
| 9th–10th Dynasties | |
| (Heracleopolis) | 2200–2015 |
| 11th Dynasty (Thebes) | 2130–2045 |
| Mentuhotep I | c. 2130 |
| Intef I | c. 2125–2112 |
| Intef II | 2112–2053 |
| Intef III | 2053–2045 |

## MIDDLE KINGDOM

| | |
|---|---|
| 11th Dynasty | 2045–1974 |
| Mentuhotep II | 2045–1994 |
| Mentuhotep III | 1994–1981 |
| Mentuhotep IV | 1981–1974 |
| 12th Dynasty | 1974–1781 |
| Amenemhat I | 1974–1944 |
| Senwosret I | |
| (Sesostris I) | 1944–1900 |
| Amenemhat II | 1900–1865 |
| Senwosret II | |
| (Sesostris II) | 1865–1856 |
| Senwosret III | |
| (Sesostris III) | 1856–1838 |
| Amenemhat III | 1838–1794 |
| Amenemhat IV | 1794–1785 |
| Sobekneferu | 1785–1781 |
| 13th Dynasty | 1781–1700 |

## SECOND INTERMEDIATE PERIOD

| | |
|---|---|
| 13th Dynasty (cont.) | |
| (Lisht; Thebes) | 1700–1650 |
| 14th Dynasty (Avaris) | 1730–1700 |
| 15th Dynasty | |
| (Hyksos at Avaris) | 1700–1520 |
| 16th Dynasty | |
| (Thebes; Abydos) | 1650–1600 |
| 17th Dynasty (Thebes) | 1600–1539 |

## NEW KINGDOM

| | |
|---|---|
| 18th Dynasty | 1539–1295 |
| 19th Dynasty | 1295–1188 |
| 20th Dynasty | 1188–1069 |

## THIRD INTERMEDIATE PERIOD

| | |
|---|---|
| 21st Dynasty | |
| (Tanis; Thebes) | 1069–943 |
| 22nd Dynasty | |
| (Bubastis; Thebes) | 943–731 |
| 23rd Dynasty (Tanis) | 730–725 |
| 24th Dynasty (Sais) | 725–720 |
| 25th Dynasty (Kushite) | 770–655 |

## LATE PERIOD

| | |
|---|---|
| 26th Dynasty (Sais) | 680–526 |
| 27th Dynasty | |
| (First Persian) | 526–404 |
| 28th Dynasty (Sais) | 404–399 |
| 29th Dynasty (Mendes) | 399–380 |
| 30th Dynasty | |
| (Sebennytos) | 380–342 |
| 31st Dynasty | |
| (Second Persian) | 342–332 |
| Greco-Roman Period | 332 BC–AD 395 |

# BIBLIOGRAPHY

## ABBREVIATIONS

*ASAE: Annales du Service des Antiquités de l'Égypte*

*BÄBA: Beiträge zur Ägyptischen Bauforschung und Altertumskunde*

*BASOR: Bulletin of the American Schools of Oriental Research in Jerusalem and Baghdad*

BdE: Bibliothèque d'Étude

*BIE: Bulletin de l'Institut d'Égypte*

*BIFAO: Bulletin de l'Institut Français d'Archéologie Orientale*

*BMSAES: British Museum Studies in Ancient Egypt and Sudan*

*BSEHGIS: Bulletin de la Société d'Études Historiques et Géographiques de l'Isthme de Suez*

*BSFE: Bulletin de la Société Française d'Égyptologie*

*CRAIBL: Comptes Rendus de l'Académie des Inscriptions et Belles-Lettres*

*EDAL: Egyptian and Egyptological Documents, Archives, Libraries*

*ENiM: Égypte Nilotique et Méditerranéenne*

*FIFAO: Fouilles de l'Institut Français d'Archéologie Orientale*

*GM: Göttinger Miszellen*

IFAO: Institut Français d'Archéologie Orientale

*JAEA: Journal of Ancient Egyptian Architecture*

*JAEI: Journal of Ancient Egyptian Interconnections*

*JARCE: Journal of the American Research Center in Egypt*

*JEA: Journal of Egyptian Archaeology*

*JRGS: Journal of the Royal Geographical Society*

*LÄ: Lexikon der Ägyptologie*

*MDAIK: Mitteilungen des Deutschen Archäologischen Instituts, Kairo*

*MIFAO: Mémoires publiés par les membres de l'Institut Français d'Archéologie Orientale*

*SAGA: Studien zur Archäologie und Geschichte Altägyptens*

*SAK: Studien zur Altägyptischen Kultur*

*SAOC: Studies in Ancient Oriental Civilization*

*TMOM: Travaux de la Maison de l'Orient et de la Méditerranée*

*WdO: Die Welt des Orients*

## GENERAL HISTORY OF EGYPT

Baud, M. *Djeser et la IIIe dynastie* (Paris, 2002).

Kemp, B. J. *Ancient Egypt: Anatomy of a Civilization*, 2nd ed. (London, 2005).

Malek, J. and W. Forman, *In the Shadow of the Pyramids: Egypt during the Old Kingdom* (London & Norman, OK, 1986).

Manuelian, P. Der and T. Schneider, *Towards a New History for the Egyptian Old Kingdom* (Leiden & Boston, 2015).

Radner, K., N. Moeller and D. T. Potts (eds), *The Ancient Near East. From the Beginnings to Old Kingdom Egypt and the Dynasty of Akkad* (Oxford, 2020).

Strudwick, N. and H. Strudwick, *Old Kingdom, New Perspectives* (Oxford, 2011).

Tallet, P. et al. *L'Égypte pharaonique: Histoire, société, culture* (Paris, 2019).

Wilkinson, T. A. *Early Dynastic Egypt* (London & New York, 1999).

## DESERT EXPEDITIONS    CHAPTER 1

Darnell, J. C. *Theban Desert Road Survey in the Egyptian Western Desert* 1 (Chicago, 2002).

— *Theban Desert Road Survey in the Egyptian Western Desert* 2 (New Haven, 2013).

Eichler, E. *Untersuchungen zum Expeditionswesen des ägyptisches Alten Reiches* (Wiesbaden, 1993).

Förster, F. *Der Abu Ballas Weg*, Heinrich-Barth Institut (Cologne, 2015).

— and H. Riemer (eds), *Desert Road Archaeology in Ancient Egypt and Beyond*, Heinrich-Barth Institut (Cologne, 2013).

Hikade, T. *Das Expeditionswesen im ägyptischen Neuen Reich*, SAGA 21 (Heidelberg, 2001).

Seyfried, K. J. *Beiträge zu den Expeditionen des Mittleren Reiches in die Ost-Wüste* (Hildesheim, 1981).

## THE RED SEA: PUNT    CHAPTER 2

Diego-Espinel, A. *Abriendo los Caminos de Punt* (Barcelona, 2011).

Meeks, D. 'Coptos et les chemins de Pount', *Topoi Suppl.* 3 (2002), 267–335.

Tallet, P. 'Les "ports intermittents" de la mer Rouge à l'époque pharaonique: caractéristiques et chronologie', *Nehet* 3 (2015), 31–72.

Tallet, P. and E. Mahfouz (eds), *The Red Sea in Pharaonic Times*, BdE 155 (2012).

## AYN SUKHNA    CHAPTERS 2, 5

Abd el-Raziq, M. et al. *Les inscriptions d'Ayn Soukhna* (Cairo, 2002).

—, *Ayn Soukhna II. Les ateliers métallurgiques du Moyen Empire*, FIFAO 66 (Cairo, 2011).

—, *Ayn Soukhna III. Le complexe de galeries magasins*, FIFAO 74 (Cairo, 2016).

Castel, G. and P. Tallet (eds), *Ayn Soukhna IV. Le matériel des galeries magasins*, FIFAO 82 (2020).

Somaglino, C., G. Castel and P. Tallet, *Ayn Soukhna V. La zone basse du site*, IFAO (Forthcoming).

## MERSA GAWASIS    CHAPTERS 2, 5

Bard, K. and R. Fattovich, *Harbor of the Pharaohs to the Land of Punt* (Naples, 2007).

—, *Seafaring expeditions to Punt in the Middle Kingdom* (Leiden, 2018).

Sayed, A. M. 'Discovery of the site of the 12th Dynasty port at Wadi Gawasis on the Red Sea shore', *Revue d'Égyptologie* 29 (1977), 136–78.

## WADI EL-JARF    CHAPTERS 2, 5

Bissey, F. 'Vestiges d'un port ancien dans le golfe de Suez', *BSEHGIS* 5 (1953–54), 266.

Lacaze, G. and L. Camino, *Mémoires de Suez. François Bissey et René Chabot-Morisseau à la découverte du désert oriental d'Égypte (1945–1956)* (Pau, 2008).

Tallet, P. 'Ayn Sukhna and Wadi el-Jarf: Two newly discovered pharaonic harbours on the Suez Gulf', *BMSAES* 18 (2012), 147–68.

—. 'The Wadi el-Jarf site: a harbor of Khufu on the Red Sea', *JAEI* 5/1 (2013), 76–84.

— and D. Laisney, *Ouadi el-Jarf I. Les installations maritimes*, IFAO (Forthcoming).

— and G. Marouard, 'An early pharaonic harbour on the Red Sea coast', *Egyptian Archaeology* 40 (2012), 40–43.

—, 'The harbor of Khufu on the Red Sea coast at Wadi al-Jarf, Egypt', *Near Eastern Studies* 77 (2014), 4–14.

— 'The harbor facilities of King Khufu on the Red Sea shore: The Wadi el-Jarf / Tell Ras-Budran System', *JARCE* 52 (2016), 168–76.

Tallet, P., G. Marouard and D. Laisney, 'Un port de la IVe dynastie au Ouadi el-Jarf (mer Rouge)', *BIFAO* 112 (2012), 399–446.

Tallet, P., et al. *Ouadi el-Jarf II. Le premier système de galeries-magasins (G1-G17)*, IFAO (Forthcoming).

Wilkinson, J. G. 'Notes on a part of the Eastern Desert of Upper Egypt', *JRGS* 2 (1832), 28–34.

## BOATS AND SAILING CHAPTERS 2, 5

Bradbury, L. 'Reflections on Traveling to "God's Land" and Punt in the Middle Kingdom', *JARCE* 25 (1988), 127–56.

Cooper, J. *The Medieval Nile: Route, Navigation, and Landscape in Islamic Egypt* (Cairo, 2014).

Jones, D. *A Glossary of Ancient Egyptian Nautical Titles and Terms* (London & New York, 1988).

Landström, B. *Ships of the Pharaohs* (New York, 1970).

Sauvage, C. *Routes maritimes et systèmes d'échanges internationaux au Bronze Récent en Méditerranée Orientale*, *TMOM* 62 (2012).

Zazzaro, C. and C. Calcagno, 'Ship components from Mersa Gawasis: Recent finds and their archaeological context' in P. Tallet and E. Mahfouz (eds), *The Red Sea in Pharaonic Times*, BdE 155 (2012), 65–85.

Zazzaro, C. and M. Abd el-Maguid, 'Ancient Egyptian stone anchors from Mersa Gawasis' in P. Tallet and E. Mahfouz (eds), *The Red Sea in Pharaonic Times*, BdE 155 (2012), 87–103.

## SOUTH SINAI CHAPTER 3

Gardiner, A. H., T. E. Peet and J. Cerny, *Inscriptions of Sinai* I, 2 vols (Oxford, 1952–55).

Giveon, R. *The Stones of Sinai Speak* (Tokyo, 1978).

Petrie, W. M. F. *Researches in Sinai* (London, 1906).

Rothenberg, B. *Sinai: Pharaohs, Miners, Pilgrims and Soldiers* (Bern, 1979).

— *The Egyptian Mining Temple at Timna* (London, 1988).

Tallet, P. *La zone minière du Sud-Sinaï* I. *Catalogue complémentaire des inscriptions du Sinaï*, MIFAO 130, (Cairo, 2013).

— *La zone minière du Sud-Sinaï* II. *Les inscriptions pré et protodynastiques du ouadi Ameyra*, MIFAO 132 (Cairo, 2015).

— *La zone minière du Sud-Sinaï* III. *Les expéditions égyptiennes dans la zone minière du Sud-Sinaï du prédynastique à la fin de la XXe dynastie*, MIFAO 138 (Cairo, 2018).

Valbelle, D. and C. Bonnet, *Le sanctuaire d'Hathor, maitresse de la turquoise. Serabit el-Khadim au Moyen Empire* (Paris, 1996).

— (eds), *Le Sinaï durant l'Antiquité et le Moyen Age* (Arles, 1997).

## Tell Ras Budran /El-Markha

Mumford, G. 'Operations in South Sinai during the Late Old Kingdom (Early EBIV/MB1)', *BASOR* 342 (2006), 13–67.

— 'Ongoing investigations at a Late Old Kingdom coastal fort at Ras Budran in South Sinai', *JAEI* 4/4 (2012), 20–28.

— 'Ras Budran and the Old Kingdom Trade in Red Sea shells and other exotica', *BMSAES* 18 (2012), 107–45.

— 'Explorations in El-Markha Plain, South Sinai: Preliminary findings at Tell Markha (Site 346) and elsewhere', *JAEI* 7/1 (2015), 91–115.

Tallet, P. 'Bat and the fortress of Khufu in the Wadi el-Jarf logbooks', *Actes du colloque Old Kingdom Art and Archaeology 7*, *EDAL* VI (2019), 56–63.

## COPPER AND EGYPTIAN MINING AND MATERIALS CHAPTER 3

Ben-Yosef, E. (ed.), *Mining for Ancient Copper: Essays in Memory of Beno Rothenberg* (Tel Aviv, 2018).

Lechtman, H. 'Arsenic bronze: Dirty copper or chosen alloy? A view from the Americas', *Journal of Field Archaeology* 23.4 (Winter 1996), 477–514.

Lucas, A. *Ancient Egyptian Materials and Industries*, 4th ed. (London, 1962).

Moores, R. G. 'Evidence for the use of a stone-cutting drag saw by the Fourth Dynasty Egyptians', *JARCE*, vol. 28 (1991), 139–48.

Odler, M. *Old Kingdom Copper Tools and Model Tools* (Oxford, 2016).

— *The Social Context of Copper in Ancient Egypt Down to the End of the Middle Kingdom*. Ph.D. dissertation, Institute of Egyptology, Charles University (2020).

Stocks, D. *Experiments in Egyptian Archaeology: Stoneworking Technology in Ancient Egypt* (London, 2003).

Tallet, P., G. Castel and P. Fluzin, 'Metallurgical sites of South Sinai in the Pharaonic era: New discoveries', *Paléorient* 37 (2012), 79–89.

## WADI EL-JARF AND OLD KINGDOM PAPYRI CHAPTERS 6–8

Collombert, P. and P. Tallet (eds), *Les archives administratives de l'Ancien Empire Egyptien, Orient et Mediterranée 37* (Leuven, 2021).

Posener-Krieger, P. *Les archives du temple funéraire de Néferirkarê-Kakaï*, BdE 65, IFAO (Cairo, 1976).

— and J. L. De Cenival, *Hieratic Papyri in the British Museum* V. *The Abu Sir Papyri*, (London, 1968).

— and S. Demichelis, *I Papiri di Gebelein* (Turin, 2004).

— , M. Verner and H. Vymazalová, *The Pyramid Complex of Raneferef: The Papyrus Archive*, Abusir X (Prague, 2006).

Tallet, P. *Les papyrus de la mer Rouge* I. *Le 'journal de Merer' (papyrus Jarf A et B)*, MIFAO 136 (Cairo, 2017).

— 'Du pain et des céréales pour les équipes royales. Le grand papyrus comptable du ouadi el-Jarf (papyrus H)' in A. Bats (ed.), *Les céréales dans le monde antique*, *Nehet* 5 (2017) 99–117.

— 'Les journaux de bord du règne de Chéops au ouadi el-Jarf (P. Jarf A-F): état des lieux', *BSFE* 198 (2018), 8–19.

— 'Des nains, des étoffes et des bijoux. Le papyrus de Nefer-Irou au Ouadi el-Jarf' in S. Vuilleumier and P. Meyrat (eds), *Sur les pistes du désert. Mélanges offerts à Michel Valloggia* (Gollion, 2019), 217–26.

— 'Un papyrus de l'année après le 13e recensement de Chéops (ouadi el-Jarf, papyrus G), Mélanges' in J. Kamrin et al. (eds), *Guardian of Ancient Egypt: Studies in Honor of Zahi Hawass* (Prague, 2020), 1545–54.

— *Les papyrus de la mer Rouge* II, *Le 'journal de Dedi' et autres fragments de journaux de bord (papyrus Jarf C, D, E, F)*, MIFAO (Cairo, 2021).

## PYRAMIDS CHAPTER 4

Edwards, I. E. S. *The Pyramids of Egypt*, rev. ed. (London, 1993).

Lehner, M. *The Complete Pyramids* (London & New York, 1997).

Maragioglio, V. and C. Rinaldi. *L'Architettura delle piramidi Menfite. Parte III, Il Complesso di Meydum, la piramide a Doppia Pendenza e la piramide*

Settentrionale in Pietra di Dahsciur (Rapallo, 1964).

Monnier, F. L'ère des géants: Une description détaillée des grandes pyramides d'Égypte (Paris, 2017).

Stadelmann, R. 'Das Dreikammernsystem der Königsgraber der Frühzeit und des alten Reiches', MDAIK 47 (1991), 373–87.

—, Die ägyptischen Pyramiden: vom Ziegelbau zum Weltwunder, 2nd ed. (Mainz am Rhein, 1991).

—, 'Snofru – builder and unique creator of the pyramids of Seila and Meidum', in O. El-Aguizy and M. Sherif Ali (eds), Echoes of Eternity: Studies Presented to Gaballa Aly Gaballa (Wiesbaden, 2010), 31–38.

Verner, M. The Pyramids. The Mystery, Culture, and Science of Egypt's Great Monuments (New York, 2006).

## The Step Pyramid at Saqqara

Deslandes, B. 'Travaux récents menés dans la pyramide à degrés de Saqqara', CRAIBL 151e année, n. 4 (2007), 1475–82.

— 'Travaux récents menés dans la pyramide à degrés de Djéser (Necropole royale de Saqqarah – Égypte)', Académie des beaux-arts 1 (2012), 109–121.

Lauer, J.-P. Fouilles à Saqqara, La pyramide à degrés (Cairo, 1936).

— Saqqara: The Royal Cemetery of Memphis (London & New York, 1974).

## Provincial step pyramids

Dreyer, G. and W. Kaiser, 'Zu den kleinen Stufenpyramiden Ober- und Mittelägyptens', MDAIK 36 (1980), 43–59.

Lauer, J.-P. 'Les petites pyramides a degrés de la IIIe dynastie', Revue archéologique (July–December 1961), 5–15.

Marouard, G. 'The Edfu pyramid project', The Oriental Institute News and Notes 213 (Spring 2012), 3–9.

## The Seila Pyramid

Muhlestein, K. 'Transitions in pyramid orientation: New evidence from the Seila Pyramid', SAK 44/1 (2015), 249–58.

— 'Excavations at the Seila Pyramid and ritual ramifications', in K. Muhlestein et al. (eds), Excavations at the Seila Pyramid and Fag el-Gamous Cemetery (Leiden, 2019), 48–75.

Swelim, N. 'An aerial view of the layer monument of SNFRW at Seila', in E.-M.

Engel et al. (eds), Zeichen aus dem Sand (Wiesbaden, 2008), 647–53.

— 'Reconstructions of the layer monument of Snfrw at Seila', in O. El-Aguizy and M. Sherif Ali (eds), Echoes of Eternity (Wiesbaden, 2010), 39–56.

## The Meidum Pyramid

Borchardt, L. Die Entstehung der Pyramide an der Baugeschichte der Pyramide von Mejdum Nachgewiesen (Berlin, 1928).

Dormion, G. and J.-Y. Verdhurt, La chambre de Meïdoum (Geneva, 2013).

El-Khouli, A. 'Archaeological report on the work at Meidum', in A. el-Khouli and G. Martin (eds), Meidum (Sydney, 1991), 11–15.

Monnier, F. 'The satellite pyramid of Meidum and the problem of the pyramids attributed to Snefru', JAEA 3 (2018), 1–23.

Petrie, W. M. F. Medum (London, 1892).

— 'General results at Meidum', in W. M. F. Petrie, et al. Meydum and Memphis vol. III (London, 1910), 1–6.

— 'The quarry marks', in W. M. F. Petrie et al. Meydum and Memphis, vol. III (London, 1910), 9.

Reader, C. 'The Meidum Pyramid', JARCE 51 (2015), 203–24.

Rowe, A. 'Excavation of the Eckley B. Coxe, Jr. Expedition at Meydûm, Egypt, 1929-30', The Museum Journal (Philadelphia, 1931), 5–46.

Verd'hurt, J.-Y. and G. Dormion, 'New discoveries in the pyramid of Meidum', in Z. Hawass and L. Pinch Brock (eds), Egyptology at the Dawn of the Twenty-first Century (Cairo & New York, 2003), 541–46.

## The Bent Pyramid at Dahshur

Fakhry, A. The Monuments of Sneferu at Dahshûr I. The Bent Pyramid (Cairo, 1959).

Monnier, F. 'New light on the architecture of the Bent Pyramid', Nile 20 (June-July 2019), 46–52.

— 'A new survey of the upper chambers of Sneferu's pyramids at Dahshur', JAEA 4 (2020), 1–17.

— and A. Puchkov, 'The construction phases of the Bent Pyramid at Dahshur, a reassessment', ENiM 9 (2016), 15–36.

Nuzzolo, M. 'The Bent Pyramid of Sneferu at Dahshur, A project failure or an intentional architectural design?' SAK 44 (2015), 259–82.

## Dahshur hub and harbour

Alexanian, N. and F. Arnold, 'The complex of the Bent Pyramid as a landscape design project', in M. Ullmann (ed.), 10. Ägyptologische Tempeltagung: Ägyptische Tempel zwischen Normierung und Individualität (Munich, 2016), 1–16.

Arnold, F. 'A ceremonial building of king Snofru at Dahshur', in M. Bietak and S. Prell (eds), Ancient Egyptian and Ancient Near Eastern Palaces, vol. I (Vienna, 2018), 113–24.

Fakhry, A. The Monuments of Sneferu at Dahshûr II. The Valley Temple (Cairo, 1961).

Rosenow, D. 'Die Siedlung nördlich des Taltempels der Knickpyramide in Dahschur', Archäologie in Ägypten 5 (November 2019), 48.

Stadelmann, R. 'The Heb-Sed Temple of Senefru at Dahshur', in M. Barta et al (eds), Abusir and Saqqara in the year 2010 (Prague, 2011), 736–46.

## The North Pyramid at Dahshur

Stadelmann, R. and H. Sourouzian, 'Die Pyramiden des Snofru in Dahshur. Erster Bericht über die Ausgrabungen an der nördlichen Steinpyramide', MDAIK 38 (1982), 379–93.

Stadelmann, R. et al. 'Pyramiden und Nekropole des Snofru in Dahshur. Dritter Vorbericht über die Grabungen des Deutschen Archäologischen Instituts in Dahschur', MDAIK 49 (1992), 259–94.

## GIZA: GENERAL CHAPTERS 4, 9–15

Jánosi, P. Die Pyramidenanlagen der Königinnen. Untersuchungen zu einem Grabtyp des Alten und Mittleren Reiches (Vienna, 1996).

— Giza in der 4. Dynastie, die Baugeschichte und Belegung einer Nekropole des alten Reiches. Band I: Die Mastabas der Kernfriedhöfe und die Felsgräber (Vienna, 2005).

— 'Old Kingdom tombs and dating – problems and priorities', in M. Bárta (ed.), The Old Kingdom Art and Archaeology (Prague, 2006), 175–83.

Lehner, M. 'The development of the Giza Necropolis: The Khufu Project', MDAIK 41 (1985), 109–43.

— 'Giza', Archiv für Orientforschung 32 (1985), 136–58.

— and Z. Hawass, Giza and the Pyramids (London & Chicago, 2017).

Perring, J. S. *The Pyramids and Temples of Gizeh*, 3 vols (London, 1839–42).

Petrie, W. M. F. *The Pyramids and Temples of Gizeh* (London, 1883).

Reisner, G. A. *A History of the Giza Necropolis*, vol. I (Cambridge, MA, 1942).

Smith, W. S. and G. Reisner, *A History of the Giza Necropolis,* vol. II: *The Tomb of Hetep-heres the Mother of Cheops* (Cambridge, MA, 1955).

Vyse, H. *Operations Carried On at the Pyramids of Gizeh in 1837*, 3 vols (London, 1840).

## THE GREAT PYRAMID AT GIZA CHAPTERS 4, 9–15

Borchardt, L. *Einiges zur dritten Bauperiode der grossen Pyramide bei Gise, BÄBA* 1, 3 (Berlin, 1932).

Dormion, G. *La pyramide de Chéops: Architecture des appartements funéraires* (Irigny, 1996)

— *La chamber de Chéops: Analyse architecturale* (Paris, 2004).

Maragioglio, V. and C. Rinaldi, *L'Architettura delle piramidi Menfite. Parte IV: Le Grande Piramide di Cheope* (Rapallo, 1965).

Monnier, F. 'À propos du couvrement de la chambre dite "du Roi" dans la pyramide de Khéops', *GM* 231 (2011), 81–96.

— 'Masons' marks upon the saddle vault of the upper chamber in the pyramid of Khufu', *GM* 245 (2015), 73–78.

— and D. Lightbody, *The Great Pyramid* (Yeovil, 2019).

Morishima, K. et al. 'Discovery of a big void in Khufu's Pyramid by observation of cosmic-ray muons', *Nature* 552 (7685, 21/28 December 2017), 386–90.

Romer, J. *The Great Pyramid: Ancient Egypt Revisited* (Cambridge, 2007).

### Great Pyramid layout and survey

Borchardt, L. *Längen und Richtungen der vier Grundkanten der Großen Pyramide bei Gise* (Berlin, 1926).

Cole, J. H. *Determination of the Exact Size and Orientation of the Great Pyramid of Giza*, Survey of Egypt Paper No. 39 (Cairo, 1925).

Dash, G. 'The Great Pyramid's footprint: results from our 2015 survey', *Aeragram* 16/2 (2015), 8–14.

Dorner, J. 'Das Basisviereck der Cheops Pyramide', in P. Jánosi (ed.), *Structure and Significance: Thoughts on Ancient Egyptian Architecture* (Vienna, 2005), 275–81.

Goyon, G. 'Quelques observations effectuées autour de la pyramide de Khéops', *BIFAO* 47 (1969), 71–86.

Lauer, J.-P. 'À propos de l'orientation des grandes pyramides', *BIE* (1960), 7–15.

Lehner, M. 'Some observations on the layout of the Khufu and Khafre Pyramid', *JARCE* 20 (1983), 7–25.

### Great Pyramid 'air shafts'

Bergdoll, S. 'Die Dixon-Relikte und die Geheimnisse der kleinen Schachte der Cheopspyramide', *GM* 248 (2016), 53–90.

Hawass, Z. 'The secret doors inside the Great Pyramid', in Z. Hawass (ed.), *The Treasures of the Pyramids* (Cairo, 2003), 156–59.

— 'The so-called secret doors inside Khufu's Pyramid', in J. Kondo et al. (eds), *Quest for the Dream of the Pharaohs*, (Cairo, 2014), 1–14.

— et al. 'First report: Video survey of the southern shaft of the Queen's Chamber in the Great Pyramid', *ASAE* 84 (2010), 202–17.

Richardson, R. et al. 'The "Djedi" Robot exploration of the southern shaft of the Queen's Chamber in the Great Pyramid of Giza, Egypt', *Journal of Field Robotics* 30 (2013), 323–48.

Stadelmann, R. 'Die sogenannten Luftkanäle der Cheopspyramide, Modelkorridore für den Aufsteige des Königs zum Himmel', *MDAIK* 50 (1994), 285–94.

### Closing the Great Pyramid

Goyon, G. 'Le mécanisme de fermeture a la pyramide de Khéops', *Revue Archéologique* 2 (1963), 1–24.

Haase, M. 'Die Verschlussstein der Cheopspyramide', *Sokar* 19 (2009), 6–14.

Lauer, J.-P. 'Raison première et utilisation pratique de la "grande galerie" dans le pyramide de Kheops', in *Aufsätze zum 70. Geburtstag von Herbert Ricke. BÄBA* 12 (Wiesbaden, 1971), 133–43.

Lehner, M. 'Niches, slots, grooves and stains: Internal frameworks in the Khufu Pyramid?', in H. Guksch and D. Polz (eds), *Stationen: Beiträge zur Kulturgeschichte Ägyptens* (Mainz, 1998), 101–13.

Wheeler, Noel F. 'Pyramids and Their Purpose', *Antiquity* 9/34 (June 1935), 161–88.

### Great Pyramid Temple

Lauer, J.-P. 'Le temple funéraire de Khéops à la grande pyramide de Guizeh', *ASAE* 46 (1947), 245–59.

— 'Note complémentaire sur le temple funéraire de Khéops', *ASAE* 49 (1949), 111–23.

### Khufu's funerary boats

Abubakr, A. M. and A. Y. Moustafa, 'The funerary boat of Khufu', in *Festschrift Ricke. BÄBA* 12 (Wiesbaden, 1971), 1–16.

El-Baz, F. 'Finding a pharaoh's bark', *National Geographic* 173, no. 4 (1988), 512–33.

Jenkins, N. *The Boat Beneath the Pyramid* (London & New York, 1980).

Lipke, P. *The Royal Ship of Cheops*, BAR International 225 (Oxford, 1984).

Nour, M. Z. et al. *The Cheops Boats, Part I* (Cairo, 1960).

Takahashi, K. and A. Nishisaka. 'Some notes on the graffiti written on the cover stones from the second boat pit of Khufu', *Bulletin of the Society for Near Eastern Studies in Japan* 59(1) (2016), 2–13.

### Khufu's satellite pyramid

Dorner, J. 'The revised and complete article on the pyramidion of the satellite pyramid of Khufu', (1995) http://nabilswelim.com/downloads/GiD_pyr.pdf (accessed 15 June 2020).

Hawass, Z. 'The discovery of the pyramidion of the satellite pyramid of Khufu,' in C. C. Van Siclen (ed.), *Iubilate Conlegae: Studies in Memory of Abdel Aziz Sadeq, Part I. Varia Aegyptiaca* 10/2-3 (1995), 105–24.

— 'The discovery of the satellite pyramid of Khufu (GI–d)', in P. Der Manuelian (ed.), *Studies in Honor of William Kelly Simpson* (Boston, 1996), 379–98.

— 'The satellite pyramid of Khufu', in Z. Hawass (ed.), *The Treasures of the Pyramids* (Cairo, 2003), 150–51.

### Khufu's causeway, valley temple and port

El-Nagar, S. 'Le port funéraire de Khéops', *Dossiers d'archéologie* 265 (July-August 2001), 122–31.

Goyon, G. 'La chaussée monumentale et le temple de la vallée de la pyramide de Khéops', *BIFAO* 67 (1969), 49–69.

Hawass, Z. 'The discovery of the harbors of Khufu and Khafre at Giza', in C. Berger and B. Mathieu (eds), *Études sur l'ancien empire et la nécropole de Saqqara* (Montpellier, 1997), 245–56.

Jones, M. 'The remains of the causeway and pyramid temple of Khufu: Rescue archaeology and preservation through documentation', in J. Kamrin et al. (eds), *Guardian of Ancient Egypt: Studies in Honor of Zahi Hawass,* vol. II (Prague, 2020), 771–92.

Messiha, H. 'The valley temple of Khufu (Cheops)', *ASAE* 65 (1983), 9–18.

## FROM WORKERS' VILLAGE TO PORT CITY     CHAPTER 11

Lehner, M. 'The pyramid age settlement of the Southern Mount at Giza', *JARCE* 39 (2002), 27–74.

— 'The lost port city of the pyramids', *Aeragram* 14/1 (Spring 2013), 2–7.

— 'On the waterfront: Canals and harbors in the time of Giza pyramid-building', *Aeragram* 15/1-2 (Spring-Fall 2014), 14–23.

— 'Labor and the pyramids: The Heit el-Ghurab "workers town" at Giza', in P. Steinkeller and M. Hudson, *Labor in the Ancient World,* vol. 5 (Dresden, 2015), 397–522.

— 'The name and nature of the Heit el-Ghurab Old Kingdom site: Workers' town, pyramid town, and the port hypothesis', in I. Hein et al. (eds), *The Pyramids: Between Life and Death* (Uppsala, 2016), 99–160.

— 'Lake Khufu: On the waterfront at Giza: modelling water transport infrastructure at Dynasty IV Giza', in M. Bárta and J. Janák (eds), *Profane Landscapes, Sacred Spaces* (Sheffield, 2020), 191–292.

— 'Merer and the Sphinx', in J. Kamrin et al. (eds), *Guardian of Ancient Egypt: Studies in Honor of Zahi Hawass,* vol. II (Prague, 2020), 895–925.

— and A. Tavares, 'Walls, ways, and stratigraphy: signs of social control in an urban footprint at Giza', in M. Bietak et al. (eds), *Cities and Urbanism in Ancient Egypt* (Vienna, 2010), 171–216.

— and W. Wetterstrom (eds), *Giza Reports. The Giza Plateau Mapping Project,* vol. 1: *Project History, Survey, Ceramics and Main Street and Gallery III.4 Operations* (Boston, 2007).

Tavares, A. 'Village, town, and barracks: A Fourth Dynasty settlement at Heit-el-Ghurab, Giza', in N. Strudwick and H. Strudwick (eds), *Old Kingdom, New Perspectives* (Oxford, 2011), 271–77.

## PRINCE ANKH-HAF     CHAPTER 12

Bolshakov, A. 'What did the bust of Ankh-haf originally look like?', *Journal of the Museum of Fine Arts* 3 (1991), 4–15.

Brovarski, E. 'Giza Mastabas Project, report on the 1989 field season', *Newsletter of the American Research Center in Egypt* 145 (1989), 1–3.

Dunham, D. 'The portrait bust of Prince Ankh-haf', *Bulletin of the Museum of Fine Arts* 37, no. 221 (1939), 42–46.

— 'An experiment with an Egyptian portrait: Ankh-haf in modern dress', *Bulletin of the Museum of Fine Arts* 41, no. 243 (February 1943), 10.

Flentye, L. 'The mastabas of Ankh-haf (G7510) and Akhethetep and Meretites (G7650) in the Eastern Cemetery at Giza: A reassessment', in Z. Hawass and J. Richards (eds), *The Archeology and Art of Ancient Egypt: Essays in Honor of David B. O'Connor,* vol. 1 (Cairo, 2007), 291–308.

## RAISING THE STONES     CHAPTER 14

Arnold, D. 'Überlegungen zum Problem des Pyramidenbaues', *MDAIK* 37 (1981), 15–28.

— *Building in Ancient Egypt, Pharaonic Stone Masonry* (New York & Oxford, 1991).

Brichieri-Colombi, S. 'Engineering a feasible ramp for the Great Pyramid of Giza', *PalArch's Journal of Archaeology of Egypt/Egyptology* 12/1 (2015), 1–15.

— 'A spurred spiral ramp for the Great Pyramid of Giza', *PalArch's Journal of Archaeology of Egypt/Egyptology* 17/3 (2020), 1–20.

Dunham, D. 'Building an Egyptian Pyramid', *Archaeology* 9, no. 3 (1956), 159–65.

Goyon, G. *Le secret des bâtisseurs des grandes pyramides. Khéops* (Paris, 1977).

Isler, M. 'Ancient Egyptian methods of raising weights', *JARCE* 13 (1976), 31–41.

— 'Concerning the concave faces on the Great Pyramid', *JARCE* 20 (1983), 27–32.

— 'On pyramid building', *JARCE* 22 (1985), 129–42.

— 'On pyramid building II', *JARCE* 24 (1987), 95–112.

Lauer, J.-P., 'Comment furent construites les pyramides?', *Historia* 86 (1954), 57–66.

Müller-Römer, F. *Der Bau der Pyramiden im alten Ägypten* (Munich, 2011).

Petrie, W. M. F. 'The building of a pyramid', *Ancient Egypt* (1930), 33–39.

## CREATING THE STATE     CHAPTER 15

### Internal colonization

Baer, K. 'The low price of land in ancient Egypt', *JARCE* 1 (1962), 25–45.

Butzer, K. W. *Early Hydraulic Civilization in Egypt: A Study in Cultural Ecology* (Chicago, 1976).

Helck, W. 'Die Bedeutung der Felsinschriften' *SAK* 1 (1974), 215–25.

— *Die altägyptischen Gaue. Beihefte zum Tübinger Atlas des Vorderen Orients,* Reihe B, Nr. 5 (Wiesbaden, 1974).

— 'Fremdarbeit', *LÄ* II (1977), 304–306.

Jacquet-Gordon, H. K. *Les nomes des domaines funéraires sous l'ancien empire Égyptien* (Cairo, 1962).

Kemp. B. J. 'Old Kingdom, Middle Kingdom, and Second Intermediate Period', in B. Trigger et al. (eds), *Ancient Egypt: A Social History* (Cambridge, 1983), 71–182.

Menu, B. 'Captifs de guerre et dépendance rurale dans l'Égypte du nouvel empire', in B. Menu (ed.), *La dépendance rurale dans l'Antiquité: Égyptienne et proche-orientale,* BdE 140 (Cairo, 2004), 187–209.

Moreno García, J. C. 'La population *mrt,* une approche du problème de la servitude dans l'Égypte du IIIe millénaire', *JEA* 84 (1998), 71–83.

— *Hwt et le milieu rural égyptien du IIIe millénaires: Économie, administration et organisation territorial* (Paris, 1999).

Wilkinson, T. A. H. *The Royal Annals of Ancient Egypt: The Palermo Stone and its Associated Fragments* (London, 2000).

### Mobilization – gangs, phyles and divisions

Andrássy, P. 'Builders' graffiti and administrative aspects of pyramid and temple building in ancient Egypt', in R. Preys (ed.), *7. Ägyptologische Tempeltagung: Structuring Religion* (Wiesbaden, 2009), 1–16.

Helck, W. 'Die Handwerker- und Priesterphylen des alten Reiches in Ägypten', *WdO* 7 (1973), 1–7.

— 'Arbeiterabteilungen und -organisation', *LÄ* I (1975), 371–73.

Posener-Kriéger, P. 'Les Papyrus de Gébélein, remarques préliminaires', *Revue d'Égyptologie* 27 (1975), 211–21.

Roth, A. *Egyptian Phyles in the Old Kingdom: The Evolution of a System of Social Organization*, SAOC 48 (Chicago, 1991).

Tallet, P. 'Des serpents et des lions. La flotte stupéfiante de Chéops sur la mer Rouge', in *Mélanges Dominique Valbelle* (Paris, 2017), 243–53.

Verner, M. 'Zur Organisierung der Arbeitskräfte auf den Großbaustellen der Alten Reichs-Nekropolen', in E. Endesfelder (ed.), *Probleme der frühen Gesellschaftsentwicklung im alten Ägypten* (Berlin, 1991), 61–91.

— 'The Abusir Builders' Crews', in N. Kloth et al. (eds), *Festschrift für Hartwig Altenmüller* (Hamburg, 2003) 445–51.

## Institutionalization

Alexanian, N. and T. Herbich, 'The workmen's barracks south of the Red Pyramid at Dahshur', *MDAIK* 70/71 (2016), 13–24.

Hillier, B. and J. Hanson, *The Social Logic of Space* (Cambridge, 1984).

## Socialization

Engelbach, R. *The Aswan Obelisk, with Some Remarks on the Ancient Engineering* (Cairo, 1922).

— *The Problem of the Obelisk, From a Study of the Unfinished Obelisk at Aswan* (London, 1923).

Kadish, G. 'Observations on time and work-discipline in Ancient Egypt', in P. Der Manuelian (ed.), *Studies in Honor of William Kelly Simpson* (Boston, 1996), 439–49.

Gabriele, P. '"Rhythm is it!" Special motif as part of wine-making scenes', in P. Jánosi and H. Vymazalová (eds), *The Art of Describing the World of Tomb Decoration as Visual Culture of the Old Kingdom* (Prague, 2018), 273–88.

## Intensification – economy of scale

Rice, P. *Pottery Analysis: A Sourcebook* (Chicago, 1987).

Sahlins, M. *Stone Age Economics* (London, 1974).

## Bureaucratization – administration

Baud, M. *Famille royale et pouvoir sous l'Ancien Empire égyptienne*, 2 vols. BdE 126 (Cairo, 1999).

Dorman, P. F. 'The biographical inscription of Ptahshepses from Saqqara: A newly identified fragment', *JEA* 88 (2002), 95–110.

Helck, W. *Untersuchungen zu den Beamtiteln des ägyptischen alten Reiches* (Glückstadt, 1954).

Jones, D. *An Index of Egyptian Titles, Epithets and Phrases of the Old Kingdom* (Oxford, 2000).

Lehner, M., 'Neighborhood to national network: Pyramid settlements of Giza', *Archaeological Papers of the American Anthropological Association 30/1, special issue* (July 2019), 20–38.

Moreno García, J. C. (ed.), *Ancient Egyptian Administration* (Leiden, 2013).

—, *The State in Ancient Egypt: Power, Challenges and Dynamics* (London, 2020).

Nolan, J. *Mud Sealings and Fourth Dynasty Administration at Giza*, Ph.D. dissertation, Dept. of Near Eastern Languages and Civilizations, University of Chicago (2010).

Schmitz, B. *Untersuchungen zum Titel S3-NJSWT 'Königssohn'* (Bonn, 1976).

Strudwick, N. *The Administration of Egypt in the Old Kingdom* (London, 1985).

# SOURCES OF ILLUSTRATIONS

a = above, b = below, c = centre, l = left, r = right

# ACKNOWLEDGMENTS

The authors wish to thank all those without whom the work on the various excavation sites referred to in this book would not have been possible, and first and foremost the Egyptian ministers of antiquities who have succeeded each other in recent years, in particular Drs Zahi Hawass, Mamdouh el-Damaty and Khaled el-Enani.

Our thanks also go to Dr Moustafa Waziri, Secretary General of the Supreme Council of Antiquities; Dr Nashwa Gaber, Director of the Department of Foreign Missions; Ashraf Mohedein, Director of Giza and to all the officials of the Giza Inspectorate, as well as those of Suez, successively Dr Nubi Mahmoud Ahmed and Dr Mahmoud Ragab, who have facilitated our work on the Ayn Sukhna and Wadi el-Jarf sites for many years.

Mark would like to thank all the supporters and team members of Ancient Egypt Research Associates (AERA), who have made possible the work and discoveries at Giza reported here. For major support, I thank Charles Simonyi and Microsoft, Dr Walter Gilbert, and Ann Lurie. I thank AERA Board members Dr James Allen, Ed Fries, Janice Jerde, Lou Hughes, Piers Litherland, Bruce Ludwig, Ann Lurie, Matthew McCauley, and Dr Richard Redding. A special thanks to Douglas C. Rawles and Reed Smith LLP for legal counsel. I want to thank Dr Mohsen Kamel, Executive Director of AERA Egypt; Dr Richard Redding, Chief Research Officer; Dr Claire Malleson, Archaeological Science and AERA Lab Director; Dan Jones, Senior Archaeologist, Sayed Salah Abd el-Hakim, and all AERA staff members in Boston and Giza. For the development of images in this book, I thank Rebekah Miracle, AERA's GIS Director, and Dr Wilma Wetterstrom, AERA's Art and Science Editor.

My gratitude (Pierre) also goes to Sheikh Rabia Barakat, chief of the Bedouin tribe of Aleigat of South Sinai, as well as to many Egyptian colleagues, whose friendship has never wavered: Dr El-Sayed Mahfouz – former colleague at the University of the Sorbonne - Moustafa Resk Ibrahim, accomplice of several missions in Sinai, and our intendant Adel Farouk, of the Suez inspectorate, who has always been able to facilitate the often complex procedure of obtaining military permits required for work on the Red Sea coast. Finally, I would like to thank both the successive directors of IFAO, Bernard Mathieu, Laure Pantalacci, Béatrix Midant Reynes, Laurent Bavay and Laurent Coulon for their help at all levels in the organization of these missions, as well as Professors Nicolas Grimal, from the Collège de France, and Dominique Valbelle, from the University of the Sorbonne, for the decisive help they gave through their funding. I do not want to forget either the very many collaborators who accompanied me in the work at Sinai, Ayn Sukhna and Wadi el-Jarf, to whom are due many of the documents, plans, photos of these different missions that appear in this book – and in particular, without being exhaustive: Damien Laisney, Grégory Marouard, Severine Marchi, Georges Castel, Patrice Pomey, Aurore Ciavatti, Claire Somaglino, Yann Tristant, Gael Pollin, Eve Menei, Emmanuel Laroze, Franck Burgos, Adeline Bats, Camille Lemoine, Hassan Mohamed Ahmed, Ihab Mohamed and Marie-Hélène Barrière. For more than 20 years, the team of Luxor workers has been led by reis Gamal Nasr el-Din, assisted by Gaalan Meabad: nothing would have been possible without them. Finally, my thanks go to Robert Emery, Stéphane Campedelli (Vinci company) and Pedro Herrera (Colas-rail company), who allowed the launch of these various projects through regular and benevolent sponsorship, as well as to the Honor Frost Foundation, the Académie des Inscriptions et Belles Lettres and the French Foreign Office for their constant support.

The publisher would like to thank Ian Shaw for his invaluable help in rendering Pierre Tallet's French text into English, and Sarah Vernon-Hunt for her expert editing of the whole text.

# INDEX

First published in the United Kingdom in 2021
by Thames & Hudson Ltd, 181A High Holborn,
London WC1V 7QX

First published in the United States of America
in 2021 by Thames & Hudson Inc., 500 Fifth Avenue,
New York, New York 10110

British Library Cataloguing-in-Publication Data
A catalogue record for this book is available from
the British Library

Library of Congress Control Number 2021939584

ISBN 978-0-500-05211-2

Printed and bound in China by 1010 Printing
International Ltd